Buying Time

Buying Time

The Delayed Crisis
of Democratic Capitalism

Wolfgang Streeck

Translated by Patrick Camiller

VERSO

London • New York

This English-language edition first published by Verso 2014
Translation © Patrick Camiller 2014
First published as *Gekaufte Zeit*
© Suhrkamp Verlag Berlin 2013

1 3 5 7 9 10 8 6 4 2

Verso
UK: 6 Meard Street, London W1F 0EG
US: 20 Jay Street, Suite 1010, Brooklyn, NY 11201
www.versobooks.com

Verso is the imprint of New Left Books

ISBN-13: 978-1-78168-548-8 (PBK)
ISBN-13: 978-1-78168-549-5 (HBK)
eISBN-13: 978-1-78168-550-1 (US)
eISBN-13: 978-1-78168-551-8 (UK)

British Library Cataloguing in Publication Data
A catalogue record for this book is available from the British Library

Library of Congress Cataloging-in-Publication Data
Streeck, Wolfgang, 1946–
[Gekaufte Zeit. English]
Buying time : the delayed crisis of democratic capitalism / Wolfgang Streeck ; translated by Patrick Camiller.
    pages cm
'First published as Gekaufte Zeit, Suhrkamp Verlag, Berlin, 2013.'
    ISBN 978-1-78168-549-5 (hardback) — ISBN 978-1-78168-619-5 (ebook)
1. Capitalism. 2. Neoliberalism. 3. Democracy—Economic aspects. 4. Economic policy.
5. Financial crises. I. Title.
HB501.S919513 2014
330.12'2—dc23
                                    2014003057

Typeset in Minion Pro by Hewer Text UK Ltd, Edinburgh
Printed and bound by CPI Group (UK) Ltd, Croydon, CR0 4YY

Contents

Crisis Theory: Then and Now

Buying Time is an expanded version of the Adorno Lectures I gave in June 2012 at the Institut für Sozialforschung, almost exactly forty years after I graduated in sociology from Frankfurt University.[1] I cannot say that I was a 'disciple' of Adorno. I attended some of his lectures and seminars, but did not understand much; that's how it was in those days, and people accepted it. Only later, more or less by chance, did it become clear to me how much I had missed as a result. Thus, my strongest memory of Adorno has remained the deep existential seriousness of his work – in stark contrast to the indifference with which so much social science is conducted today, after decades of professionalization.

Fortunately, no one will think me qualified to assess Adorno's work. I have in any case refrained from seeking specific links between what I have to say and what Adorno left behind; that would appear forced and presumptuous. If there are things in common, they are of a very general nature. One is my intuitive refusal to believe that crises will always turn out well in the end – an intuition that I certainly think I can find in Adorno too. He lacks the kind of 'functionalist' sense of security that one sees in Talcott Parsons, for example; there is never any guarantee that everything will sooner or later automatically return to equilibrium. He could not bring himself to share

1   I am grateful to the Institute and its director, Axel Honneth, for the invitation and the challenge it posed to work out and systematize my ideas; and to Sidonia Blättler who organized my stay in Frankfurt. In the collection of material and data, both before and after the lectures, I received various forms of help from my students and assistants at the Max Planck Institute for the Study of Societies in Cologne – among others, Annina Assmann, Lea Elsässer, Lukas Haffert, Daniel Mertens and Philip Mehrtens. Lea Elsässer made a special contribution with the numerous diagrams. Without my colleagues in Cologne – Jens Beckert, Renate Mayntz, Fritz Scharpf, Martin Höpner, Armin Schäfer and others – I would never have been able to sort out and give shape to my ideas. Naturally I alone am to blame for any misconceptions.

Hölderlin's basic confidence: 'But where danger threatens / That which saves from it also grows.'[2] Nor am I able to believe it, for whatever reason. In my eyes, social orders are normally fragile and precarious; unpleasant surprises may turn up at any moment. I also think it wrong to demand that someone who identifies a problem should immediately offer a solution as well.[3] I do not bow to such prescriptions in this book, even if, in chapter 4, I offer a (not very realistic) proposal to address a partial aspect of the crisis. Problems may be such that there is no solution to them – or anyway, none achievable here and now. If someone were to ask me reproachfully where was 'the positive', this would then indeed be a case where I could appeal to Adorno. For his reply, much better formulated, would doubtless have been: what if there is nothing positive?

My book treats the financial and fiscal crisis of contemporary democratic capitalism in the light of Frankfurt School crisis theories of the late 1960s and early 1970s – a period when Adorno was still active and when, of course, I was studying in Frankfurt. The theories I address were attempts to grasp the incipient radical changes in the postwar political economy as aspects of a process encompassing the whole of society, in which more or less eclectic use was made of elements of the Marxist tradition. The accounts from which I set out were anything but uniform; many were no more than sketches and, as one might expect, changed with the course of events, in ways often unnoticed by the authors themselves. On looking back at them, one also repeatedly finds a stubborn insistence on minor differences within the same theoretical family, which today appear irrelevant or

---

2   'Wo aber Gefahr ist, wächst das Rettende auch': 'Patmos', in Friedrich Hölderlin, *Poems and Fragments*, translated by Michael Hamburger, London: Anvil Press, 1994, p. 482.

3   Economists tend to demand this of other economists, arguing that a diagnosis that does not include a therapy is inadequate. Take, for example, the so-called 'economists' dispute' over the euro crisis, which raged in the German press in summer 2012. One signatory of a 'Eurosceptical' letter addressed to 'dear fellow-citizens' that caused widespread public outrage justified as follows his endorsement of a counter-appeal just a few days later: 'I believe economists have a duty to come up with constructive suggestions. If you're a professional firefighter, merely shouting at the flames isn't good enough' (*Guardian* online, 15 July 2012). Some fires, however, cannot (or cannot yet) be extinguished.

even incomprehensible. For this reason alone, the point at issue cannot be who then was more right than others.

The theoretical endeavours of the Frankfurt years also demonstrate how social-scientific knowledge is unavoidably tied to its time. Nevertheless, it might be possible to link up with 1970s theories of the crisis of 'late capitalism' in grappling with present-day events – and not only because we now know again, and are again able to voice, what was forgotten for decades or dismissed as irrelevant: that the economic and social order of the wealthy democracies is still a capitalist order and can be understood, if at all, only with the help of a theory of capitalism. In retrospect, we can also see what was then *imperceptible* (because it was *still self-evident* or had already *become self-evident*) or what people were *unwilling* to perceive (because it stood in the way of their political projects). If, despite all the theoretical efforts, there was a failure to see important aspects of the real world, not to mention foresee what was coming, this may serve to remind us that society faces an open future and that history is unpredictable – a fact which the social sciences have not always fully appreciated.[4] On the other hand, however great the changes, much that was seen in the past and then forgotten can be recognized in the present. Little as we can rely upon static observation of the world, a social formation may appear identical with itself for decades if it is conceived as a developmental process containing structures that change over time, whose logic can be understood retrospectively even if it does not lend itself to prediction.

My analyses treat the financial and fiscal crisis of contemporary capitalism as part of the developmental continuum of society as a whole. The starting point is the end of the 1960s, and I describe the process, from today's vantage, as a dissolution of the regime of post-war democratic capitalism.[5] As I said, my contribution will link up

---

4   This is true in so far as they still think of themselves, and present themselves outwardly, as nomothetic sciences. The same accusation cannot be made against Frankfurt sociology.

5   It is inevitably more or less arbitrary where one situates the beginning of a process, because history is always interconnected and everything has a prehistory. There are decisive

with a theoretical attempt around that time, undertaking to explain new developments by reference to older, primarily Marxist, traditions. Some of these went back to earlier research conducted by the Institut für Sozialforschung, although Adorno himself had not been directly involved in it. The crisis theory of the 'Frankfurt School' heuristically assumed a relationship of tension between social life and an economy ruled by the imperatives of capital valorization and capital growth – a tension which, in the postwar formation of democratic capitalism, was mediated by government policy in a number of historically unfolding ways. Social institutions, especially in the spheres of politics and economics, thus appeared as constant objects of contention, inherently contradictory, unstable and only provisionally, if at all, in equilibrium, involving no more than temporary compromises between fundamentally incompatible action orientations and social systems. In keeping with the tradition of political economy, the 'economy of society' was understood as a social system (not simply a technical system, or one determined by laws of nature), which consisted of power-backed interactions between parties with different interests and resources.

By taking up theories of the 1970s and attempting to update them in the light of four decades of later capitalist development, I treat the current crisis of democratic capitalism within a dynamic perspective embedded in a sequence of development.[6] That this is the right way to conduct macrosociology or political economy, I believe I have learned over the years from numerous investigations of various social fields.[7] What is most revealing for social science is not states of affairs but

---

breaks and formative moments, however. That the 1970s marked the end of one era and the beginning of another has become a commonplace which I have no reason to doubt.

6   W. Streeck, 'Institutions in History: Bringing Capitalism Back In', in John Campbell et al. (eds), *Handbook of Comparative Institutional Analysis*, Oxford: Oxford University Press, 2010, pp. 659–86.

7   See my study of the liberalization of German political economy since the 1970s: W. Streeck, *Re-Forming Capitalism: Institutional Change in the German Political Economy*, Oxford: Oxford University Press, 2009. On the analysis of capitalism as a developmental process, see W. Streeck, 'Taking Capitalism Seriously: Towards an Institutional Approach to Contemporary Political Economy', *Socio-Economic Review*, vol. 9, 2011, pp. 137–67.

processes – or states of affairs as they are connected with and within processes. Theories that treat structures or events as unique, in the sense of detached from previous structures or events, can be fundamentally misleading. For everything social takes place in time, unfolds over time, becomes more self-same in and over time. We can understand what we see today only if we know how it looked yesterday and where it might be heading. Everything at hand is always moving along a path of development – which is why the three main parts of this book contain so many diagrams and stylized narratives representing historical processes.

The fact that everything needs time is not the only important point: there is also the question of *when* and *where* it takes place *in* time. Space – the social context constituted by propinquity – is no less fundamental than time for society, and the time that counts is not only chronological[8] but also historical. Social-scientific knowledge really comes about only when it has been provided with a time and space index. The crisis at issue here is a crisis of capitalism in the wealthy democracies of the Western world – a context that took shape after the experiences of the Great Depression, the relaunch of capitalism and liberal democracy following the Second World War, the breakdown of the postwar order in the 1970s, the 'oil price shocks' and high inflation, and so on. This crisis has implications for other societies too, both present and future, but their precise nature, which only empirical research can elucidate, will be decided by historically specific practical action. What we know in general about political and economic crises may prove useful. But at least as significant is the distinctive, unprecedented character of *this* crisis, which must be worked out and interpreted on the basis of its spatio-temporal context.

The inclusion of time in our study of the contemporary financial and fiscal crisis will be revealing in a number of respects. First of all, the historical context will put into perspective many of the national

---

8   As in the concept of path dependence (see P. Pierson, 'Increasing Returns, Path Dependence, and the Study of Politics', *American Political Science Review*, vol. 94/2, 2000, pp. 251–68; and *Politics in Time: History, Institutions, and Social Analysis*, Princeton, NJ: Princeton University Press, 2004).

differences among democratic capitalist societies that have been identified by cross-sectional studies in the social sciences and held to
indicate distinctive models or 'varieties of capitalism'.[9] If the crisis is
treated as an intermediate stage in a protracted developmental
sequence, it turns out that the parallels and interactions among capitalist countries far outweigh their institutional and economic
differences. The underlying dynamic, allowing for local variations, is
the same – even for countries considered as far apart from each other
as Sweden and the United States. What becomes particularly visible in
a study over time is the leading role of the largest and most capitalist
of all the capitalist countries, the United States, where all the trend-
setting developments originated: the ending of the Bretton Woods
system and of inflation, the growth of budget deficits as a result of tax
resistance and tax cuts, the rise of debt-financing of government
activity, the wave of fiscal consolidations in the 1990s, finance market
deregulation as part of a policy of privatizing government functions,
and, of course, the financial and fiscal crisis of 2008.

The causal links and mechanisms of interest to sociologists also
operate in a temporal dimension, and indeed over long periods of
time as far as the adaptation and change of institutions or whole societies are concerned. We tend to underestimate how long societal
causes take to produce their effects. If we ask too soon whether or not
a theory concerning the change or end of a social formation is accu-
rate, we run the risk of seeing it refuted before it has had a chance to
prove itself. A good example is the literature on globalization in the
comparative political science of the 1980s and 1990s, which, basing
itself on empirical observations of the time, concluded that the opening of frontiers between national economies was not likely to have
negative effects on the welfare state. Today we know that things simply

9   P. Hall and D. Soskice, 'An Introduction to Varieties of Capitalism', in Peter A. Hall
et al. (eds), *Varieties of Capitalism: The Institutional Foundations of Comparative Advantage*,
Oxford: Oxford University Press, 2001, pp. 1–68. For a critique of the 'varieties of capitalism'
approach, see Streeck, *Re-Forming Capitalism*; W. Streeck, 'E Pluribus Unum? Varieties and
Commonalities of Capitalism', in Mark Granovetter et al. (eds), *The Sociology of Economic
Life*, 3rd edition, Boulder, CO: Westview, 2011, pp. 419–55.

took longer – and that the solidly established, inert institutions such as European welfare states could not have been expected to disappear, or to become something fundamentally different, after just a few years of economic internationalization. Institutional change often, probably mostly, takes place as gradual change,[10] which may for a long time be dismissed as marginal, even after the marginal has become the core and the principal force shaping the dynamic of development.[11]

In addition to the long, incremental nature of social and institutional change – but how long is long? – social trends of development repeatedly come up against *counteracting factors* that may slow them down or divert, modify or halt them.[12] Societies observe the trends at work in them and react to them. In doing so, they display an inventiveness far beyond anything imagined by social scientists, even by those who have correctly identified the (socially contentious)

---

10   W. Streeck and K. Thelen, 'Introduction: Institutional Change in Advanced Political Economies', in W. Streeck and K. Thelen (eds), *Beyond Continuity: Institutional Change in Advanced Political Economies*, Oxford: Oxford University Press, 2005, pp. 1–39.

11   See the literature on changes to the 'German model' of labour relations. In the 1980s, early departures from industry-level wage setting could still be interpreted as a flexible adaptation to changed conditions that aimed at, and resulted in, the preservation of the system as a whole. As the process continued, the view began to prevail that it was leading to a 'dualization' of the system, such that the old regime remained the same but lost its universal character (B. Palier and K. Thelen, 'Institutionalizing Dualism: Complementarities and Change in France and Germany', *Politics and Society*, vol. 38/1, 2010, pp. 119–48). But the more the trend persists and the more the margins eat, however slowly, into the core of the system, the more one finds onself forced to give up this interpretation and describe the process as what it can now be seen to have been from the beginning: the liberalization of a social domain hitherto regulated by politics rather than market forces (A. Hassel, 'The Erosion of the German System of Industrial Relations', *British Journal of Industrial Relations*, vol. 37/3, 1999, pp. 483–505; Streeck, *Re-Forming Capitalism*).

12   The concept of 'counteracting factors' is central to Marx's theorem of the tendential fall of the rate of profit (K. Marx, *Capital, Volume Three*, London: Penguin/New Left Books, 1981, pp. 339ff.). Marx's 'law' is not deterministic because it allows that the postulated tendency of the rate of profit to decline may be held back by countervailing forces. These would then be explained as the effect of a cause – the 'tendential fall' itself – that cannot be empirically observed because of the counteraction preventing it from being effective. This is also a central idea for Karl Polanyi, when he speaks of the 'countermovement' of society against the expansion of markets and their spreading to the 'fictitious commodities' of land, labour and capital (K. Polanyi, *The Great Transformation: The Political and Economic Origins of Our Time*, Boston: Beacon Press, 1944, ch. 11).

underlying trends. The crisis of late capitalism in the 1970s must have been visible even to those who had no interest in its downfall or self-destruction. They too sensed the tensions more or less accurately diagnosed by crisis theory, and acted in response. From today's vantage, such reactions appear as successful attempts – stretching over more than four decades – *to buy time*. While the common expression 'buying time' does not necessarily imply an outlay of money, it clearly does in this case – and on a large scale. Money, the most mysterious institution of capitalist modernity, served to defuse potentially destabilizing social conflicts, at first by means of inflation, then through increased government borrowing, next through the expansion of private loan markets, and finally (today) through central bank purchases of public debt and bank liabilities. As I will show, the 'buying of time' that postponed and extended the crisis of postwar democratic capitalism is closely related to the epochal process of capitalist development that we call 'financialization'.[13]

With a sufficiently large time frame, the development of the current crisis may be understood as an evolutionary, and also dialectical, process.[14] Within a long developmental sequence, that is, what may have repeatedly looked in the short run like the end of the crisis – and hence a refutation of the prevailing version of crisis theory – may turn out to be merely a change in the outward manifestation of the underlying conflicts and integration deficits. Ostensible solutions never took more than a decade to become problems – or rather, the old problem in a new form. Each victory over the crisis sooner or later became the prelude to a new crisis, through complex and unpredictable shifts that, each for a time, concealed the fact that all stabilization mechanisms can only be provisional, as long as the expansion of

---

13   G. Krippner, *Capitalizing on Crisis: The Political Origins of the Rise of Finance*, Cambridge, MA: Harvard University Press, 2011.

14   On the revival of the concept of dialectical change in modern institutional theory, see A. Greif, *Institutions and the Path to the Modern Economy*, Cambridge: Cambridge University Press, 2006; and A. Greif and D. Laitin, 'A Theory of Endogenous Institutional Change', *American Political Science Review*, vol. 98/4, 2004, pp. 633–52.

capitalism – the 'land-grabbing' by the market[15] – clashes with the logic of the social lifeworld.

One of the less agreeable memories from my student years in Frankfurt is of lectures and seminars which, to my taste at least, focused too much on 'approaches' and too little on what the actual research was meant to help us understand. More often than not I missed the kind of worldly realism to be found in a book such as C. Wright Mills's *The Power Elite*; and to this day I soon become bored with sociology from which histories, local colour and the exotic, often absurd, side of social and political life are absent. Although I therefore travel light in terms of theory, my theme here – the financial and fiscal crisis of the wealthy capitalist democracies – does require me to connect with the rich theoretical tradition of political economy. This is because, unless the sociology of social crises and the political theory of democracy learn to conceive of the economy as a field of social-political activity, they inevitably fall wide of the mark, as does any conception of the economy in polity and society that leaves out of account their present capitalist form of organization. After what has happened since 2008, no one can understand politics and political institutions without closely relating them to markets and economic interests, as well as to the class structures and conflicts arising from them. Whether or not this is 'Marxist' or 'neo-Marxist' is a matter of complete indifference to me, and I have no wish to enter into it. But one outcome of historical developments is that we can no longer say for sure where, in the effort to shed light on current events, non-Marxism ends and Marxism begins. Besides, social science – especially when it concerns itself with whole societies and their development – has never really been able to do without recourse to central elements of 'Marxist' theories, even as it defines itself in opposition to them.[16]

---

15 B. Lutz, *Der kurze Traum immerwährender Prosperität: Eine Neuinterpretation der industriell-kapitalistischen Entwicklung des Europa des 20. Jahrhunderts*, Frankfurt/ Main: Campus, 1984; R. Luxemburg, *The Accumulation of Capital*, London: Routledge & Kegan Paul, 1951.

16 Of course, this applies especially to someone like Max Weber, who refrained all his life – probably wisely – from openly tackling Marx or even quoting from his work. In

In any event, I am convinced that present trends in modern societies cannot be even approximately understood without the help of key concepts from the Marxian tradition – and that this will become all the more the case, the more plainly the capitalist market economy becomes the driving force of the emergent global society.

My considerations on the crisis of democratic capitalism range far and wide; the picture they show is drawn with a broad brush on a large canvas. Context and sequence occupy centre stage, with individual events more to the side; rough commonalities overshadow subtle distinctions; particular cases receive less attention than the links between them; synthesis trumps analysis; and boundaries between disciplines are continually disregarded. The argument spans wide arcs: from the strike wave in the late 1960s to the introduction of the euro, from the end of inflation in the early 1980s to the rapid growth of income inequality around the end of the century, from 'containment policy' in the age of Eurocommunism to the present fiscal crises of the Mediterranean countries, and much more besides. Probably not everything will stand up to more specialized research; that is the risk I run, a risk that affects any synoptic treatment of current events. But, of course, I am hopeful that most of the book will endure in the end.

The book is divided into three main parts that correspond to the three lectures. This results in some overlap and sometimes surprising transitions that would not have occurred in a more systematic treatment. But perhaps such a book would also have been less readable. The facts and data used to demonstrate or illustrate various points are

---

Germany, 'Marxist approaches' were purged or separated off from the core social sciences, far more sharply than in the original capitalist countries, Britain and the USA, where terms such as 'capitalism' or 'class' have always been part of the everyday language of the social sciences. One need only skim the main works of American 'modernization theory' (e.g., W. Rostow, *The Stages of Economic Growth: A Non-Communist Manifesto*, Cambridge: Cambridge University Press, 1960; C. Kerr et al., *Industrialism and Industrial Man: The Problems of Labor and Management in Economic Growth*, Cambridge, MA: Harvard University Press, 1960) to realize how the academic-political establishment of the leading capitalist power in the 1950s and 1960s thought it natural to draw on key concepts (whether correctly or incorrectly understood) of Marxian political economy.

all more or less familiar, at least in the specialist literature; my contribution, if any, has been to organize them within a larger historical and theoretical context. Each of the three lectures has been expanded beyond what was possible to fit into an hour of oral presentation, with the purpose of greater clarity and concreteness. To maintain the flow of the text, I have made copious use of footnotes – often quoting from the remarkably straightforward reporting in the *New York Times*, or presenting particularly grotesque facts that make one unsure whether to laugh or cry at what has come to appear normal. Sometimes I use footnotes to allow myself to engage in risky (but potentially all the more productive) speculations, without giving them *droit de cité* in the main body of the text.

Buying Time, then, is divided into three main chapters. Chapter 1 begins with a short, by now almost commonplace, account of the nexus linking financial, fiscal and growth crises, a nexus which has so far resisted successful management and confronts politics with unending mysteries. I then look at theories that postulated in the 1970s an impending 'legitimation crisis' of 'late capitalism' and try to explain why they were only insufficiently prepared for the social trends that appeared to disprove their intuitions in the coming decades. One of these trends was the long-drawn-out shift away from postwar social capitalism to the neoliberalism of the early twenty-first century. I also outline how the crisis diagnosed in the 1970s actually unfolded and changed over time, until it acquired its present form in 2008.

Chapter 2 focuses mainly on the crisis in public finances and its origins and consequences. Starting with a critique of theories in 'institutional economics' that trace the rise of public debt since the 1970s to a surfeit of democracy, it argues that rising debt levels should rather be seen as one aspect among others of the neoliberal transformation, or 'involution',[17] of the democratic capitalism that emerged after 1945. It is that which has brought back the notion of a 'crisis of the tax state', which already had a central position in economic debates around the

17 J. Agnoli, *Die Transformation der Demokratie*, Berlin: Voltaire Verlag, 1967.

time of the First World War.[18] I then go on to examine the 'debt state' as an actual institutional formation, which replaced the classical tax state at the latest in the 1980s. Among my concerns here is the relationship between the debt state and the class structure or distribution of life chances in society, as well as the conflicts and power relations that develop between citizens and 'markets' within the socio-political formation of the debt state. I conclude with a discussion of the (systematically central) *international dimension* of the debt state and of the role of international financial diplomacy in its governance.

Chapter 3 turns to the form of political organization that has begun to replace the debt state: what I call the 'consolidation state'. For contingent reasons its development in Europe is inseparably bound up with the progress of European integration, which for some time has operated as a liberalization machine for national economies. My analysis describes the consolidation state as a European multilevel governance regime and conceives of fiscal consolidation as a fundamental recasting of the European state system. The chapter ends with reflections on the potential for, and limits of, political opposition to this process of political restructuring.

In chapter 4, the concluding section, I summarize my main theses and – partly on the basis of public discussions in summer and autumn 2012 – explore, with European monetary union and the future of the euro as the main focus, a possible answer to the crisis that might perhaps slow the capitalist expansion process ('globalization', for short) and thereby keep open the option of democratic control over 'the markets'.

---

18   J. Schumpeter, 'The Crisis of the Tax State' [1918], in Richard Swedberg, ed., *The Economics and Sociology of Capitalism*, Princeton, NJ: Princeton University Press, 1991, pp. 99–141.

CHAPTER ONE

From Legitimation Crisis to Fiscal Crisis

There is much to suggest that the neo-Marxist crisis theories circulating in Frankfurt in the 1960s and 1970s were wrongly thought to have been refuted in subsequent decades. Perhaps the transformation and dissolution of a major social formation such as capitalism simply takes rather longer – too long for impatient theorists who would like to know in their lifetime whether they have been right to hold the theories they did. Social change also seems to involve time-consuming detours which theoretically should not occur, and which can therefore be explained, if at all, only post hoc and ad hoc. In any event, I would argue that the crisis weighing capitalism down at the beginning of the twenty-first century – a crisis of its economy as well as its politics – can be understood only as the climax of a development which began in the mid-1970s and which the crisis theories of that time were the first attempts to interpret.

In retrospect, it is no longer disputed that the 1970s marked a turning-point:[1] they brought the end of postwar reconstruction; the incipient breakdown of the international monetary system, which had been nothing less than a political world order for postwar capitalism;[2] and the return of crisis-like disturbances and interruptions of economic activity as steps in capitalist development. Frankfurt sociologists,

---

1   For the Federal Republic of Germany, see among many others the studies of A. Doering-Manteuffel and L. Raphael, *Nach dem Boom. Perspektiven auf die Zeitgeschichte seit 1970*, Göttingen: Vandenhoeck und Ruprecht, 2008; and T. Raithel et al., *Auf dem Weg in eine neue Moderne? Die Bundesrepublik Deutschland in den siebziger und achtziger Jahren*, Munich: Oldenbourg Wissenschaftsverlag, 2009. On the Western world as a whole, see, e.g., T. Judt, *Postwar: A History of Europe Since 1945*, London: Penguin, 2005; and A. Glyn, *Capitalism Unleashed: Finance Globalization and Welfare*, Oxford: Oxford University Press, 2006; and the Trilateral Commission report on the 'governability' of the democracies: M. Crozier et al., *The Crisis of Democracy: Report on the Governability of Democracies to the Trilateral Commission*, New York: New York University Press, 1975.

2   J. Ruggie, 'International Regimes, Transactions and Change: Embedded Liberalism in the Postwar Economic Order', *International Organization*, vol. 36/2, 1982, pp. 379–99.

inspired by Marxism in various ways, were better placed than others to gain intuitive access to the political and economic drama of the times. Yet their attempts to grasp the distortions of the time – from the strike waves of 1968[3] to the first so-called oil crisis – within the broader historical context of modern capitalist development were soon all but forgotten, and so too were the practical ambitions invariably associated with crisis theory as critical theory. Too many surprising things had happened. The theory of 'late capitalism'[4] had tried to redefine the tensions and fractures in the political economy of the time. But the subsequent development of these, including their apparent resolution, eluded its theoretical grasp. One problem seems to have been that it essentially took over the characterization of the 'golden years' of post-war capitalism as a period of joint technocratic management by governments and large corporations, based upon and suited for the maintenance of stable growth and the eventual elimination of systemic crisis tendencies. What appeared critical to them was not the technical governability of modern capitalism but its social and cultural *legitimation*. Underestimating capital as a political actor and a strategic social force, while at the same time overestimating the capacity of government policy to plan and to act, they thus replaced economic theory with theories of the state and democracy; the penalty they paid was to forgo a key part of Marx's legacy.

The crisis theory of the period around 1968 was partly or totally unprepared for three main developments. The first was that capitalism soon began, with astonishing success, its reversal to 'self-regulated markets', in the course of the neoliberal quest to revive the dynamic of capitalist accumulation through all manner of deregulation, privatization and market expansion. Anyone who experienced this at

---

3   C. Crouch and A. Pizzorno, *The Resurgence of Class Conflict in Western Europe Since 1968*, 2 vols, London: Macmillan, 1978.

4   J. Habermas, *Legitimation Crisis*, Boston: Beacon Press, 1975; J. Habermas, *Zur Rekonstruktion des Historischen Materialismus*, Frankfurt/Main: Suhrkamp, 1975; C. Offe, 'Structural Problems of the Capitalist State', in Klaus Von Beyme (ed.), *German Political Studies*, vol. 1., London: Sage, 1974, pp. 31–54; C. Offe, *Berufsbildungsreform: Eine Fallstudie über Reformpolitik*, Frankfurt/Main: Suhrkamp, 1975.

close quarters in the 1980s and 1990s soon ran into difficulties with the concept of late capitalism.⁵ The same was true, second, of predictions of a legitimation and motivation crisis. Already the 1970s saw a high and fast-spreading cultural acceptance of market-adjusted and market-driven ways of life, as expressed in particular in the eager demand of women for 'alienated' wage-labour or in the growth of the consumer society beyond all expectations.⁶ And, third, the economic crises accompanying the shift from postwar to neoliberal capitalism (especially the high inflation of the 1970s and the public debt of the 1980s) remained quite marginal to legitimation crisis theory⁷ – unlike for the Durkheim-inspired explanations of inflation as an expression of anomie resulting from distributional conflict,⁸ or for an author like James O'Connor, who as early as the late 1960s, albeit in the categories of an orthodox Marxist worldview, had predicted a 'fiscal crisis of the state' and an ensuing revolutionary-socialist alliance of unionized public employees and their clientele in the discarded surplus population.⁹

I would like to propose a historical narrative of capitalist development since the 1970s that links what I consider the revolt of capital against the postwar mixed economy with the broad popularity of expanding labour and consumer goods markets after the end

---

5 This is why it was gradually modified and stripped of its eschatological connotation. Looking back, Claus Offe thought it had been a 'terminological error' (C. Offe, 'Erneute Lektüre: Die "Strukturprobleme" nach 33 Jahren', in Jens Borchert et al. [eds], *Strukturprobleme des kapitalistischen Staates. Veränderte Neuausgabe*, Frankfurt/Main: Campus, 2006, pp. 181–96), especially once there appeared to be no alternative to capitalism after 1989 and the only question seemed to be how to regulate rather than how to overcome it.

6 W. Streeck, 'Citizens as Customers: Considerations on the New Politics of Consumption', *New Left Review*, vol. 76, July–August 2012.

7 The reason for this was probably that the economic crises were felt less strongly in Germany, where the theory of a legitimation crisis originated. One thinks of the government rhetoric concerning the 'German model' in the 1970s and 1980s.

8 J. Goldthorpe, 'The Current Inflation: Towards a Sociological Account', in Fred Hirsch et al. (eds), *The Political Economy of Inflation*, Cambridge, MA: Harvard University Press, 1978, pp. 186–216.

9 J. O'Connor, 'Inflation, Fiscal Crisis, and the American Working Class', *Socialist Revolution*, vol. 2/2, 1972, pp. 9–46; J. O'Connor, *The Fiscal Crisis of the State*, New York: St Martin's Press, 1973.

of the short 1970s, and with the sequence of economic crisis phenomena from then until today (which has come to a head in a triple crisis of banking, public finances and economic growth). My account sees the 'unleashing'[10] of global capitalism in the last third of the twentieth century as a successful resistance on the part of those who own and dispose of capital – the 'profit-dependent' class – against the multiple constraints that post-1945 capitalism had had to endure in order to become politically acceptable again under the conditions of system competition. I explain this success, and the wholly unexpected revitalization of the capitalist system as a market economy, by reference *inter alia* to government policies that bought time for the existing economic and social order. This they achieved by generating mass allegiance to the neoliberal social project dressed up as a consumption project, first through inflation of the money supply, then through an accumulation of public debt, and finally through lavish credit to private households – something the theory of late capitalism could never have imagined. It is true that, after a time, each of these strategies burned itself out, in ways familiar to neo-Marxist crisis theory, in that they began to undermine the functioning of the capitalist economy, which requires expectations of a 'just return' to be privileged over all others. Legitimation problems therefore arose time and again, though not among the masses but among capital, in the shape of accumulation crises, which in turn posed dangers for the legitimation of the system with its democratically empowered populations. As we shall see, these could be overcome only by continued economic liberalization and the immunization of policy against pressure from below, so as to win back the confidence of 'the markets' in the system.

With hindsight, the crisis history of late capitalism since the 1970s appears as an unfolding of the old fundamental tension between capitalism and democracy – a gradual process that broke up the forced marriage arranged between the two after the Second World War. In so far as the legitimation problems of democratic capitalism turned into

---

10   Glyn, *Capitalism Unleashed.*

accumulation problems, their solution called for a progressive emancipation of the capitalist economy from democratic intervention. The securing of a mass base for modern capitalism thus shifted from the sphere of politics to the market, understood as a mechanism for the production of *greed and fear*,[11] in a context of increasing insulation of the economy from mass democracy. I shall describe this as the transformation of the Keynesian political-economic institutional system of postwar capitalism into a neo-Hayekian economic regime.

My conclusion will be that, unlike the 1970s, we may now really be near the end of the postwar political–economic formation – an end which, albeit in a different way, was foretold and even wished for in the crisis theories of 'late capitalism'. What I feel sure about is that the clock is ticking for democracy as we have come to know it, as it is about to be sterilized as redistributive mass democracy and reduced to a combination of the rule of law and public entertainment. *This splitting of democracy from capitalism through the splitting of the economy from democracy* – a process of de-democratization of capitalism through the de-economization of democracy – has come a long way since the crisis of 2008, in Europe just as elsewhere.

It must remain an open question, however, whether the clock is also ticking for capitalism. Institutionalized expectations in a transformed democracy under neoliberalism to make do with the justice of the market are evidently by no means incompatible with capitalism. But, despite all the efforts at re-education, diffuse expectations of social justice still present in sections of the population may resist channelling into laissez-faire market democracy and even provide an impetus for anarchistic protest movements. Such a possibility was indeed repeatedly considered in the old crisis theories. It is not clear, though, that protests of that kind are a threat to the capitalist 'two-thirds society' looming on the horizon or to global 'plutonomy';[12]

---

11 According to the self-understanding of finance capitalism, greed and fear are the decisive behavioural motives in stock markets and in the capitalist economy as a whole (H. Shefrin, *Beyond Greed and Fear: Understanding Behavioral Finance and the Psychology of Investing*, Oxford: Oxford University Press, 2002).

12 The Citibank research department developed this as a positive concept, to

various techniques for managing an abandoned underclass, developed and tested in the United States, appear thoroughly exportable also to Europe. More critical could be the question of whether, if monetary doping with its potentially dangerous side effects has to be abandoned at some point, other growth drugs will be available to keep capital accumulation under way in the rich countries of the world. On this we can only speculate – as I do in the concluding remarks of this book.

A NEW TYPE OF CRISIS

Capitalism in the rich democratic countries has for several years now been in the throes of a threefold crisis, with no end in sight: a *banking crisis*, a crisis of *public finances*, and a crisis of the '*real economy*'. No one foresaw this unprecedented coincidence – not in the 1970s, but also not in the 1990s. In Germany, because of special conditions[13] that had arisen more or less by chance and seem rather exotic to the outside world, the crisis hardly registered with people for years, and there was a tendency to warn against 'hysteria'. In most of the other rich democracies, however, including the United States, the crisis cut deep into the lives of whole generations and by 2012 was in the process of turning the conditions of social existence upside down.

---

dispel fears among the select customers of the bank's private banking department that their future prosperity would depend, as in the Keynesian world, on the material welfare of the broad masses (Citigroup Research, *Plutonomy: Buying Luxury, Explaining Global Imbalances*, 16 October 2005; Citigroup Research, *Revisiting Plutonomy: The Rich Getting Richer*, 5 March 2006).

13   Against the advice of any number of people who claimed to know better, Germany had defended its industrial base and moved only slowly, in the 1980s and 1990s, in the direction of an American or British-style 'service society'. After 2008 it was therefore able to continue exporting goods such as luxury cars and machinery that no one else could offer at the same quality level, profiting from the high growth-rates in China and the ever more unequal distribution of income in the crisis-torn United States. Moreover, the currency was fixed across the eurozone, with an exchange-rate lower than that of a purely German currency would have been. The European financial and fiscal crisis then put even greater pressure on the euro exchange rate.

1) The *banking crisis* stems from the fact that, in the financialized capitalism of the Western world, too many banks had extended too much credit, both public and private, and that an unexpectedly large part of this suddenly turned bad. Since no bank can be sure that the bank with which it does business will not collapse overnight, banks are no longer willing to lend to one another.[14] There also is the possibility that customers may feel compelled at any moment to start a run on banks and withdraw their deposits for fear they may otherwise lose them. Furthermore, since regulatory authorities expect banks to increase their capital reserves in proportion to the sums owed them, so as to reduce their risk exposure, the banks must cut back on their lending. It would help if states took over the bad loans, gave unlimited deposit protection and recapitalized the banks. The sums required for such a rescue operation could well prove astronomical, however, and governments are already overburdened with debt. At the same time, it might be as expensive, or even more expensive, if individual banks collapsed and others were dragged down with them. Here too, though – and this is the core of the problem – no more than guesses are possible.

2) The *fiscal crisis* is the result of budget deficits and rising levels of government debt, which go back to the 1970s (Fig 1.1),[15] as well as

---

14   In the nature of things, there can be no exact statistical data on the scale of a bank crisis. Even the bank that issued certain loans cannot be sure which of them are bad, and if it does know it must try to keep it secret (unless it has the option of shifting worthless securities into a state-supported 'bad bank'). The same applies to the mutual exposure of national banking systems, about which governments and international organizations can only speculate. The published results of 'stress tests' conducted by national or international authorities are inherently unreliable, because the announcement of problems inevitably makes it more likely that they will develop into crises. Stress tests are therefore usually designed in such a way as to produce reassuring results – a good example is the (until recently) inconspicuous European findings on the state of the Spanish banks.

15   Fig. 1.1 shows the build-up of debt over four decades, for the OECD as a whole and for seven selected OECD countries, each representing a specific group of countries: the USA and UK, English-speaking democracies with a high degree of financialization; Sweden, the Scandinavian democracies; Germany and France, large continental European countries; Italy, a Mediterranean country; and Japan, a developed Asian industrial society. One is struck by the low variance, especially if one disregards Japan and its extremely high levels of new debt since the end of the property bubble in the late 1980s.

FIGURE I.I

Public debt as percentage of national product: OECD average

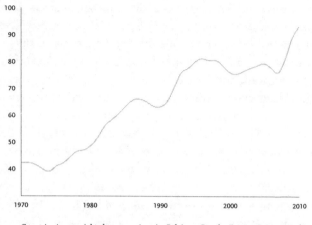

Countries in unweighted average: Austria, Belgium, Canada, France, Germany, Italy, Netherlands, Norway, Sweden, UK, USA

Public debt as percentage of national product: seven countries

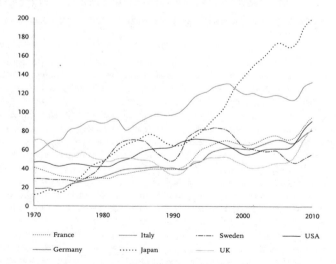

| ·········· France | ———— Italy | —·—·— Sweden | ———— USA |
| ———— Germany | ······ Japan | ·········· UK | |

Source: OECD Economic Outlook: Statistics and Projections

the borrowing required since 2008 to save both the finance industry (through the recapitalization of financial institutions and the acquisition of worthless debt securities) and the real economy (through fiscal stimuli). The increased risk of government insolvency in a number of countries is reflected in the higher costs of old and new debt. To regain the 'confidence' of 'the markets', governments impose harsh austerity measures on themselves and their citizens, with mutual supervision within the European Union, going as far as a general ban on new borrowing. That does not help to alleviate the banking crisis, or *a fortiori* the recession in the real economy. It is even debatable whether austerity reduces the debt burden, since it not only fails to promote growth but probably has a negative impact on it. And growth is at least as important as balanced budgets in lowering the national debt.

3) Finally, the *crisis of the real economy* manifest in high unemployment and stagnation (Fig. 1.2)[16] partly stems from the fact that firms and consumers have difficulty in obtaining bank loans – because many of them are already deep in debt and the banks are risk-averse and short of capital – while governments have to curb their expenditure or, if it can no longer be avoided, raise taxes. Economic stagnation thus reinforces the fiscal crisis and, via resulting defaults, the crisis of the banking sector.

It is clear that the three crises are closely interlinked: the first with the second through *money*; the first with the third through *credit*; and the second with the third through *government spending and revenue*. They continually reinforce one another, although their scale, urgency and interdependence vary from country to country. At the same time, multiple interactions occur between countries: failed banks in one

---

16 A detailed discussion of the impact of the financial and fiscal crisis on the real economy would require a separate monograph and would also be beyond my competence. For the five years after 2007, the last before the crisis, Fig. 1.2 shows economic stagnation or even a decline in GNP for all the selected countries, with the possible exception of Germany and Sweden. The situation is particularly dramatic in the four European crisis countries (Greece, Ireland, Portugal and Spain), where the recession was accompanied by falling employment and rising unemployment. The picture is quite similar in Britain and, particularly, the United States.

country may drag down banks in others; a general rise in interest rates on government bonds, triggered by one country's insolvency, may ruin the public finances of many other countries; national booms and busts have international repercussions, and so on. In Europe, as we shall see, the institutional system of monetary union imparts a special shape and dynamic to these interactions.

By the summer of 2012 the present crisis of the capitalist democracies had lasted more than four years. Its appearance has continuously changed as new countries and new combinations of problems come to the fore. No one knows what will happen next; the issues change from month to month, sometimes from week to week, but nearly all return at some point or another. The policy field is mined with an array of unpredictable side effects, as complex as anything that deserves to be called such. Whatever governments do to solve a problem sooner or later produces another; that which ends one crisis makes the others worse; for every hydra head that is lopped off, two more grow in its place. Too many things have to be tackled at once; short-term fixes get in the way of long-term solutions; long-term solutions are not even attempted because short-term problems take priority; holes keep appearing that can be plugged only by making new holes elsewhere. Never since the Second World War have the governments of the capitalist West looked so clueless; never behind the façades of equanimity and tried political craftsmanship have there been so many indications of blind panic.

TWO SURPRISES FOR CRISIS THEORY

Banks and finance markets do not feature in the neo-Marxist crisis theories that were developed in Frankfurt in the years around 1968.[17] No wonder – for no one then foresaw the 'financialization' of modern capitalism. But nor do those theories speak of economic cycles, growth

---

17   In the following, in summarizing these theories, I concentrate on what they have in common rather than on their undeniable differences. The latter seem trivial in comparison with the actual developments in later years, and that is the only difference that concerns me here.

FIGURE I.2. *Effects of the 2008 crisis on the real economy*

		2005	2006	2007	2008	2009	2010	2011
Germany	GDP	100.0	103.9	107.4	108.3	102.8	106.4	109.7
	employment	65.5	67.2	69.0	70.1	70.3	71.1	72.5
	unemployment	11.2	10.3	8.7	7.5	7.7	7.1	5.9
France	GDP	100.0	102.7	105.0	104.7	102.0	103.4	105.2
	employment	63.7	63.6	64.3	64.9	64.0	63.8	63.8
	unemployment	8.9	8.8	8.0	7.4	9.1	9.4	9.3
Italy	GDP	100.0	102.3	103.9	102.6	97.0	98.7	99.2
	employment	57.6	58.4	58.7	58.8	57.5	56.9	57.0
	unemployment	7.7	6.8	6.1	6.7	7.8	8.4	8.4
Japan	GDP	100.0	101.7	103.9	102.8	97.1	101.4	100.7
	employment	69.4	70.1	70.9	71.1	70.5	70.6	71.2
	unemployment	4.4	4.1	3.8	4.0	5.1	5.1	4.6
Sweden	GDP	100.0	104.6	108.1	107.3	102.0	107.9	112.2
	employment	72.3	73.1	74.2	74.3	72.2	72.7	74.1
	unemployment	7.5	7.1	6.2	6.2	8.3	8.4	7.5
UK	GDP	100.0	102.6	106.2	105.0	100.4	102.5	103.2
	employment	71.8	71.6	71.5	71.5	69.9	69.5	69.5
	unemployment	4.8	5.4	5.3	5.6	7.6	7.8	8.0
USA	GDP	100.0	102.7	104.6	104.3	100.6	103.7	105.5
	employment	71.5	72.0	71.8	70.9	67.6	66.7	66.6
	unemployment	5.1	4.6	4.6	5.8	9.3	9.6	9.0
Greece	GDP	100.0	105.5	108.7	108.5	105.0	101.3	94.3
	employment	60.1	61.0	61.4	61.9	61.2	59.6	55.6
	unemployment	9.9	8.9	8.3	7.7	9.5	12.5	16.0
Spain	GDP	100.0	104.1	107.7	108.7	104.6	104.5	105.3
	employment	64.3	65.7	66.6	65.3	60.6	59.4	58.5
	unemployment	9.2	8.5	8.3	11.3	18.0	20.1	20.3
Portugal	GDP	100.0	101.4	103.8	103.8	100.8	102.2	100.6
	employment	67.5	67.9	67.8	68.2	66.3	65.6	64.2
	unemployment	7.7	7.7	8.0	7.6	9.5	10.8	11.7
Ireland	GDP	100.0	105.3	110.8	107.5	100.0	99.5	100.2
	employment	67.5	68.5	69.2	68.1	62.5	60.4	59.6
	unemployment	4.8	4.7	4.7	5.8	12.2	13.9	14.6

Sources: OECD (2012), 'Public expenditure on active labour market policies', *Employment and Labour Markets: Key Tables from OECD Economic Outlook: Statistics and Projections*, No. 9

crises, limits to growth, underconsumption or overproduction. The reason may be that their authors wanted to mark their distance from the economic determinism that many Marxist traditions, especially the Soviet orthodoxy, read into Marx's theory of capitalism. Probably more important, however, was a zeitgeist that stretched surprisingly far into the Left: the idea of the capitalist economy having been turned into a prosperity machine which, with the help of the Keynesian toolkit, could be kept stable and crisis-free through orderly cooperation between governments and large corporations. The material reproduction of capitalist industrial society thus seemed assured, crisis tendencies overcome, and the 'pauperization' of the working class predicted by orthodoxy was no longer visible even on the most distant horizon.

No doubt this reflected the experience of two decades of rapid and nearly uninterrupted growth – and, as far as Germany was concerned, the overcoming in 1966 of what could scarcely be called a crisis, by means of the 'modern', anti-cyclical economic policy of the Christian Democrat (CDU)/Social Democrat (SPD) 'Great Coalition'. In the view of many at the time, the Bundesrepublik had then finally moved beyond its 'ordoliberal' misconceptions and joined the 'mixed economies' of the capitalist West, with their public enterprises, planning authorities, industrial branch councils, regional development boards, negotiated incomes policy, and so on, as detailed in Andrew Shonfield's *Modern Capitalism* (1965) and popularized in Germany by the economics expert of the SPD, Karl Schiller. The same *Steuerungsoptimismus* – a term that first came into circulation when its referent had already disappeared – prevailed in the United States under Kennedy and Johnson, whose interventionist economic advisers had been trained in the school of Keynesianism. Planning was anything but anathema, and even the possibility of convergence between capitalism and communism was a legitimate theme of political-economic debate: the capitalist market needed more planning and communist planning more market, so that capitalism and communism might be able to meet halfway.[18] In contem-

---

18   Kerr, *Industrialism and Industrial Man.*

porary theories, the economy as mechanism replaced capital as class; 'technology and science as ideology'[19] occupied a space previously reserved for power and interests. The belief that the economy had become essentially a technical matter was no less widespread among sociologists than among economists. Amitai Etzioni's *The Active Society* (1968) – probably the most ambitious attempt to define the conditions under which modern democratic societies would freely choose their path of development and put their choice into practice – may serve as one of many possible examples: it mentions the economy only once in its 666 pages, and then only to state that 'Western nations' could have 'confidence in their capacity to control societal processes with the wide use of Keynesian and other controls for preventing wild inflations and deep depressions and for spurring economic growth.'[20]

As far as Frankfurt was concerned, the reinterpretation of modern capitalism as a system of technocratic economic administration – a new kind of 'state capitalism' – was the work of Friedrich Pollock, a member of the Institut für Sozialforschung both before and after its emigration, who functioned as its economic expert until his death in 1970. In his view, capitalism had become thoroughly state-planned in the course of its development, 'so that nothing essential was left to the laws of the market or other "economic laws"'.[21] Even after the war and the end of fascism and the war economy, Pollock found no reason to change his judgement: the development of large corporations and ever more sophisticated instruments of state planning meant that the age of laissez-faire was well and truly over, and that advanced capitalism had mutated into a politically regulated and essentially crisis-free economic machinery. Under fascism and state socialism as well as the New Deal, the three post-capitalist

19   J. Habermas, *Technik und Wissenschaft als Ideologie*, Frankfurt/Main: Suhrkamp, 1969.

20   A. Etzioni, *The Active Society*, New York: The Free Press, 1968, p. 10. In the 1980s, Etzioni did try to fill this gap with a social science theory of the economy and economic action (A. Etzioni, *The Moral Dimension: Toward a New Economics*, New York: The Free Press, 1988).

21   F. Pollock, 'State Capitalism: Its Possibilities and Limitations' [1941], in Stephen Eric Bronner and Douglas MacKay Kellner (eds), *Critical Theory and Society: A Reader*, London: Routledge, 1989, p. 100.

economic systems, the primacy of politics had succeeded the old primacy of economics and had thereby overcome the crisis tendencies inherent in the original, chaotically disorganized, competitive form of capitalism. For Adorno and Horkheimer, according to Helmut Dubiel in his introduction to a collection of Pollock's essays, 'Pollock's theory of state capitalism [was] the detailed account of a social order in which state bureaucracies have gained such a hold over the economic process that one may speak of a primacy of politics over economics under non-socialist conditions.' And further: 'Pollock's thesis of a new kind of domination that was once more purely political, no longer mediated by economics, offered . . . Horkheimer and Adorno the political-economic justification to regard political economy as no longer a top priority.'[22]

Although the Frankfurt crisis theories of the 1970s expected the economic collapse of capitalism as little as did Keynesian economists in the United States, they were still crisis theories, and critical theories to boot. The capitalist line of fracture, however, was no longer its economy but its polity and society: located in the field of democracy rather than the economy, of labour rather than capital, of social integration rather than system integration.[23] Rather than the production of surplus-value – its 'contradictions', it was thought, had become controllable – the problem was the legitimacy of capitalism as a social system; not whether capital, converted into the economy of the society, would be able to keep society supplied, but whether what it was able to supply

---

22   In F. Pollock, *Stadien des Kapitalismus*, Munich: Beck, 1975, pp. 18f. This is not contradicted by the fact that Adorno introduced 'late capitalism' into social theory as a 'Frankfurt School' concept, using it in the title he chose for the German Sociological Congress in 1968 and in his opening report 'Late Capitalism or Industrial Society?' (T. Adorno, 'Late Capitalism or Industrial Society?', in Volker Merja et al., *Modern German Sociology*, New York: Columbia University Press, 1987). Adorno distinguished 'late capitalism' from what he called 'liberal capitalism', which, following Pollock, he regarded as a historically prior form of capitalism now superseded by state intervention and organization. Late capitalism was thus essentially identical with what others had been calling 'organized capitalism'. The possibility of a looming crisis of organized (late) capitalism, or of a return to its liberal past in the shape of a neoliberal future, does not appear anywhere in Adorno's writings.

23   D. Lockwood, 'Social Integration and System Integration', in George K. Zollschan et al. (eds), *Explorations in Social Change*, London: Houghton Mifflin, 1964, pp. 244–57.

would be enough to make its recipients continue playing the game. Thus, for the crisis theories of the 1960s and 1970s, the impending crisis of capitalism was one not of *production* but of *legitimation*. With hindsight and from afar, the intuitions of the time are reminiscent of concepts like Maslow's hierarchy of needs:[24] once material existence is assured, non-materialist demands such as those for self-fulfilment, emancipation, recognition or authentic community will be released and demand to be satisfied.[25] The assumption was that, under the new historical conditions of assured prosperity, neither the repressive discipline required by capitalism as a social organization nor the coercive regime of alienated wage-labour could in the long run continue to be enforced. With the end of scarcity made possible by the development of the productive forces, it would be less and less possible to reproduce capitalist domination, as institutionalized for example in superfluous workplace hierarchies and pay differentials geared to an economically obsolete performance principle.[26] Worker

---

24 A. Maslow, 'A Theory of Human Motivation', *Psychological Review*, vol. 50/4, 1943, pp. 370–96.

25 There also seems to be an affinity with theories such as Daniel Bell's on the cultural contradictions of capitalism (D. Bell, *The Cultural Contradictions of Capitalism*, New York: Basic Books, 1976). Bell, too, assumed that the development of capitalism would bring forth motives and needs incompatible with its social organization – except that, as a conservative, he tended to regard such new cultural orientations as decadent or hedonistic, whereas in the Frankfurt crisis theories they appeared as progressive or emancipatory, furthering the development of humanity. Both Bell and the Frankfurt theorists, however, believed that capitalist societies would become increasingly unmanageable: either because people were, so to speak, outgrowing them; or because they had lost their minds and needed to be brought back within the bounds of the possible. In either case what was seen to be coming was an overstretching of the democratic state, and this either had to be parried through institutional reforms (so Crozier et al., *The Crisis of Democracy* [the Trilateral Commission report]) or else led, by the exercise of democracy, to the incorporation of ever more elements into the political-economic system that were alien to capitalism and and would in the end collectively overcome it. On the overlaps between theories of late capitalism and ungovernability, see A. Schäfer, 'Krisentheorien der Demokratie: Unregierbarkeit, Spätkapitalismus und Postdemokratie', *Der modern Staat*, vol. 2/1, 2009, pp. 159–83.

26 In his dissertation of 1967, Claus Offe wrote: 'The concept of a social order based on performance is actually becoming *senseless* . . . in view of the fact that advanced forms of industrial work make irrelevant the category of individual capacities manifested in competition' (C. Offe, *Leistungsprinzip und industrielle Arbeit: Mechanismen der*

participation and democracy, emancipation in and even from work, were waiting to be discovered as possibilities and put into practice.[27] The commodification of human beings, and competition instead of solidarity, were outdated ways of life and would be increasingly recognized as such. Demands for the democratization of all areas of life and for political participation beyond the limits of existing institutions would grow into a rejection of capitalism as a society and explode from within an obsolete organization of work and life based on private property. The empirical research of the Frankfurt School in those years therefore concentrated mainly on the political consciousness of students and workers and on the potential of trade unions to become more than wage-machines. Markets, capital and capitalists hardly figured, however, and democratic theory and communication theory took the place of political economy.

Actually, of couse, it was not the masses that refused allegiance to postwar capitalism and thereby put an end to it, but rather capital in the shape of its organizations, its organizers and its owners. As to the legitimacy of the capitalist wage-and-consumption society in the view of large parts of the population – in Helmut Kohl's words, 'ordinary citizens up and down the country' – it experienced an upturn in the decades after the long late 1960s that the theorists of late capitalism had never expected in their worst nightmares. Whereas the struggle against 'consumption terror' still had some resonance among students in 1968, the great majority of the generation that had fought the marketization of life under capitalism actively took part in the unprecedented wave of consumerism and commercialism that began shortly afterwards.[28] Markets for goods such as cars, clothing, cosmetics, food and consumer electronics, and for services such as body care, tourism or entertainment, expanded with a dynamism never seen before and

---

Statusverteilung in Arbeitsorganisationen der industriellen 'Leistungsgesellschaft', Frankfurt/Main: Europäische Verlagsanstalt, 1970, p. 166; emphasis in the original). The book prefigures later arguments for a student wage and a guaranteed basic income.

27   A. Gorz, *Strategy for Labor*, Boston: Beacon Press, 2000 [1967]; A. Gorz, *Critique de la division du travail*, Paris: Galilée, 1973.

28   Streeck, 'Citizens as Customers'.

became the foremost engines of capitalist growth. Ever faster process and product innovations, made possible by the rapid spread of micro-electronics, shortened the life-cycle of more and more consumer goods and allowed them to be geared to ever more narrowly defined groups of customers.[29] At the same time, the money economy tirelessly conquered new spheres of social existence that had previously been reserves of unpaid activity, opening them up for the production and absorption of surplus-value. One example among many was sport, which in the 1980s became a global industry worth billions of dollars.

Wage-labour too – or, in the language of 1968, wage-dependence – underwent a rehabilitation not foreseen by legitimation crisis theories. Beginning in the 1970s, women throughout the Western world poured into labour markets, and what had been branded shortly before as historically obsolete wage-slavery was now experienced as liberation from unpaid household drudgery.[30] Despite the generally lower pay, the popularity of female employment grew uninterruptedly in the following decades. In fact, women often became allies of the employers seeking labour-market deregulation, to allow 'outsiders' to undercut (male) 'insiders'. The growth in female employment was also closely bound up with simultaneous changes in family structure: the divorce rate increased and marriage became less common, as did children, while more children found themselves in unstable family relations, which further augmented the female labour supply.[31]

In the subsequent period, paid employment became the main vehicle of social integration and recognition for women as well. To be a 'housewife' is today a stigma, and colloquially the word 'work' has become synonymous with full-time employment paid market rates. Women in particular gain social prestige by combining *Kinder und*

---

29 Overwhelmed by the force with which reality sped away from the ascetic imagery of Critical Theory, sociologists generally stopped referring to 'false needs' or 'false consciousness' – concepts that had been highly popular a short time before.

30 In this respect, the role of immigrants – whose numbers steadily increased in the 1970s – was similar to that of women.

31 W. Streeck, *Flexible Employment, Flexible Families, and the Socialization of Reproduction*, MPIfG Discussion Paper No. 09/13, Cologne: Max-Planck-Institut für Gesellschaftsforschung, 2009.

Karriere (children and a career), even if the 'career' is that of a super-market cashier. Adorno, far more pessimistic than the legitimation crisis theorists, would have seen in this – as in the consumption fever of the past three to four decades – that very 'sense of well-being in aliena-tion' (*Wohlgefühl in der Entfremdung*) which he early on expected the 'culture industry' to be capable of providing. Neo-Protestantism, whose adherents are proud of their lives of constant exhaustion minutely structured around 'the compatibility of job and family',[32] and the human capital capitalism of self-commodification in contemporary labour markets, with its internalization of returns-to-education calculations in the life plans of whole generations, apparently have put an end to the 'crisis of wage-labour' and of the achievement principle, as has the 'new spirit of capitalism'[33] which, by drawing on newly created spaces of creativity and autonomy at the workplace, has deepened corporate inte-gration and served as a vehicle for personal identification with the aims of profit extraction.[34]

Whereas the loyalty of workers and consumers to postwar capital-ism held steady, the same was by no means true on the side of capital. The problem of the Frankfurt crisis theories of the 1970s was that they did not think capital capable of any strategic purpose, because they treated it as an apparatus rather than an agency, as means of production rather than a class.[35] So they had to make their calculations without it. Even for Schumpeter, not to speak of Marx, 'capital' had been a constant

---

32   J. Schor, *The Overworked American: The Unexpected Decline of Leisure*, New York: Basic Books, 1992.

33   L. Boltanski and E. Chiapello, *The New Spirit of Capitalism*, London: Verso, 2005.

34   The investment of middle-class families in school grades and university degrees, beginning with the now emblematic Chinese lessons at kindergarten, shows how strong the belief is once again in achievement as a mechanism of status and consumption-opportunity allocation.

35   This had the advantage that difficult questions of class theory could be avoided: for example, the status of managers in contrast to owners, the differences between small and large capital, the role of enterprises as organizations vis-à-vis entrepreneurs as persons, the classification of the many new middle strata, or the class position of politicians and civil servants. On the numerous problems of sociological class theory, see E. Wright, *Classes*, London: Verso, 1985. Nevertheless, a theory of capitalism in which capital is neither active nor capable of action remains inevitably anaemic.

trouble spot in modern economic society: the source of 'creative destruction'[36] until the socialism of bureaucracy would finally lay it to rest. That was how Weber saw and foresaw it too, and perhaps the peculiar lifelessness of capital in the theory of legitimation crisis goes partly back to him. So there was no way of dealing with what eventually happened in the decades after the end of the long 1960s: that is, when capital proved to be a player instead of a plaything, a predator instead of a working animal, with an urgent need to break free from the cage-like institutional framework of the post-1945 'social market economy'.

The neo-Marxist crisis theories developed in Frankfurt four decades ago were superior to other theories of the time in recognizing the fragility of social capitalism. But they misunderstood its causes, and hence the direction and dynamic of the impending historical change. Their approach ruled out the possibility that capital, not labour, would cancel the legitimacy of the democratic capitalism that had taken shape in the *trente glorieuses*.[37] In reality, the history of capitalism after the 1970s, including the subsequent economic crises, is a history of capital's escape from the system of social regulation imposed on it against its will after 1945. Its beginning was marked, in and around 1968, by a series of worker revolts that confronted employers in the mature industrial societies with a new generation of workers who took for granted the growth-rates and social advances of postwar reconstruction and the political promises of the founding years of democratic capitalism. These promises capitalism was neither able nor willing to fulfil forever.

In subsequent years, the capitalist elites and their political allies looked for ways to extricate themselves from the obligations that they had had to incur for the sake of social peace and which, broadly speaking, they had been able to meet during the reconstruction phase. New product strategies to ward off market saturation, a growing

---

36   J. Schumpeter, *The Theory of Economic Development*, London: Transaction, 1980 [1912].

37   The French term for the (approximately) thirty years of economic progress after the Second World War, corresponding to the English 'golden age'. In Germany the corresponding reference is to the years of the 'economic miracle'.

labour surplus resulting from changes in the social structure, and not least the internationalization of markets and production systems, gradually opened up ways for firms to shake off the social policies and collective bargaining regimes that after 1968 threatened to subject them to a long-term profit squeeze.[38] With time, this turned into an enduring liberalization process that brought about the powerful, wide-scale return of self-regulating markets, not anticipated in any theory and without precedent in the political economy of modern capitalism. Frankfurt crisis theory was not prepared for this: for a state which, to rid itself of social expectations it could no longer satisfy, deregulated and liberalized the capitalism it was supposed to place in the service of society; and for a capitalism which found its politically organized freedom from crises too constrictive.[39] Liberalization, as control technology, relief of government from social responsibilities and liberation of capital at the same time, in fact progressed only slowly, especially so long as memories of 1968 remained alive, and was accompanied by numerous political and economic disruptions, until it reached its highest point so far in the present crisis of public finances and the world financial system.

THE OTHER LEGITIMATION CRISIS AND
THE END OF THE POSTWAR PEACE

In view of the four decades that have passed since the heyday of crisis theory, I would like to propose a broader concept of legitimation crisis that contains not two players (the state and its citizens) but

---

38   On the dramatic scale of the profit squeeze in the years from 1965 to the nadir of 1980 (before temporary relief came in the 1990s, if only because employers managed effectively to appropriate all the productivity gains), see R. Brenner, *The Economics of Global Turbulence: The Advanced Capitalist Economies from Long Boom to Long Downturn*, London: Verso, 2006.

39   Nor did it see the potential involved in the historical expansion and stretching of what it could only regard as consumerist pseudo-satisfactions to secure the acquisitive and productive motivations on which capitalism depends – as a deflection of demands for collective political progress onto the satisfaction of individual economic wants by the booming world of commodities.

three: the state, capital and wage-earners.[40] Expectations in relation to which the political-economic system must legitimate itself exist not only among the population but also on the side of capital-as-actor (no longer just as machinery) – or, more precisely, among the profit-dependent owners and managers of capital. In fact, since this is a capitalist system, their expectations ought to be more important for its stability than those of the *capital-dependent* population; only if the former are satisfied can the latter too be satisfied, while the reverse is not necessarily true. Contrary to neo-Marxist theories, a legitimation crisis may therefore also grow out of discontent on the part of 'capital' with democracy and its associated obligations – hence *without* a progressive, *system-transcending* evolution of the demands of society on economic and social life, such as many thought to lie ahead in the 1970s.

A legitimation crisis theory that starts with capital treats firms and their owners and managers as advantage-seeking profit maximizers rather than as prosperity machines, or functionaries obediently carrying out government economic policy. 'Capital' will appear in it as a self-willed and self-interested collective actor, strategic and capable of communication but only to a limited extent predictable, which may be dissatisfied and express itself accordingly. In a class theory modelled on classical political economy, who or what belongs to capital may be determined by its main form of income. Capital interests result from income dependence on returns on invested capital; capital income is residual income that owners or managers of capital obtain by seeking to maximize the yield from the invested capital at their disposal. In this sense, 'profit-dependent' interests stand face to face with the interests of the 'wage-dependent' who, disposing of labour-power rather than capital, supply it to owners of the latter at a contractually agreed price. That price – of labour-power as a commodity – is independent of the profit that may or may not be obtained

40   My view of economic crises as crises of political confidence, and of declining investment as a communication of discontent on the part of owners and managers of capital, closely follows Michal Kalecki's theory of political business cycles (e.g. M. Kalecki, 'Political Aspects of Full Employment', *Political Quarterly*, vol. 14/4, 1943, pp. 322–31).

from its deployment. In the psychologistic worldview of labour economics, the distinction between residual capital income and contractually fixed labour income – between profits and wages – is associated with different 'risk propensities': 'risk-averse' individuals prefer to be workers, with a low but secure *labour* income, while the more 'risk-tolerant' become entrepreneurs, with a less secure but potentially high *capital* income. Whereas recipients of residual income seek the highest possible yield on their capital investment, earners of fixed income try to keep as low as possible the input required of them.[41] Distribution conflicts arise from the fact that, other things being equal, higher residual income for the profit-dependent entails lower wages for the wage-dependent, and vice versa.[42]

For a theory of political economy in which capital is an actor and not just machinery, the seemingly technical 'functioning' of the 'economy' – above all, growth and full employment – is in reality a political matter. Here lies the difference from a technocratic concept of crisis, such as we find in the years after the Second World War and also in Pollock's work and Frankfurt social theory. Both growth and full employment depend on the willingness of capital owners to invest, and that in turn depends on their aspirations for an 'adequate' rate of return, as well as on their general assessment of the security and stability of the capitalist economic order. The absence of economic crises means that

---

41   Hence it is that employers and economists axiomatically suspect workers of 'shirking' – and insist that, because of their 'opportunism with guile', they need to be kept under effective supervision or 'monitoring'.

42   Of course there is a grey area where the categories mix, today more than ever. In it we find various forms of payment by results, akin to piece-rates for manual industrial workers; small savers who rely on both wage and capital income; and the proceeds from so-called 'human capital', which may be regarded as income from both labour and capital. What matters here is the analytical distinction between the dynamic of capital accumulation geared to open-ended profit maximization and the traditionalism of a secure livelihood at a given, or predictably rising, level of income. Both economic cultures exist alongside each other in capitalism as different action orientations, represented by different social groups and institutions with conflicting, and partly overlapping, expectations and requirements (W. Streeck, 'Taking Capitalism Seriously: Towards an Institutional Approach to Contemporary Political Economy', *Socio-Economic Review*, vol. 9/1, 2011, pp. 137–67).

capital is content, while crises signal its discontent. Exactly what return on investment capital owners and managers demand is not set in stone; it varies with time and place. Investors may become more modest if they have no alternatives, or more demanding if their profits no longer seem enough in comparison with what they can obtain elsewhere. Above all, if they see their social environment as hostile and inclined to impose exaggerated obligations on them, they may 'lose confidence' and withhold their capital – for example, by developing a 'liquidity preference' – until conditions improve.

Economic crises in capitalism result from crises of confidence on the part of capital; they are not technical disturbances but *legitimation crises of a special kind*. Low growth and unemployment are results of 'investment strikes'[43] on the part of owners who could invest their capital but refuse to do so because they lack the necessary confidence. Under capitalism the capital of society is private property that its owners may in principle use or not use as they see fit. Nobody can oblige them to invest,[44] and determining when the profit-dependent class may be willing to put their capital to work is so difficult at this point that the latest economists give up their mathematics and turn to 'psychology' for an answer. Stimulating economic growth, then, involves negotiating something like an equilibrium between, on the one hand, the profit expectations of capital owners and the demands they make on society and, on the other hand, the wage and employ-ment expectations of wage-earners – a compromise that capital has to find sufficiently reasonable for it to keep engaging in the generation of prosperity. If this fails, and the insecurity and unsatisfied demands of capital make themselves felt as disturbances to 'the economy', a further, derivative legitimation crisis may ensue, this time among the wage-dependants for whom the technical functioning of the system,

---

43 This was a common term in the 1970s critiques of capitalism. The political idea was to make 'investment strikes' impossible through investment controls.

44 This is the problem with any government economic policy. 'You can lead a horse to water, but you can't make it drink' – as Karl Schiller, the Keynesian economist and SPD economic expert of the late 1960s and early 1970s, said of his efforts to revive the economy after the brief crisis of 1967.

especially its provision of growth and full employment, is the necessary condition for them to be at peace with it. *New* demands are not required for this, only non-fulfilment of the old ones.

In other words, capitalism presupposes a social contract in which the legitimate mutual expectations of capital and labour, of profit-dependants and wage-dependants, are more or less explicitly enshrined as a formal or informal economic constitution. Contrary to what economic theory and ideology would have us believe, capitalism is not a state of nature but a historical social order in need of institutionalization and legitimation: its concrete forms change with time and place and are in principle both susceptible to renegotiation and in danger of breaking down. In the 1970s, what the literature described as the political-economic postwar settlement of democratic capitalism – a social compact on the foundations of a re-established capitalism in a new form – began to unravel. After 1945, capitalism had found itself on the defensive worldwide; in all the countries of the emergent Western bloc, it had to make efforts to extend and renew its social franchise, in the face of a working class strengthened by war and the rivalry between two systems.[45] This could be achieved only through sizeable concessions that Keynesian theory had already envisaged and paved the way for: in the medium term, government intervention in the business cycle, and state planning to provide for growth, full employment, social redistribution and ever greater protection from the unpredictability of markets; in the long term, a gradual departure from capitalism in a world of permanently low interest rates and profit margins. Only under these conditions, in the service of politically defined social purposes, could a profit-oriented economic regime, after the end of the war economy, be rebuilt within a stable liberal democracy immune from fascist regression and Stalinist temptations; only then was it politically feasible to restore full property rights and managerial authority. Observance of the 'peace formula', as it was called in the theoretical discussion in Frankfurt, was negotiated and supervised by an interventionist state committed

---

45   One might speak of the need for a renewal of the capitalist *profit-hunting permit*.

to disciplining the market for planning and redistribution, a state which, on pain of losing its legitimacy, had to make sure that the social contract underlying the new capitalism was in fact kept. This political-economic peace settlement began to crumble in the 1970s. A synthetic account of this development should start with the weakening of growth in the second half of the 1960s, which suggested that the capitalist economy might not forever remain as able or willing to deliver the goods as it had been since the end of the war. Western governments, struggling to maintain social peace and political stability for as long as possible, experimented with new techniques of planning and steering the economy, while workers insisted more self-confidently than ever on their understanding of what had been agreed in the founding years of the system. Why should they continue to play along, respecting the rules of capitalism and allowing capital to make profits, if things were no longer getting better for themselves? Capital, for its part, had to fear a 'revolution of rising expectations' that it would no longer be able to satisfy, except at the price of a further decline in profitability and a conversion of the private economy, under political-electoral pressure, into a highly regulated and planned semi-public infrastructure.

All in all, the situation in the late 1960s began to resemble what Michal Kalecki had described, in a prescient article written in 1943, as the moment when the resistance of capital might sink the Keynesian model.[46] Kalecki's starting point was to ask what the employers of his time actually found objectionable in Keynesian economic policy, given that it promised to provide for constant growth of their businesses without cyclical fluctuations. His answer was that permanent full employment brought the danger that workers would become over-demanding once they had forgotten the insecurity and deprivation associated with unemployment. At that point discipline might break down at the workplace as well as in the political arena. This was why, in Kalecki's view, capital should have an interest in lasting structural unemployment, serving to warn employees of what they might

---

46   Kalecki, 'Political Aspects of Full Employment'.

face if their demands became excessive. This, of course, assumed that governments could be persuaded to renounce Keynesian measures to guarantee full employment.

To employers and governments under democratic capitalism, the global wave of wildcat strikes in 1968 and 1969 appeared to be the result of a long period of crisis-free growth and secure full employment that had fuelled excessive expectations on the part of a labour force spoiled by affluence and the welfare state.[47] Workers, on the other hand, thought they had simply been insisting on their democratic right to continuous improvements in living standards and economic security. From then on, the expectations of labour and capital were so far apart that the postwar regime of democratic capitalism could not but enter into crisis. The first half of the 1970s witnessed more and more strike waves as workers and unions stuck to their demands and capital saw its room for manoeuvre being exhausted. Its response was to begin with preparations to withdraw from the postwar social contract, overcoming its passivity, restoring its capacity for action and organization, and extricating itself from democratic political efforts to plan its activity and use it for other objectives than its own. In this it benefited from the fact that, unlike workers and trade unions, it had an alternative strategy to continuing to toil under democratic capitalism: gradually to deny it its 'confidence' together with the investment necessary for it to function.

THE LONG TURN: FROM POSTWAR CAPITALISM TO NEOLIBERALISM

Around the middle of the 'Roaring Seventies', later so called on account of the high expectations of prosperity and freedom that dominated politics

---

47   We cannot go into this in detail here, but I am convinced that in the discursive processing of the strike movements of 1968–69 one can find the origin of today's hegemonic commonsense notion that 'we' – that is, ordinary men and women – have become too demanding and must learn to content 'ourselves' with less. As we shall see, mainstream economic theory also blames exaggerated demands among the masses for the high level of public debt in later decades – an explanation ideally suited to make people forget the dramatically more unequal distribution of generated wealth.

and the public mood, the owners and managers of capital – and not, as legitimation crisis theory had hoped and expected, the broad mass of wage-earners – opened a long struggle for a fundamental restructuring of the political economy of postwar capitalism. Still reeling from the impact of 1968, capitalists and their managers were alarmed by political declarations of intent to test what further burdens could be imposed on them, as later expressed in book titles such as Korpi's *The Democratic Class Struggle* (1983) or Esping-Andersen's *Politics against Markets* (1985). In response they embarked on their exit from a regime which had enabled them after 1945, despite the experiences of the interwar period, to regain their positions on the commanding heights of industry.

Subsequently a growing number of firms, industries and business associations converted to a new common objective: the liberalization of capitalism and the expansion of its markets at home and abroad. The events of the late 1960s and the energy crisis of 1972 had made it less likely than ever that 'the economy' would be able to fulfil, under conditions it found tolerable in the long run, the obligations into which it had entered under political pressure in the postwar regime. There was no reliance any more on high growth as a democratic-capitalist peace formula. To forgo profits in order to ensure full employment, or to organize with great costs production and product-lines in such a way that they provided secure jobs with high wages and low differentials, would have required from firms and those dependent on their profits a degree of sacrifice that seemed increasingly unacceptable. Since the state could not be relied upon,[48] being almost everywhere under more or less social democratic control, the only solution that remained was an escape into the market: freeing the capitalist economy from the bureaucratic-political and corporatist

---

48   The 1970s saw the rise of public choice theory in economics. Political actors and public authorities were modelled as self-serving utility maximizers who, unlike capital, had the advantage that they could use public power for their own enrichment. See J. Buchanan and G. Tullock, *The Calculus of Consent: Logical Foundations of Constitutional Democracy*, Ann Arbor: University of Michigan Press, 1962. Buchanan, one of the school's founding fathers, characterized public choice in retrospect as 'politics without romance' (J. Buchanan, *Public Choice: The Origins and Development of a Research Program*, Fairfax, VA: Center for Study of Public Choice, 2003).

controls of the reconstruction period, with a recovery of profit margins to be achieved through free markets and deregulation[49] instead of through government policies with their danger of social obligations coming with them.

As seen from today, the rollback of state intervention and the return to the market as the prime mechanism of resource allocation appear as a breathtakingly successful strategy that did more than just surprise critical theory – far from it.[50] Beginning in the early 1980s, central elements of the social contract of postwar capitalism were gradually revoked or called into question in the societies of the West: politically guaranteed full employment, collective society-wide wage formation negotiated with free trade unions, worker participation at workplace and enterprise level, state control of key industries, a broad public sector with secure employment as a model for the private sector, universal social rights protected from competition, tax and income policies that kept inequality within tight limits, and government cyclical and industrial policies to secure steady growth. In 1979, the year of the 'second oil crisis', more or less aggressive policies to curb trade unions were introduced in all the Western democracies. At the same time, mostly gradual yet decisive reforms of labour markets and social security systems got under way worldwide, in the name of a supposedly overdue 'flexibilization' of institutions and an 'activation' of the labour force; they amounted to a fundamental revision of the postwar welfare state, increasingly defended with reference to the expansion of markets beyond national frontiers, so-called globalization. Part of this was an erosion of rights to job security, the division

---

49   On the the deregulation movement in the United States, see E. Canedo, *The Rise of the Deregulation Movement in Modern America, 1957–1980*, New York: Columbia University, 2008.

50   In different perspectives and from different normative positions, Weber, Schumpeter and Keynes all predicted a peaceful, or not so peaceful, end to free-market capitalism in the second half of the twentieth century. It is also worth recalling that, in *The Great Transformation* (1944), Karl Polanyi took it for granted that liberal capitalism was history and would not return. 'Within the nations we are witnessing a development under which the economic system ceases to lay down the law to society and the primacy of society over that system is ensured' (K. Polanyi, *The Great Transformation: The Political and Economic Origins of Our Time*, Boston: Beacon Press, p. 251).

of labour markets into core and periphery areas with different degrees of protection, the authorization and encouragement of low-pay employment, the acceptance of high structural unemployment, the privatization of public services and a cutback of public employment, and if possible the elimination of trade unions from the wage formation process.[51] At the end, over and above national differences and specificities, stood a 'lean' and 'modernized' welfare state increasingly geared to 'recommodification', whose 'employment-friendliness' and lower costs had been bought by lowering the minimum subsistence level guaranteed as a social right.[52]

Not only labour markets were deregulated from the late 1970s on; the same was increasingly true of the markets for goods, services and capital. While governments hoped that this would bring faster growth and in any case relieve them of political responsibilities, employers invoked the expansion of markets and sharper competition to justify the degrading of wages and work conditions or the widening of wage differentials.[53] At the same time, capital markets were transformed into markets for corporate control, which made of 'shareholder value' the supreme maxim of good management.[54] In many places, even in Scandinavia, citizens were referred to private education and

---

51   For a selection from the abundant literature on the subject, see H. Katz and O. Darbishire, *Converging Divergences: Worldwide Changes in Employment Systems*, Ithaca, NY: Cornell University Press, 2000.

52   For a survey of the evolution of the welfare state since the 1980s, see F. Scharpf and V. Schmidt (eds), *Welfare and Work in the Open Economy*, vol. 1, *From Vulnerability to Competitiveness*, Oxford: Oxford University Press, 2000; F. Scharpf and V. Schmidt, *Welfare and Work*, vol. 1, *Diverse Responses to Common Challenges*, Oxford: Oxford University Press, 2000; as well as the editors' introduction to Francis G. Castles et al. (eds), *The Oxford Handbook of the Welfare State*, Oxford: Oxford University Press, 2010, pp. 1–15, and the articles in the same volume by M. Kautto ('The Nordic Countries', pp. 586–600) and B. Palier ('Continental Western Europe', pp. 601–15).

53   See, among many others, P. Emmenegger et al., *The Age of Dualization: The Changing Face of Inequality in Deindustrializing Countries*, Oxford: Oxford University Press, 2012; J. Goldthorpe (ed.), *Order and Conflict in Contemporary Capitalism*, Oxford: Clarendon Press, 1984; B. Palier and K. Thelen, 'Institutionalizing Dualism: Complementarities and Change in France and Germany', *Politics and Society*, vol. 38/1, 2010, pp. 119–48.

54   See Martin Höpner, *Wer beherrscht die Unternehmen? Shareholder Value, Managerherrschaft und Mitbestimmung in Deutschland*, Frankfurt/Main: Campus, 2003.

insurance markets as a supplement or even alternative to public providers, with the option of taking up credit to pay the bills. Economic inequality grew everywhere by leaps and bounds (Fig. 1.3).[55] In this way and others, responding in more or less the same way to the pressure coming from the owners and managers of their

FIGURE 1.3. *Evolution of income inequality: Gini coefficients, seven countries*

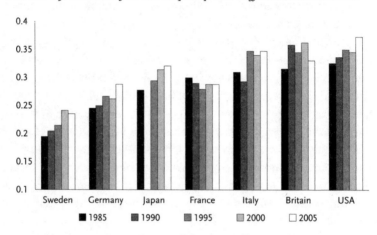

Sources: OECD *Database on Household Income Distribution and Poverty*; OECD *Factbook 2008*; *Economic, Environmental and Social Statistics 2008*; OECD *Factbook 2010*: Country Indicators, OECD *Factbook Statistics*

---

55 Fig. 1.3 shows the evolution of the Gini coefficient, the most commonly used measure of income inequality, in the seven countries used as examples (see fn. 15 in this chapter). The Gini coefficient measures the deviation of the actual distribution from equal distribution. Another measure of inequality is the share of wages – as opposed to profits – in national income. Here the picture for the sixteen main OECD countries between 1960 and 2005 is as devastating as for the Gini coefficient: 'Labour's share increased when capital's relative bargaining power was threatened by the ascendancy of social democratic projects in the aftermath of World War II. The last two decades have seen a new swing of the pendulum toward a restoration of bargaining power to the capitalist class . . . Neo-liberalism is . . . an attempt to restore the capitalist class's share of income to its pre-World War II levels' (T. Kristal, 'Good Times, Bad Times: Postwar Labor's Share', *American Sociological Review*, vol. 75/5, 2010, pp. 758f.).

'economy', the developed capitalist countries shed the responsibility they had taken on in mid-century for growth, full employment, social security and social cohesion, handing the welfare of their citizens more than ever over to the market.

In the rich countries of the West, the long turn to neoliberalism encountered remarkably weak resistance. The high structural unemployment that now became the norm was only one reason for this. The conversion of sellers' markets into customer markets, together with the burgeoning arts of marketing, ensured ever wider loyalty for the commercialization of social life and stabilized the motivation for work and performance among the general population.[56] Moreover, new forms of employment and work organization in the developing 'knowledge society' co-opted the self-fulfilment project that had been part of 1968.[57] The new labour markets also had their supporters – women, for whom a job had come to mean personal freedom, but also the younger generation who found the flexibility of their individualized, non-traditional lifestyles mirrored in the flexibility of their employment conditions. They certainly did not have to fear that their nightmare of a gold watch after fifty years in the same company would ever come true. The various rhetorical efforts of employers and politicians to obscure the distinction between freely chosen and forced mobility, between self-employed and precarious work, between giving notice and being given the sack, were by no means unproductive in a generation taught from an early age to view the world as meritocratic and the labour market as a sporting challenge, rather like mountain biking or a marathon race. Whereas in the 1940s Polanyi had seen a human need for stable social relations as the Archimedean point for a fightback against the liberal project,[58] the cultural tolerance of market uncertainty grew against all expectations in the last two decades of the twentieth century.

---

56 Streeck, 'Citizens as Customers'.
57 Boltanski and Chiapello, *The New Spirit of Capitalism*.
58 Polanyi, *The Great Transformation*.

BUYING TIME

Nevertheless, the neoliberal revolution did not succeed without political assistance. By the end of the late 1960s, the capitalist peace
formula had become unrealistic. High economic growth jointly
produced by labour and capital, which could have been used for
secure employment, rising wages and continuing progress towards
better working conditions and extended social protection, was drying
up. By the early 1970s at the latest, productive capital investment
threatened to fall short of what was needed to ensure full employment
in a context of growing wage militancy and expanding government
social policy. These were generally seen as the cornerstone of the
postwar social contract. A legitimation crisis, of parliamentary
democracy if not of the capitalist economy, therefore seemed to lie
ahead. In the following years, however, that problem was successfully
addressed, if in a way not expected by Frankfurt crisis theory: that is,
by a monetary policy that accommodated wage rises in excess of
productivity growth, resulting in high global rates of inflation, especially in the second half of the 1970s.[59]

---

59 Attempts to get by with without inflation by means of 'incomes policy' had
mixed fortunes. The greatest successes were in countries where unions and employers were
integrated into government stability policy, with a corporatist approach offering employers
negotiated wage restraint and trade unions compensation, non-monetary for the time
being, in the form of rights to organize or of improved pension entitlements. Incomes
policy featured prominently in the comparative political science and the institutional
economics of the 1970s; see, by way of an introduction, R. Flanagan and L. Ulman, *Wage
Restraint: A Study of Incomes Policy in Western Europe*, Berkeley: University of California
Press, 1971. As the extensive literature of the time was able to show, inflation rates reflected
the institutional structure of the national economy, varying not only with the mode of wage
formation but also with the status of the central bank. The lowest inflation was in West
Germany, whose wage-bargaining system was in effect highly centralized and whose
independent central bank anticipated as early as the mid-1970s the monetarist economic
policy later adopted by the USA and the UK (F. Scharpf, *Crisis and Choice in European
Social Democracy*, Ithaca, NY: Cornell University Press, 1991). Despite, or because of, these
conditions, the SPD leader Helmut Schmidt could fight the 1976 election campaign with
the slogan 'Rather 5 per cent inflation than 5 per cent unemployment'. The other side of the
stable currency, however, was that public debt began to climb earlier in Germany than
elsewhere; we shall return to this point below. The Bundesbank – which, by denying the
government control over the money supply, indirectly forced it into fiscal measures to

Following the strike wave around 1968, the inflationary mone-tary policy of the 1970s safeguarded social peace in a rapidly developing consumer society by compensating for inadequate economic growth and ensuring the continuation of full employment.[60] In this respect, it amounted to a temporary repair of the failing neocapitalist peace formula. The trick was to defuse the emergent distribution conflict between labour and capital by introducing additional resources, even if these existed only as money and not, or not yet, in reality. Inflation made the cake only seem larger, but this did not necessarily make a difference in the short term. It produced in both employees and employers a 'money illusion', as Keynes had called it, of greater affluence, as a boost for the new consumerism. But that illusion faded over time and finally disappeared when the declining value of money induced its owners either to stop investing or to seek safety in other currencies.[61]

Governments that sought social peace by means of inflation, introducing not yet existing resources into the capitalist distributional conflict, were able to draw on the magic of modern 'fiat money', the amount of which, politics commanding public power, may increase

preserve employment as well as the legitimacy of its policies and of the market economy – became a model for other European countries, including France under Mitterrand, and later for the European Central Bank too. The national institutional differences, which became especially striking in the 1970s, were the starting point for the literature on corporatism and then on 'varieties of capitalism' (W. Streeck, 'The Study of Interest Groups: Before "The Century" and After', in Colin Crouch et al. [eds], *The Diversity of Democracy: Corporatism, Social Order and Political Conflict*, London: Edward Elgar, 2006, pp. 3–45).

60   On the following, see W. Streeck, 'A Crisis of Democratic Capitalism', *New Left Review*, vol. 71, 2011, pp. 1–25.

61   In the 1970s there was agreement that inflation mainly harms the owners of monetary assets, whereas it improves the distributional position of the working class – at least so long as investment is not impaired. But in reality the latter happens at the latest when the resulting uncertainty about prices and price relations becomes too great for investors (F. Hayek, 'Full Employment, Planning and Inflation', *Studies in Philosophy, Politics, and Economics*, Chicago: University of Chicago Press, 1967 [1950], pp. 270–9). Then the solution to a *legitimation problem* becomes the cause of a *reproduction problem* – or successful social integration generates a crisis of system integration (in the sense of D. Lockwood, 'Social Integration and System Integration', in George K. Zollschan et al. [eds], *Explorations in Social Change*, London: Houghton Mifflin, 1964, pp. 244–57) that may give rise to a new crisis of social integration and thus raise again the old legitimation problems.

ad libitum. With the onset of stagflation – of stagnation despite accel-erating inflation – in the second half of the 1970s, however, the replacement of real with nominal growth lost its charm; central banks, under the leadership of the Federal Reserve, resorted to drastic stabi-lization measures, including in the American case interest rates above 20 per cent that soon brought an end to inflation that has lasted to the present day (Fig. 1.4). As deflation in capitalist economies worldwide brought a sharp recession and continuing unemployment (Fig. 1.5), the legitimation problem of what had been the capitalism of the post-war period came bouncing back, and with it the temptation to relieve it once more by conjuring up money from nowhere. So began, or continued, a development which has reached a provisional climax in today's global financial and fiscal crisis.

The monetary stabilization of the world economy in the early 1980s was a *tour de force* that came with a high political risk; it could be undertaken only by governments, such as those of Reagan and Thatcher, that were willing to trade mass unemployment for the resto-ration of 'sound money' and to crush the expected social resistance at whatever cost.[62] In fact, the deflation of capitalist national economies, backed up with lasting unemployment and neoliberal labour-market reforms, brought about a worldwide decline in union organization (Fig. 1.6) that made the strike weapon virtually unusable in distribu-tional conflicts; the incidence of strikes fell towards zero nearly everywhere and has remained there ever since (Fig. 1.7).[63] At the same time, the gap separating the promises of capitalism and the expectations of its clientele from what ever more powerful markets were willing to deliver not only persisted but tended to grow wider; once again, under changed conditions and with new instruments, it had to be politically bridged, however provisionally. *This was the beginning of the public debt era.*

---

62 Two dramatic and symbolically important turning-points were Reagan's breaking of the air traffic controllers' union in 1981 and Thatcher's defeat of the miners in 1984.
63 Fig. 1.7 leaves out Italy's very high strike rates of the 1970s, which would have made the trend in other countries invisible on the scale. In Italy too, strike activity fell dramatically after 1980.

FIGURE I.4. *Rates of inflation (%), seven countries*

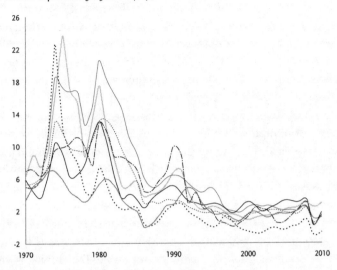

FIGURE I.5. *Unemployment (%), seven countries*

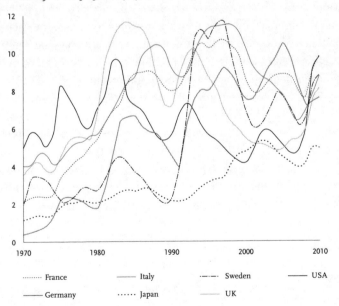

| .... France | .... Italy | –.–.– Sweden | —— USA |
| —— Germany | ...... Japan | —— UK | |

Sources: OECD *Economic Outlook: Statistics and Projections*

Like inflation, public debt enables a government to commit financial resources to the calming of social conflicts, resources which in reality are not yet available, in the sense that citizens still have to generate them and the state has to acquire that money through tax. Now, however, it is not the government printing shop but the private credit system that fills the hole, by supplying in advance the tax revenue that will have to be raised, or not raised, at a future date. In the early 1980s, demands on social security systems increased, especially as a result of high unemployment and because benefits promised in previous decades in return for wage restraint were coming due. Although 'reforms' were soon made to reduce entitlements, not all the promises or informal agreements underlying social policy could be revoked at once. Moreover, the end of inflation had also curbed the devaluation of existing public debt, so that debt burdens rose in proportion to the national product. Since tax increases would have been as politically risky as faster erosion of the social state, governments turned to debt as a way out. In the case of the United States, Krippner has shown that Reagan already began with the first liberalization of financial markets, which was supposed to raise the necessary capital, both domestically and from overseas, enabling banks to multiply credit faster and more often than in the past and thereby to cover the state's growing borrowing requirement.[64]

Even this could ensure only temporary peace for capitalism. In the 1990s, governments began to worry about the rising share of debt service in public budgets, while creditors began to have doubts about the ability of states to repay their growing debt. Again it was the United States that took the initiative, and under the Clinton administration attempts were made to balance the budget mainly through social spending cuts.[65] Most other countries in the Western world

64 G. Krippner, *Capitalizing on Crisis: The Political Origins of the Rise of Finance*, Cambridge, MA: Harvard University Press, 2011.

65 In 1991 Clinton won the presidential elections with a campaign against the 'double deficit' (in the trade balance and the federal budget) that Reagan and Bush had left behind.

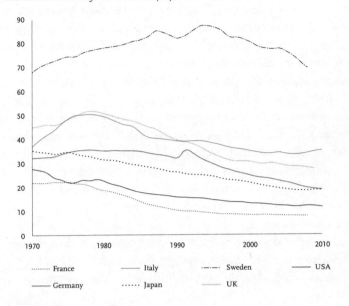

FIGURE I.6. *Level of unionization (%), seven countries*

.... France   ———— Italy   —·—·— Sweden   ———— USA

———— Germany   ······ Japan   ———— UK

FIGURE I.7. *Days not worked per 1,000 employees, six countries (three-year moving averages)*

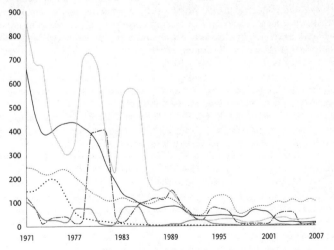

Sources: *ILO Labour Statistics*, US Bureau of Labor Statistics; Amsterdam Institute for Advanced Labour Studies, ICTWSS Database, 3 May 2011

followed suit,[66] having been brought into line by international organizations such as the OECD and the International Monetary Fund.[67] But even two decades after capitalism broke loose from its postwar casing, its further development still required legitimation through provision of additional, conflict-dampening resources – *only now what was politically necessary could ideally be matched with what was desirable from a neoliberal point of view.* Especially in the USA and UK, but also in Scandinavia,[68] budgetary consolidation threatened to depress demand and cause private income losses that would be dangerous to system legitimacy. The answer was another round of frontloading, through a second wave of capital market liberalization that this time permitted a rapid increase in private debt. Colin Crouch has called this new phase of capitalist development 'privatized Keynesianism.'[69]

Privatized Keynesianism replaces government debt with private debt, as a mechanism for expanding the resource inventory in the national economy.[70] It is the third and latest variant in which

66   Fig. 1.1 shows that what I call the first phase of budgetary consolidation was by no means unsuccessful. Germany was an exception at the time: it had to finance reunification, and Kohl had promised that this would be done without tax increases.

67   The 1990s saw the growth of a politically inspired and government-funded institutional economics literature that dealt with how 'reforms' to democratic institutions might slow down or reverse the tendency towards greater public indebtedness in the rich democracies (P. Molander, 'Reforming Budgetary Institutions: Swedish Experiences', in Rolf R. Strauch et al. [eds], *Institutions, Politics and Fiscal Policy*, Boston: Springer, 2000, pp. 191–212; J. Poterba and J. von Hagen, *Institutions, Politics and Fiscal Policy*, Chicago: University of Chicago Press, 1999; R. Strauch and J. von Hagen, *Institutions, Politics and Fiscal Policy*, Boston: Kluwer Academic Publishers, 2000).

68   On Sweden see P. Mehrtens, *Staatsentschuldung und Staatstätigkeit: Zur Transformation der schwedischen politischen Ökonomie*, Cologne: Universität Köln und Max-Planck-Institut für Gesellschaftsforschung, 2013.

69   C. Crouch, 'Privatised Keynesianism: An Unacknowledged Policy Regime', *British Journal of Politics and International Relations*, vol. 11/3, 2009, pp. 382–99.

70   The countries in question also profited from the growth of a deregulated finance industry, in the wake of the 'structural shift' towards a 'service society'. In the 1990s, Wall Street and the City of London became the most important branches of the economy and the largest taxpayers in the USA and UK respectively. In the United States, before the crisis of 2008, roughly 45 per cent of corporate profits came from the financial sector; the corresponding figure at the beginning of the 1980s had been just under 20 per cent (Krippner, *Capitalizing on Crisis*, p. 33). On the scale of the redistribution in favour of the

purchasing power is anticipated to meet the unfulfilled promises of late postwar capitalism; in it the state limits itself to regulatory policies that enable private households to supplement their income from work and benefits by taking on debt at their own risk. Here too there are parallels between countries usually classified under different, or even opposing, 'varieties' of capitalism. For example, it was not only in the USA and Britain but also in Sweden (and elsewhere in Scandinavia) that household debt increased sharply from the 1990s on, not only offsetting the decline in public debt due to consolidation policies but also raising a country's total indebtedness even where it had previously remained constant (Fig. 1.8).[71]

At the level of political ideas, a new theory underpinning the replacement of public with private debt held that capital markets were self-regulating and did not require government intervention, because their participants disposed of all the necessary information to prevent the emergence of systematic imbalances.[72] This raised the possibility of borrowing as a means to privatize public services, so that the state would finally be able to shake off its postwar responsibility for growth and social security, which had always seemed suspect in the eyes of capital, and transfer it back to the market and its axiomatically rational participants. At this point neoliberal reform would have arrived at its logical conclusion.

As we know, the hope for this proved illusory, at least for the time being. The current triple crisis results from a breakdown of the debt pyramid consisting of promises of growth that capitalism has for some time no longer been able to deliver – at least to the mass of the

finance industry and resource extraction, see D. Tomaskovic-Devy and K. Lin, 'Income Dynamics, Economic Rents and the Financialization of the US Economy', *American Sociological Review*, vol. 76/4, 2011, pp. 538–59.

71   Fig. 1.8 shows four countries where the compensation effect was especially marked. It is worth noting that Sweden too (along with other Scandinavian countries) belongs in this group.

72   Among the main names here are Eugene Fama (father of the 'efficient market hypothesis'), Merton H. Miller (co-founder of the Modigliani-Miller theorem), Harry Markowitz, Robert Merton, Myron Scholes and Fischer Black. Most have taught at the University of Chicago and appear on the list of winners of the so-called Nobel Prize in economics, awarded by the Swedish central bank (Riksbank).

population on whose cooperation or sufferance it depends more than it would like. With this, neoliberal reform, too, has reached a point of crisis. After years of privatization and deregulation, the possible collapse of the international banking system in 2008 compelled public authorities to re-enter the economic fray, wrecking all the gains in budgetary consolidation they had achieved at high political risk. Since 2008, governments have had little or no idea how to clear away the debris of the financial crisis and recreate some kind of order – a task that certainly cannot be privatized. In the measures taken by governments and central banks to save the private banking system, the distinction between public and private money has become increasingly irrelevant, and finally, with the takeover of bad loans, it became clear how seamlessly the one passed into the other. Today it is virtually impossible to tell where the state ends and the market begins, and whether governments have been nationalizing banks, or banks have been privatizing the state.[73]

To sum up, time was bought in three ways and in three successive stages. The development of the leading country of modern capitalism, the United States, is paradigmatic (Fig. 1.9). In the USA, inflation shot up in the early 1970s and, after sharp fluctuations, stood close to 14 per cent by the end of the decade. This marked the first turning-point, as inflation was suppressed and gave way to a rapid rise in *public debt* until 1993. Clinton's policy of budgetary consolidation then brought a fall in the government debt ratio of more than 10 percentage points in the space of a few years, but this was offset by a sharp increase in *private* debt. Shortly before the collapse of the finance industry private households began to experience a debt reduction, mainly as a result of insolvency and accompanied with a new increase in government debt and a fall in the rate of inflation towards zero.

---

73 This became clear in summer 2012, during the discussions on an EU 'rescue package' for Spanish banks. Of course, the dual nature of money as private property and public institution goes back a long way (G. Ingham, *The Nature of Money*, Cambridge: Polity, 2004); it underlies the mysterious nature of capitalism (D. Graeber, *Debt: The First 5,000 Years*, Brooklyn, NY: Melville House, 2011), which is ultimately unfathomable even to those dependent on profit.

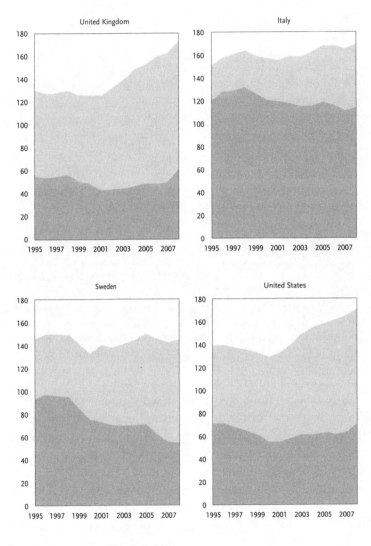

FIGURE I.8. *Government debt and household debt (% of GDP), 1995–2008, four countries*

Sources: OECD *National Accounts Statistics;* OECD *Economic Outlook: Statistics and Projections*

FIGURE 1.9. *The crisis sequence: USA*

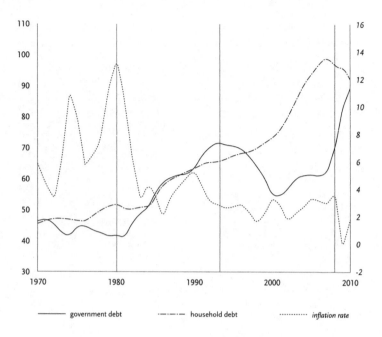

Sources: OECD *National Accounts Statistics;* OECD *Economic Outlook: Statistics and Projections*

In Germany, the sequence of crises was somewhat different because of special historical and institutional conditions, but it followed the same overall logic (Fig. 1.10). In the 1970s the Federal Republic had high inflation for a very short period only, ending with a double-digit public sector wage agreement in 1974, as a result of which Willy Brandt resigned as chancellor. On the other hand, public debt increased rapidly and, though still only 30 per cent of GDP, dominated the debate in the run-up to the general election in 1980. A further rise of public debt occurred in the early 1990s, after German reunification, now accompanied with high levels of private debt. The latter eventually fell back after the turn of the millennium, while public debt continued to rise as part of an international trend. In the first few years of the CDU–SPD coalition government (2005–2009), however, when fiscal consolidation policy was by no means wholly unsuccessful, public debt too decreased.[74] But then, as in the United States, it climbed back up again in the wake of the financial crisis.

In Sweden too, inflation and public and private debt behaved like communicating vessels over a period of forty years (Fig. 1.11). Falling inflation after 1980 coincided with rising public debt, which by the middle of the decade peaked in the first of the country's two major postwar financial crises. The debt was then reduced by more than 20 percentage points under a conservative government, but this rekindled inflation or was indeed made possible by it. Another turning-point then came at the end of the 1980s, when public debt again rose sharply against a background of falling inflation. The second financial crisis, which broke in 1994, led to a long period of budgetary consolidation together with low rates of inflation; Sweden became the model for the consolidation international.[75] Simultaneously this was offset by a sustained rise in private household debt.

The three monetary methods of generating illusions of growth and prosperity – inflation, public debt, private debt – functioned successively for a limited period and then had to be abandoned, as they began to hinder the accumulation process more than they

---

74 On the peculiarities of German household debt, see the forthcoming dissertation by Daniel Mertens (D. Mertens, *Privatverschuldung in Deutschland: Zur institutionellen Entwicklung der Kreditmärkte in einem exportgetriebenen Wachstumsregime*, Cologne: Universität Köln und Max-Planck-Institut für Gesellschaftsforschung, 2013).

75 Finansdepartementet, *An Account of Fiscal and Monetary Policy in the 1990s*, Stockholm, 2001; S. Guichard et al., 'What Affects Fiscal Consolidation? – Some Evidence from OECD Countries', conference paper, 9th Banca d'Italia Workshop on Public Finances, Rome, 2007; J. Henriksson, *Ten Lessons About Budget Consolidation*, Brussels: Bruegel, 2007; P. Molander, 'Reforming Budgetary Institutions: Swedish Experiences', in Rolf R. Strauch et al. (eds), *Institutions, Politics and Fiscal Policy*, Boston: Springer, 2000, pp. 191–212; P. Molander, 'Budgeting Procedures and Democratic Ideals: An Evaluation of Swedish Reforms', *Journal of Public Policy*, vol. 21/1, 2001, pp. 23–52.

FIGURE I.10. *The crisis sequence: Germany*

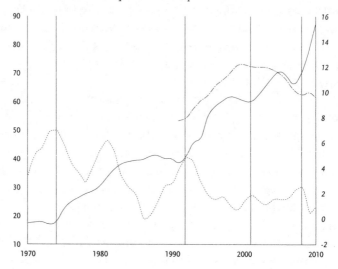

FIGURE I.11. *The crisis sequence: Sweden*

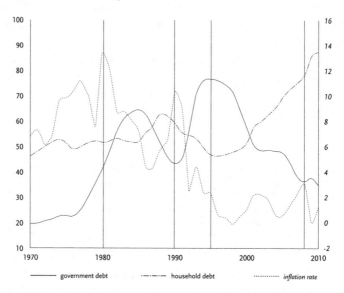

——— government debt   —·—·— household debt   ············· *inflation rate*

Sources: OECD *National Accounts Statistics*; OECD *Economic Outlook: Statistics and Projections*; Swedish National Debt Office, SCB (Statistics Sweden)

supported it.[76] Meanwhile the neoliberal revolution continued to make headway, defining the conditions for each successive attempt to patch up the capitalist peace formula. Whenever such an attempt came to an end, the damage was considerable and the measures needed to rectify it became more demanding. Today, a solution to the ongoing financial and fiscal crisis seems to require nothing less than a redefinition of the relationship between the polity and the economy involving a deep restructuring of the international state system, especially in Europe, the heartland of the modern welfare state. And it is far from certain that such fundamental change can be effected in the short time available to solve the crisis.

We may gain a rough idea of the next stage if we recall how post-war capitalism developed after the end of the *trente glorieuses*. Each of the three passages to a new mode of legitimation was associated with defeats of the wage-dependent population that made it possible to press on with the liberalization agenda: the end of inflation, ushering in structural unemployment and a long-term weakening of trade unions and their ability to engage in strike action; the consolidation of public finances in the 1990s, with deep cuts in social rights of citizenship, the privatization of public services, and various forms of commercialization through which private insurance companies replaced governments and politics as the providers of social security; and the end of '*Pumpkapitalismus*',[77] with a not even roughly predictable loss of savings and income from savings, as well as a rise in unemployment and underemployment, as well as further cuts in

---

76 Inflation or public and private debt do not necessarily lead to crises. Nominal pay increases in anticipation of future productivity increases may operate as spurs to higher productivity; public debt may finance investment in growth, which may then both pay off and devalue the debt; and credit may pull prosperity forward that is later actually produced. In all three cases, the outcome depends on the reaction of owners of investment capital: inflation that turns into galloping inflation may trigger fear of asset losses and lead to capital flight; public debt may reach a point at which there is doubt about its future servicing; and the same may happen with private debt. Each time, what is at stake is the 'confidence' of investors in the ability of economic actors to put themselves in their place and understand their 'psychology' or, which is the same, their profit expectations.

77 R. Dahrendorf, 'Vom Sparkapitalismus zum Pumpkapitalismus', *Cicero online*, 23 July 2009.

public services following a new wave of budgetary consolidation. At the same time, political-economic conflict over distribution moved ever further outside the experience of the man or woman in the street and their capacity to influence it politically: that is, it gradually shifted from the annual wage struggle at enterprise level towards parliamentary elections, from there to private loan and insurance markets, and then to a realm of international financial diplomacy completely remote from everyday life, whose issues and strategies were a closed book for everyone except those directly involved, and perhaps even for them too.

I argue that to continue along the road followed for the last forty years is to attempt to free the capitalist economy and its markets once and for all – not from governments on which they still depend in many ways, but from the kind of mass democracy that was part of the regime of postwar democratic capitalism. Today, the means to tame legitimation crises by generating illusions of growth seem to have been exhausted. In particular, the money magic of the past two decades, produced with the help of an unfettered finance industry, may have finally become too dangerous for governments to dare to buy more time with it. Unless there is another growth miracle, the capitalism of the future may well have to manage without the peace formula of credit-based consumerism. The utopian ideal of present-day crisis management is to complete, with political means, the already far-advanced depoliticization of the economy; anchored in reorganized nation-states under the control of international governmental and financial diplomacy insulated from democratic participation, with a population that would have learned, over years of hegemonic re-education, to regard the distributional outcomes of free markets as fair, or at least as without alternative.

CHAPTER TWO

Neoliberal Reform:
From Tax State to Debt State

The standard economic theory of politics – which should not be confused with the political theory of the economy in the Marxian tradition – explains the crisis of public finances in terms of a failure of democracy. It is a more or less formalized version of the 'overstretching' or 'ungovernability' postulate to be found in conservative theories of legitimation crisis. Its favourite narrative is of excessive demands on the 'common pool'[1] – an old, though perhaps not venerable, concept invented in the nineteenth century to justify in the name of efficiency the usually forcible privatization of the medieval commons in the transition to modern capitalism.[2] Marx described this process of 'primitive accumulation' in *Capital Volume 1*.[3]

FINANCIAL CRISIS: A FAILURE OF DEMOCRACY?

In short, the many different variants of the story of the 'tragedy of the commons'[4] boil down to the idea that if a resource is not individually owned and freely available to all the members of a community, it will soon be exhausted through overgrazing, overfishing, and so on. People acting in accordance with individual rationality will not be able to resist the temptation to take more

---

1   A. Alesina and R. Perotti, 'Budget Deficits and Budget Institutions', in James M. Poterba and Jürgen von Hagen (eds), *Institutions, Politics and Fiscal Policy*, Chicago: Chicago University Press, 1999.

2   D. North and R. Thomas, *The Rise of the Western World: A New Economic History*, Cambridge: Cambridge University Press, 1973.

3   K. Marx, *Capital, Volume One*, London: Penguin/New Left Books, 1976 [1867], Part 8.

4   G. Hardin, 'The Tragedy of the Commons', *Science*, vol. 162/3859, 1968, pp. 1243–8.

from the common pool than they give to it, and more than that pool is able to provide in the long run. In this way of thinking, public finances are the commons and democracy is a licence for citizens to exploit it at will. Since politicians, whose jobs depend on elections, act rationally in the sense of standard economics – that is to say, selfishly – they will cede to the pressure and demands of electoral majorities; the contest for votes will nurture the illusion that the 'pool' is inexhaustible. Once in office, their desire to be re-elected will lead them to spend more than the government raises in revenue, with the result that chronic deficits pile up into a mountain of debt.

For mainstream economics, the crisis of public finances is due to unclear property relations, and thus unclear responsibilities, the latter in turn being attributable to a failure of democracy: or, to be more precise, an extension of democratic decision-making to issues for which it is not appropriate. Consequently, if the fiscal crisis is to be overcome, public finances must be shielded from democratically generated demands and the social commons resting upon taxation must ultimately be trimmed to size. As we shall see, this is a doctrine of considerable power. I will argue against it by suggesting an alternative history of today's public debt that is more in accordance with reality. This too will ultimately come down to a version of the theory of the 'common pool' and the failure of democracy, but one placed on its feet instead of standing on its head.

Do the public finances of democratic capitalism suffer from an excess of democracy? If we trace the roots of the current fiscal crisis, we find that since the Second World War the most dramatic leap in indebtedness, which took place after 2008 (Fig. 2.1), has obviously nothing at all to do with a democratically empowered inflation of demand on the part of the electorate. If any inflated demands were in play, they came from banks that got into difficulties but managed to present themselves as 'too big to fail', as so important to the system that they deserved to be rescued politically, not least by their agents in the state apparatus such as Hank Paulson, the former boss of Goldman

Sachs and treasury secretary under George W. Bush.[5] In doing so, they played on the fear of people and governments about a collapse of the real economy, paving the way for a costly rescue-Keynesianism that had nothing to do with frivolous enrichment of the mass of voters with ownerless assets but was believed to be necessary for the prevention of collective impoverishment. The lost growth that nevertheless ensued raised the debt ratio for many countries, in addition to the extra spending on stimulus packages and bank bailouts. That the intensification of the fiscal crisis after 2008 is attributable to the financial crisis rather than a surfeit of democracy is borne out by quantitative studies that have found a positive correlation between the size of a country's financial sector and the scale of new debt taken on in the wake of the crisis.[6]

As we have seen, the proliferation of the finance industry in the last third of the twentieth century was connected in many ways with the fiscal crisis of the rich democracies. The deregulation and the bloated growth of the sector in the United States began in the 1980s, when the Reagan administration had to cope with a decline in economic performance and the fiscal consequences of its tax cuts.[7] Greater freedom for the money industry was supposed, first, to correct the chronic balance-of-payments shortfall by attracting capital imports and to secure the living standards of the population;[8] and, second, to make it possible for the government to finance its own

---

5   On the 'inflated demands of the economic system', see J. Beckert, *Die Anspruchsinflation des Wirtschaftssystems*, Cologne: Max-Planck-Institut für Gesellschaftsforschung, 2009. By now the literature on Goldman Sachs would fill whole book shelves. A well-researched journalistic article is M. Taibbi, 'The Great American Bubble Machine', *Rolling Stone*, 9 July 2009. See also W. Streeck, 'Wissen als Macht, Macht als Wissen: Kapitalversteher im Krisenkapitalismus', *Merkur*, vol. 65/9–10, 2012.

6   M. Schularick, *Public Debt and Financial Crises in the Twentieth Century*, Discussion Paper, No. 2012/1, Berlin: Free University, School of Business and Economics, 2012.

7   G. Krippner, *Capitalizing on Crisis: The Political Origins of the Rise of Finance*, Cambridge, MA: Harvard University Press, 2011.

8   This had already begun under Richard Nixon, in the shape of efforts to persuade countries such as Saudi Arabia to invest their surplus oil revenue in the United States (see D. Spiro, *The Hidden Hand of American Hegemony: Petrodollar Recycling and International Markets*, Ithaca, NY: Cornell University Press, 1999).

FIGURE 2.1. *Growth of public debt since 2007 (% of GDP)*

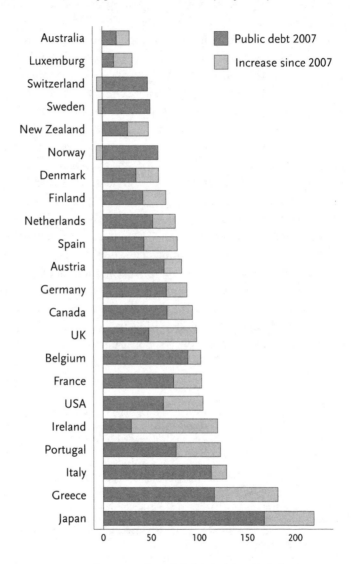

Source: OECD *Economic Outlook: Statistics and Projections*

deficits. The latter were partly related to the choking of inflation in the early 1980s and the Federal Reserve's high interest policy, which put an end to the devaluation of government debt and, in the wake of the resulting economic downturn and jobs crisis, triggered greater demands on the social welfare systems. At the same time, deregulation of the finance sector was supposed to fuel 'structural change' to a service and knowledge economy, giving rise to renewed economic growth and, no less important, higher tax revenue.

A further spurt of financialization then came with the Clinton administration and its spectacularly if only temporarily successful measures to shore up public finances.[9] The budget surpluses briefly recorded around the turn of the millennium were due *inter alia* to sharp cuts in social spending. Financial deregulation made it possible to plug the gaps resulting from deficit reduction, by means of a rapid extension of loan facilities for private households at a time when falling or stagnant wages and transfer incomes, combined with rising costs of 'responsible self-provision', might otherwise have jeopardized support for the policy of economic liberalization. Credit expansion to replace collective provision and compensate for stagnant household incomes amounted to a crossroads in the economic history of democratic capitalism, which under the presidency of George W. Bush found its sequel in the loose money policy following September 11 and the promotion of home ownership through 'subprime mortgages' for poorer sections of the population.

CAPITALISM AND DEMOCRACY IN THE NEOLIBERAL REVOLUTION

Against this background, and contrary to the claims of the 'common pool' theory, it is hard to see the debt accumulated in Western democracies since the second half of the 1970s as a result of democratic pressure on parties and governments. In fact, the rise, decline and new rise of public debt prove to be closely bound up with the victory

---

9 J. Stiglitz, *The Roaring Nineties: A New History of the World's Most Prosperous Decade*, New York and London: W. W. Norton & Company, 2003.

of neoliberalism over postwar capitalism, a victory accompanied by a political *emasculation* of mass democracy. The first serious budget deficits in the 1980s followed the disciplining of trade union militancy and the move to high levels of unemployment. Joblessness served in turn to legitimate radical labour-market reforms and cuts in social protection, which, in the name of a supposedly overdue 'flexibilization' of market-regulating institutions, involved a fundamental revision of the postwar social contract. These developments have already been outlined in Chapter 1 above.

The most visible expression of the sweeping success of the neoliberal revolution is the ever greater inequality of income and property in the countries of democratic capitalism. Had the rise in public debt been due to the rising power of mass democracy, it would be impossible to explain how prosperity and opportunities for prosperity could have been so radically redistributed from the bottom to the top of society. As regards income, it has become ever more skewed over the years, not only in countries with a relatively high degree of inequality such as Italy, Britain or the United States, but also in comparatively egalitarian countries such as Sweden or Germany (see above, Fig. 1.3).[10] For Germany, I have argued that this trend is closely bound up with the gradual disintegration of the system of industry-wide wage formation and the resulting decline of union power.[11] In the case of the United States, Bruce Western and Jake Rosenfeld have demonstrated with much more quantitative precision the negative correlation between union bargaining power and income inequality.[12]

Thomas Kochan, one of the leading labour-market researchers in the United States, views the evolution of pay since the late 1970s as a breach of the American social contract. Previously, productivity,

10   The only real exception was France, where the Gini coefficient fell slightly from 1985 until 1995 and then held steady at an only slightly higher level. The current, market-driven 'reforms' in France suggest, however, that the situation will soon be normalized in this country, too, despite the political complexion of the sitting president and his government.

11   Streeck, *Re-Forming Capitalism*, pp. 41ff.

12   B. Western and J. Rosenfeld, 'Unions, Norms, and the Rise in US Wage Inequality', *American Sociological Review*, vol. 76/4, 2011, pp. 513–37.

household income and average hourly wage-rates had grown at the same rate (1945 = 100, 1975 = 200), but then productivity continued on a steep upward curve, reaching 400 by the year 2010, while average hourly wages remained stuck at approximately 200. It is true that household income rose to just under 250, but only because longer hours and increased female participation in the workforce meant that families were devoting more and more time to the labour market.[13] The figures show that, when measured against productivity rises, working households in the United States have gained next to nothing since the 1980s, in spite of increased labour input, higher labour intensity, greater flexibility requirements, and a constant worsening of employment conditions.

The situation looks very different for the residual incomes of owners and managers of large capital. On 26 March 2012, Steven Rattner reported in the *New York Times* that no less than 93 per cent of the additional US income created in 2010 – $288 billion – had gone to the top 1 per cent of taxpayers, and 37 per cent to the top 0.1 per cent, raising their income by 22 per cent. In good part as a result of successive tax cuts, 'the top 1 per cent has done progressively better in each economic recovery of the past two decades. In the Clinton era expansion, 45 per cent of the total income gains went to the top 1 per cent; in the Bush recovery, the figure was 65 per cent; now it is 93 per cent.'[14] As to property, according to the *New York Times* of 12 June 2012, the inflation-adjusted net assets of the average American family in 2010, after the housing market collapse, were back at the level of 1990.

Whichever figures one uses to describe this unparalleled upward redistribution, the conclusion is the same. Larry Mishel of the Economic Policy Institute has calculated that 81.7 per cent of the asset

---

13   T. Kochan, 'A Jobs Compact for America's Future', *Harvard Business Review*, March 2012, pp. 64–73; T. Kochan, 'Resolving the Human Capital Paradox: A Proposal for a Jobs Compact', policy paper no. 2012–011, Kalamazoo, MI: W. E. Upjohn Institute for Employment Research.

14   Slightly older, but equally astonishing, figures may be found in J. Hacker and P. Pierson, 'Winner-Take-All Politics: Public Policy, Political Organization, and the Precipitous Rise of Top Incomes in the United States', *Politics and Society*, vol. 38, 2010, pp. 152–204; J. Hacker and P. Pierson, *Winner-Take-All Politics: How Washington Made the Rich Richer – and Turned Its Back on the Middle Class*, New York: Simon & Schuster, 2011.

increase in the United States between 1983 and 2009 went to the top
5 per cent, while the bottom 60 per cent *lost* the equivalent of 7.5 per
cent of the total asset increase. As to the 'compensation' of corporate
leaders, the *New York Times* of 7 April 2012 put the amount received
by the hundred highest-paid managers at an average of $14.4 million
in the crisis year of 2011 – that is, 320 times the average American
income. Comparative figures for the 1970s are not easy to obtain, but
there can be no doubt that top corporate incomes have skyrocketed in
the last two to three decades, and not only in the United States.[15]

The extent to which neoliberalized capitalism is displacing the
democratic welfare-state capitalism of the 1960s and 1970s can be
gauged from the fact that electoral participation is in constant and often
dramatic decline, especially among those who should have the greatest
interest in social benefits and in redistribution from the top to the
bottom of society.[16] Voter turnout increased in all the Western democracies in the 1950s and 1960s, but since then it has fallen by an average
of no less than 12 percentage points (Fig. 2.2). The trend is universal,
and there are no signs that it is about to change. More than one-half of
national elections with the lowest postwar turnout took place after the
year 2000; the more recent an election, the more likely it is that a smaller
proportion of people voted than at any time since the war. Participation
in regional and local elections is regularly lower than in national elections and, at least in Germany (Fig. 2.3), has declined even more. The
lowest turnout has been for elections to the European Parliament.

Contrary to revisionist theories of democracy current in the
1960s,[17] low electoral participation does not mean that citizens are

15   See the figures in W. Streeck, 'German Capitalism: Does it Exist? Can it Survive?',
New Political Economy, vol. 2/2, 1997, pp. 237–56. The case of Volkswagen chairman Martin
Winterkorn, who received a total income of 18.3 million euros in 2011, shows that Germany
is catching up fast with the USA.

16   A. Schäfer, 'Die Folgen sozialer Ungleichheit für die Demokratie in Westeuropa',
Zeitschrift für vergleichende Politikwissenschaft, vol. 4/1, 2010, pp. 131–56; A. Schäfer and
W. Streeck, 'Introduction', in Armin Schäfer et al. (eds), *Politics in the Age of Austerity*, Cam-
bridge: Polity, 2013.

17   S. Lipset, *Political Man: The Social Bases of Politics*, Garden City, NY: Anchor
Books, 1963 [1960].

content with how things are going. As Armin Schäfer has shown,[18] those from lower income groups and social strata are the least likely to vote; their turnout has also been declining the most sharply. What we see as a result is a strong negative correlation between electoral participation and regional unemployment or welfare dependence. In large German cities, the district-by-district variation in turnout has increased in every election since the 1970s and, in less affluent areas (with a high proportion of immigrants, high unemployment, low incomes, etc.), electoral participation has fallen so low that parties increasingly refrain from any campaigning there[19] – which further reduces the numbers at the lower end of society who turn out to vote, nudging party platforms more and more to 'the centre'.

Everything suggests that declining electoral participation in the capitalist democracies is a sign not of contentment but of resignation. The losers from the neoliberal turn cannot see what they might get from a change of government; the TINA ('There is no alternative') politics of 'globalization' has long arrived at the bottom of society where voting no longer makes a difference in the eyes of those who would have most to gain from political change. The less hope they invest in elections, the less those who can afford to rely on the market have to fear from political intervention. The political resignation of the underclasses consolidates the neoliberal turn from which it derives, further shielding capitalism from democracy.

EXCURSUS: CAPITALISM AND DEMOCRACY

At this point I should like to interpolate a few general considerations on the relationship between capitalism and democracy, markets and democratic politics, and neoliberalism and public authority. It has been shown many times that neoliberalism needs a *strong* state to

18 Schäfer, 'Die Folgen sozialer Ungleichheit für die Demokratie in Westeuropa'; A. Schäfer, *Republican Liberty and Compulsory Voting*, MPIfG Discussion Paper No. 11/17, Cologne: Max-Planck-Institut für Gesellschaftsforschung, 2011.
19 For a journalistic account of this correlation, see M. Schlieben, 'Die wählen sowieso nicht', *Zeit online*, 13 May 2012.

FIGURE 2.2. *Participation in national parliamentary elections (%), 1950s to 2011*

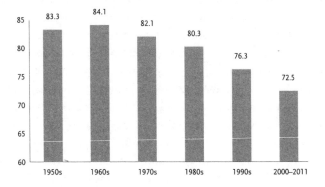

Countries: Australia, Austria, Belgium, Canada, Denmark, Finland, France, Germany, Greece, Ireland, Italy, Japan, Luxemburg, Netherlands, New Zealand, Norway, Portugal, Spain, Sweden, Switzerland, UK, USA

Source: Voter Turnout Database, International Institute for Democracy and Electoral Assistance (IDEA)

FIGURE 2.3. *Electoral participation in Germany (%), 1950s to 2000s*

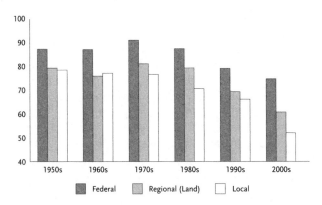

Source: Armin Schäfer, 'Demokratie im Zeitalter wirtschaftlicher Liberalisierung', www.mpifg.de

suppress demands from society, and especially from trade unions, for intervention in the free play of market forces; this is convincingly argued in relation to the Thatcher government, for example, by Andrew Gamble's *The Free Economy and the Strong State* (1988). On the other hand, neoliberalism is incompatible with a *democratic* state, in so far as democracy involves a regime which, in the name of its citizens, deploys public authority to modify the distribution of economic goods resulting from market forces – a regime regarded critically also by the 'common pool' theory of fiscal government failure.

In the end, we are speaking here of a very old tension between capitalism and democracy. At the time of the Cold War, it was a political commonplace to argue that democracy was impossible without capitalism (or, what came to the same thing, without economic progress), just as capitalism was claimed to be impossible without democracy.[20] In the interwar years, things were still seen differently: whereas the bourgeoisie, being a natural minority, feared dispossession at the hands of a democratically elected majority government, which could not be anything other than a workers' government, the radical Left was constantly on the alert for an anti-democratic putsch by a coalition of capital, army and aristocracy; the fascist regimes of the 1920s and 1930s evinced a fundamental incompatibility between democratic politics and capitalist economy. Mirroring the 'bourgeois' solution of a right-wing dictatorship, the Left tended to believe in the necessity of a workers' council, or soviet, regime, a 'dictatorship of the proletariat' or a 'people's democracy', changing its terminology in accordance with the theoretical and political conjuncture. It was thus by no means a matter of course that a capitalist economy came to be combined in the postwar West with a democratic political system – one, moreover, that derived its legitimacy from continuous intervention in the functioning of the market economy, in pursuit of democratically

---

20 A prominent representative of this position, which was closely linked to 'modernization' theory, was Seymour Martin Lipset (*Political Man: The Social Bases of Politics*). Recent counter-examples include post-Allende Chile and China since Deng Xiaoping.

established collective goals that favoured the wage-dependent majority of its citizens.

Two competing principles of distribution were institutionalized in the political economy of postwar democratic capitalism: what I shall call *market justice* on the one hand and *social justice* on the other. By *market justice*, I mean distribution of the output of production according to the market evaluation of individual performance, expressed in relative prices; the yardstick for remuneration according to market justice is marginal productivity, the market value of the last unit of output under competitive conditions.[21] *Social justice*, on the other hand, is determined by cultural norms and is based on status rather than contract. It follows collective ideas of fairness, correctness and reciprocity, concedes demands for a minimum livelihood irrespective of economic performance or productivity, and recognizes civil and human rights to such things as health, social security, participation in the life of the community, employment protection and trade union organization.

Neither market nor social justice is uncontroversial. Émile Durkheim already considered the question of what was required for competition to be fair and its outcome to count as just.[22] In practice, standard economics assumes that most markets are sufficiently 'perfect' that what emerges from them can be considered both just and efficient. Things are more complicated with social justice, whose substance is 'socially constructed' and therefore subject to cultural–political discourse as well as historical change. What is just in market terms is decided by the market and expressed in prices; what is socially just is decided in a political process where power and mobilization enter the balance, and finds its expression in formal and informal institutions. To the extent that a society sees itself through the lens of standard economics, or surrenders to its way of thinking, it may in the marginal case accept market justice as social justice and thereby

---

21   E. Böhm-Bawerk, *Control or Economic Law?*, Auburn, AL: Ludwig von Mises Institute, 2012 [1914].

22   E. Durkheim, *The Division of Labour in Society*, London: Palgrave Macmillan, 1974 [1893].

eliminate the tension between the two.[23] One variant of this solution is to declare, with Friedrich von Hayek, the concept of social justice nonsensical,[24] and to configure political and economic institutions in such a way that demands for social justice which interfere with market justice are excluded from the outset.

Be that as it may, from the point of view of market justice there is a constant danger that ideas of social justice will usurp the public power through the formation of a democratic majority and then regularly distort the operation of the market. Social justice is material, not formal, in nature – and so it cannot but appear irrational, arbitrary and unpredictable in terms of the formal rationality of the market.[25] Politics, to the extent that it is driven by demands for social justice, therefore confuses the market process, muddies its outcomes,

23 At an individual level, the economic theory taught at most university economics departments achieves this with astonishing effectiveness in most of its disciples. Organized business pursues the same objective with its demand for school classes in 'economics' – which amounts to nothing other than moral re-education rewarded with school grades and presented as initiation into positive, 'value-free' science. See also the report in the *Frankfurter Allgemeine Zeitung* (9 August 2012) on a lecture entitled 'Markets Are Wonderful', given by Ben Bernanke, the head of the US Federal Reserve, to a group of selected teachers.

24 'What we have to deal with in the case of "social justice" is simply a quasi-religious superstition of the kind which we should respectfully leave in peace so long as it merely makes those happy who hold it, but which we must fight when it becomes the pretext of coercing other men. And the prevailing belief in "social justice" is at present probably the gravest threat to most other values of a free civilization' (F. A. Hayek, *Law, Legislation and Liberty: A New Statement of the Liberal Principles of Justice and Political Economy*, Abingdon: Routledge, 2013 [1976], vol. 2, 230).

25 This idea may already be found in Max Weber. 'The concept of "substantive rationality", on the other hand, is full of ambiguities. It conveys only one element common to all "substantive" analyses: namely, that they do not restrict themselves to note the purely formal and (relatively) unambiguous fact that action is based on "goal-oriented" rational calculation with the technically most adequate available methods, whether they be ethical, political, utilitarian, hedonistic, feudal (*ständisch*), egalitarian, or whatever, and measure the results of the economic action, however formally "rational" in the sense of correct calculation they may be, against these scales of "value rationality" or "substantive" goal rationality". There is an infinite number of possible value scales for this type of rationality, of which the socialist and communist standards constitute only one group. The latter, although by no means unambiguous in themselves, always involve elements of social justice and equality' (M. Weber, *Economy and Society*, 2 vols, Berkeley: University of California Press, 1978 [1956], pp. 85–6).

creates false incentives and 'moral hazards', undermines the performance principle and is generally alien to the 'business world'. On the other hand, from the point of view of social justice, the 'democratic class struggle'[26] is an indispensable corrective in a system which, resting upon unequal contracts between wage-earners and profit-makers, gives rise to a cumulative advantage in line with what has been called the Matthew principle: 'For to all those who have, more will be given, and they will have an abundance; but from those who have nothing, even what they have will be taken away' (Matt. 25:29). While correctives to the market based on social–political ideas of justice are disturbances to capitalist practice, they must be considered inevitable so long as it is possible that the born losers of the market refuse to play ball. Without losers there can be no winners, and without permanent losers, no permanent winners.[27]

Furthermore, capital could always react to social encroachments in the market that seemed to go too far. Crises develop if those who control essential means of production fear they will not eventually be rewarded in accordance with their ideas of market justice; their 'confidence' then sinks below the minimum level necessary for investment. Holders and handlers of capital may transfer it abroad or park it somewhere in the money economy, withdrawing it forever or temporarily from circulation in the economy of a polity in which they no longer trust. The result is unemployment and low growth – more than ever under today's conditions of unfettered capital markets.

---

26   W. Korpi, *The Democratic Class Struggle*, London: Routledge and Kegan Paul, 1983.

27   The political correction of market justice by social justice in order to protect social cohesion has interesting precursors. Medieval English legal theory distinguished between 'justice' and 'equity'. It was the responsibility of common law courts to produce justice. Their judgements, however, even when formally unassailable, could clash with substantive ideas of justice. Those involved in such cases could appeal to the 'court of equity', which resided at the chancellery of the royal court and could overturn or modify the judgements of common law courts. Such interventions tended to appear systematically incoherent to defenders of the common law, until centuries later the law of equity was incorporated into the common law (M. Illmer, 'Equity', in Jürgen Basedow et al., *Handbuch des Europäischen Privatrechts*, vol. 1, Tübingen: Mohr Siebeck, 2009, pp. 400–4). In relation to the contractual regime of the free market, the interventionist state of today plays the role of a court of equity – or did so in the postwar period attuned to decommodification.

Market justice too involves normative standards – those of the owners and managers of capital – but is in this sense social justice, albeit one that presents itself, with the help of standard economics, as natural rather than social justice. The fact that the 'psychological' trust of capital in political conditions is the main *technical* prerequisite for the functioning of a capitalist economy sets narrow limits to the correction of market justice by democratically empowered social justice. A basic asymmetry of a capitalist political economy consists in the fact that the demands of 'capital' for an adequate return operate in effect as empirical preconditions for the functioning of the whole system, whereas the corresponding demands of 'labour' count as disruptive.

Max Weber, like Schumpeter and others after him, feared that substantive justice, driven by 'the bureaucracy' and its socialist supporters, would gradually superimpose itself on the formal justice of the market, eventually resulting in the downfall of capitalism and the freedom of the bourgeois individual associated with a capitalist economic order.[28] The neoliberal turn we have witnessed since the 1970s has removed this danger for the foreseeable future. Today the liberalization of capitalism has reached a point where the final liberation of market justice from its historical remodelling by social justice is coming closer and closer, due to the fact that it is becoming ever less possible to simulate social justice by feeding fictive resources into the distributional conflict while allowing market justice to prevail. I shall go into this in greater detail below.

The market could be made immune from democratic correctives either through the neoliberal re-education of citizens or through the elimination of democracy on the model of 1970s Chile; the first involves an attempt to indoctrinate the public in standard economic theory, while the second is not available as things stand at present. A strategy to dispel the tension between capitalism and democracy, and to establish the long-term primacy of the market over politics, must therefore centre on incremental 'reforms' of political-economic

---

28   C. Offe, *Reflections on America: Tocqueville, Weber and Adorno in the United States*, Cambridge: Polity, 2006.

institutions:[29] the move towards a rule-bound economic policy, independent central banks and a fiscal policy safe from electoral outcomes;
the transfer of economic policy decisions to regulatory bodies and
'committees of experts'; and debt ceilings enshrined in the constitution that are legally binding on governments for decades to come, if
not forever. In the course of this, the states of advanced capitalism are
to be constructed in such a way that they earn the enduring trust of
the owners and movers of capital, by giving credible guarantees at the
level of policy and institutions that they will not intervene in 'the
economy' – or that, if they do, it will only be to protect and enforce
market justice in the shape of suitable returns on capital investments.
A precondition for this is the neutralization of democracy, in the
sense of the social democracy of postwar capitalism, and the successful completion of a programme of Hayekian liberalization.

In their rhetoric and ideational policy, the champions of market
justice seek to gain the upper hand by denouncing social justice as
'political' (in the sense of particularist) and therefore as dirty or corrupt.
In contrast, it is claimed that market justice, with its ostensible imper-
sonality and price-theoretical calculability, functions in accordance
with universalist principles, in a 'clean' manner in the sense of untouched
by politics. Such distinctions and equations have long entered deep into
everyday language: the statement that something was decided 'politically' is often enough to make it appear that the aim was to enrich some
defined interest group.[30] Capitalist PR experts tirelessly hawk around
the view that, whereas markets distribute according to general rules,
politics does so with an eye to power and connections. The fact that
markets, in assessing efficiency and allocating rewards, disregard the
initial endowment that participants bring to them can be ignored more
easily than redistributive policies, which must be publicly debated and
actively implemented. Also, *policy decisions* can be attributed to

---

29   W. Streeck and K. Thelen, 'Introduction: Institutional Change in Advanced
Political Economies', in W. Streeck and K. Thelen (eds), *Beyond Continuity: Institutional
Change in Advanced Political Economies*, Oxford: Oxford University Press, 2005, pp. 1–39.
30   In the 'public choice' view of the world, this is self-evident because axiomatically
true.

FIGURE 2.4. *Government spending and revenue, seven countries (% of GDP)*

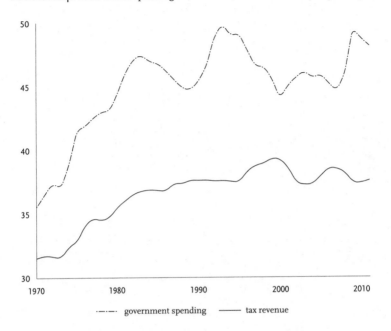

----- government spending   ——— tax revenue

Source: OECD *Economic Outlook: Statistics and Projections*

particular individuals or institutions, which can therefore be held accountable for them, whereas *market judgements* – especially if the market is assumed to be a state of nature – seem to fall from the sky without human intervention and have to be accepted as a fate behind which lurks a higher meaning intelligible only to experts.

STARVING THE BEAST!

If the growth of public debt correlates with the neoliberal turn and the downward trend in political participation, and not with a democratic mass mobilization, what is its actual cause? As I see it, today's crisis of public finances is the contemporary form of a functional problem of

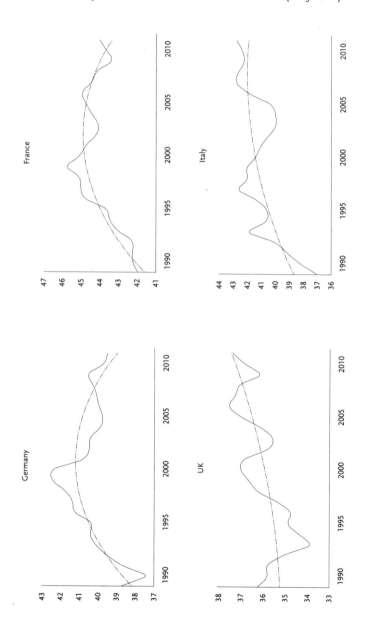

FIGURE 2.5. *Tax revenue 1989–2011, seven countries (% of GDP)*

Sweden

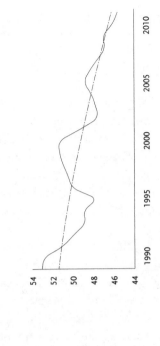

Japan

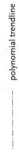

USA

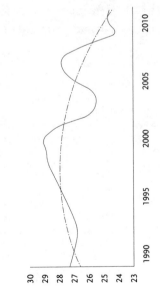

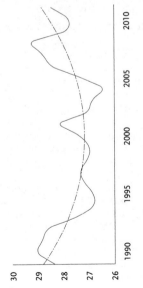

tax revenue

polynomial trendline

the modern state that was diagnosed in the early twentieth century: namely, its tendency to fall short in extracting from a society of private owners the means it requires to perform its growing tasks. Not *high spending* but *low receipts* are the cause of government debt, to be explained by economy and society, organized around the principle of possessive individualism, setting limits to their taxation while at the same time making more and more demands on the state.

It is indeed apparent that the debt surge of the rich democracies in the 1970s coincided with the increase in tax revenue lagging behind that of public spending. Whereas the two had previously kept pace with each other, the total tax take remained basically constant from the mid-1980s at the latest (Fig. 2.4), and in a number of countries (most notably Sweden, France, Germany and the United States) it actually declined with the forward march of neoliberalism around the turn of the century (Fig. 2.5).[31] Here too the trend was roughly uniform and the causes similar. The end of the growth phase brought to a close so-called cold progression, or 'bracket creep', whereby payers of income tax kept moving up into higher brackets. In part, the effect of this on state revenue was offset by the inflation of the 1970s, but soon middle-class losses in real income, in particular, led to mounting tax resistance[32] and demands

---

31   Japan, starting from a very low level, has registered a rising trend in recent years. The tax take also slightly increased in Britain under the Labour government, but there are currently strong efforts at a trend reversal. For the European Monetary Union, the years from 2000 until the present crisis saw a link between greater openness to foreign direct investment and a fall in tax revenue from capital and work income, in the latter case as a result of lower wages at the bottom end of the labour market. Because of the deficit limits set by the EU stability pact, this led to a decline in public expenditure (I. Rademacher, *National Tax Policy in the EMU: Some Empirical Evidence on the Effects of Common Monetary Policy on the Distribution of Tax Burdens*, unpublished thesis, social sciences faculty, Frankfurt/Main, 2012).

32   F. Block, 'Read Their Lips: Taxation and the Right-Wing Agenda', in Isaac William Martin et al. (eds), *The New Fiscal Sociology: Taxation in Comparative and Historical Perspective*, Cambridge: Cambridge University Press, 2009, pp. 68–85; J. Citrin, 'Do People Want Something for Nothing? Public Opinion on Taxes and Government Spending', *National Tax Journal*, vol. 32/2, Supplement, 1979, pp. 113–29; J. Citrin, 'Proposition 13 and the Transformation of California Government', *The California Journal of Politics and Policy*, vol. 1/1, 2009, pp. 1–9; C. Steuerle, *The Tax Decade: How Taxes Came to Dominate the Public Agenda*, Washington, DC: The Urban Institute Press, 1992.

for reforms such as the indexation of tax bands. Together with the successful stabilization of money, this meant that government revenue could rise only through visible rather than politically less risky invisible tax increases.

In the 1990s, other factors entered the picture. The fast-growing internationalization of the economy opened up new scope for large corporations to shift their tax obligations to less demanding countries. Even where this did not involve actual relocation, it exposed the nation-states of democratic capitalism to more intense fiscal competition with one another and pushed their governments to lower the top rates of corporate taxation.[33] True, the withdrawal of various exemptions was supposed to 'broaden' the national tax base and to make the overall outcome revenue-neutral, but the fact remains that it was no longer possible to contemplate *raising* taxes. Besides, the pervasive neoliberal insistence on 'incentives' to kick-start economic growth entailed higher pay and lower tax rates at the top, along with cuts in wages and benefits at the bottom of the income ladder. In this respect too, the 'varieties' of capitalism differed only in degree: the combination of tax reforms and labour-market reform (Hartz IV!) under Schröder's Red-Green government in Germany[34] was matched by Clinton's abolition of 'welfare as we know it' and Bush's notorious tax cuts after 2001.[35]

The American case offers convincing evidence that the origins of the public financial crisis have at least as much to do with revenue as with expenditure. For strategists of the organized tax resistance going back to the late 1970s, which celebrated its first victories in California, the popular demand for lower taxes served the more

---

33 S. Ganghof, *Wer regiert in der Steuerpolitik? Einkommenssteuerreform zwischen internationalem Wettbewerb und nationalen Verteilungskonflikten*, Frankfurt/Main: Campus, 2004; S. Ganghof and P. Genschel, 'Taxation and Democracy in the EU', *Journal of European Public Policy*, vol. 15, 2008, pp. 58–77; P. Genschel and P. Schwarz, 'Tax Competition and Fiscal Democracy', in Schäfer et al. (eds), *Politics in the Age of Austerity*.

34 Ganghof, *Wer regiert in der Steuerpolitik?*, esp. pp. 98–117.

35 Hacker and Pierson (*Winner-Take-All Politics*) examine in impressive detail the role that tax cuts played in shaping the American 'winner takes all' economy and the high public debt that came with it in the 1990s and early 2000s.

far-reaching aim of making it impossible for the government to continue with equally popular social programmes. The slogan of this hugely successful movement, 'Starving the Beast', was spread around by one of the most influential figures in American politics, the anti-taxation activist Grover Norquist.[36] That the main objective of the movement was not to balance the budget but to roll back the state along neoliberal lines is shown by the fact that its political standard-bearer in the first decade of the new century, George W. Bush, who had inherited a budget surplus from his predecessor, found nothing more pressing to do than to convert this into a record deficit by greatly reducing the tax bill for the super-rich – while at the same time unleashing two wars that dug further holes on the expenditure side.[37]

Furthermore, the fact that state revenue began to stagnate after the 1970s, while expenditure continued to increase until the first neoliberal wave of fiscal consolidation around the end of the century, need not be attributed to democratic empowerment of insatiable electorates. Rather, there is much to be said for the functionalist view that it expressed a growing need for public investment and curative measures to accompany capitalist development – measures that repaired the damage caused by capital accumulation as well as creating the conditions for further growth.[38] An example of curative expenditure

---

36   R. Kuttner, *Revolt of the Haves: Tax Rebellions and Hard Times*, New York: Simon & Schuster, 1980; I. Martin, *The Permanent Tax Revolt: How the Property Tax Transformed American Politics*, Stanford, CA: Stanford University Press, 2008; D. Tarschys, 'The Scissors Crisis in Public Finance', *Policy Sciences*, vol. 15/3, 1983, pp. 205–24.

37   The German situation is very similar, in that the budget would have been balanced before 2008 had it not been for Schröder's tax reform. In a speech to the Frankfurt Chamber of Industry and Commerce in January 2006, the newly appointed finance minister in Angela Merkel's Grand Coalition (2005–9) praised the previous SPD–Green government for carrying out 'the most extensive tax reform in our country's history' (P. Steinbrück, 'Lobbyisten in der Produktion', *Frankfurter Allgemeine Zeitung*, 12 January 2006). At the beginning of 2005, German income tax rates were lower than ever before, and the tax burden on the national economy had been far below the long-term average. The finance minister of the time was in 2012 the candidate for chancellor of the Social Democratic Party of Germany (SPD).

38   There are many similar classifications of public expenditures: J. O'Connor (*The Fiscal Crisis of the State*, New York: St Martin's Press, 1973), for example, distinguishes

might be the increased outlay on social benefits associated with the return of structural unemployment,[39] or the rising costs of health care and new environmental protection policies. Oriented to investment, rather, is all the public expenditure on the building and maintenance of physical infrastructure, the formation of human capital, and scientific-technological research indispensable for private capital accumulation. In a broader sense, it also includes spending on the so-called peaceful use of nuclear energy, without which private electricity generation by nuclear reactors would apparently be unprofitable; public childcare facilities to enable the spread of female employment and thereby contribute to economic growth; the upkeep of aircraft-carriers and the development and deployment of drones and similar technologies to secure oil imports at acceptable prices; or the, as we now know, highly risky deregulation of the private finance industry, in order to expand the volume of credit as the last remaining means of generating economic (pseudo-)growth.[40]

---

between 'social capital expenditures' (further subdivided into 'social investment' and 'social consumption') and 'social expenses of production'; and also between legitimation and accumulation as two functions of public spending.

39   On the other hand, the necessity for this – as for any measure of social justice – is open to dispute and subject to political negotiation. A society may always draw the neoliberal conclusion that support for those out of work is unfair to those in work, and in doing so it may save a lot of public money. But social policy may also be thought to 'pay', by maintaining the capacity for work and the 'good will' of wage-earners; it would then no longer be curative or even 'decommodifying', but would represent investment rather than consumption. There are social and cultural conditions – such as, to an increasing extent, those prevailing at present – in which this is the only effective justification for social policy in general.

40   Social policy has the character of investment when it promotes the willingness of wage-earners to remain in dependent employment and to act in accordance with the corresponding expectations. Capitalism cannot function if employees behave in ways permitted to, and even expected of, their employers: that is, in radical and unconditional pursuit of utility maximization. (The expectation of distributive moderation contradicts the model of Homo oeconomicus and can be reconciled with it only on the assumption, axiomatic in labour economics, that workers are 'risk-averse'.) Without pay restraint in return for the security of a steady wage, the employer–employee relation would collapse. In the tripartite agreements of the 1970s involving government, employers and unions (P. Schmitter and G. Lehmbruch (eds), Trends Towards Corporatist Intermediation, London: Sage, 1979), the government often provided pension increases in return for union wage restraint – increases which would only apply later when they would have to be defrayed from the public purse.

THE CRISIS OF THE TAX STATE

It is hard not to think here of a classical trope which, since the replacement of 'public finance' with 'public choice', has been dismissed from economic theory as lacking in rigour. I am referring to Adolph Wagner's 'law' of rising state activity and public expenditure, which was formulated in the closing decades of the nineteenth century[41] and still served as a major inspiration for Richard Musgrave in the 1950s.[42] Wagner, a statist *Kathedersozialist* and rector of Berlin university, who was one of Bismarck's advisers on economic and social policy and from 1910 a member of the Prussian Upper Chamber, expected the state's share of a modern growing economy to move constantly upward, both to provide for a higher level of civilization in general and to cover what would today be called the 'externalities' of expanding markets and a privatized mode of production.[43] The echoes of Marx's notion of an increasing socialization of the capitalist mode of production despite its private organization are hardly accidental, even though there is nothing in Wagner to match Marx's central idea of the internally contradictory nature of capitalist development and the need for a revolutionary political breakthrough to bring the relations of production into line with the mode of production.

Wagner's ideas were all the more important for the 'sociology of finance' developing around the time of the First World War. The Austrian socialist Rudolf Goldscheid, a prominent adversary of Max Weber in the early period of the Deutsche Gesellschaft für Soziologie, saw the development of the feudal 'domain state' into the modern 'tax

---

Thus, a large part of the social spending increases of the 1980s and later was in reality a form of labour remuneration deferred to reduce the burden on employers. This explains why unions and employees were and are so insistent that it should be paid.

41   See A. Wagner, 'Staat in nationalökonomischer Hinsicht', in Ludwig Elster et al. (eds), *Handwörterbuch der Staatswissenschaften*, Jena: Fischer, 1911, pp. 727–39.

42   R. Musgrave, *The Theory of Public Finance*, New York: McGraw-Hill, 1958.

43   'Furthermore, the history of progressive nations – comparisons both across time and between countries and economies at different stages of development – allows us to derive a tendency or so-called "law" of the development of state activities for civilized countries: the law of the increasing scale of "public" or state activities among advancing civilized nations' (A. Wagner, *Grundlegung der politischen Oekonomie*, 3rd edn, Leipzig: C. F. Wintersche Verlagshandlung, 1892, pp. 883f.; see also pp. 892–908).

state' – its revenue being raised from a society of private property-owners – as a phenomenon accompanying the advance of capitalism.[44] In a fiscal-sociological reformulation of Marx's theorem of a growing contradiction between mode and relations of production, he expected that the ability of the tax state to wrest the resources it needed from its citizens – or, to be more precise, from a civil society dominated by property owners – would sooner or later become inadequate. At this point the tax state would come up against its limits, since in a capitalist socio-economic order it operated as an 'expropriated state' devoid of the resources it needed to carry out its tasks. What would then be required was a 'recapitalization' of the state that replaced the tax-funding of its expenditures with revenue from public economic activities. According to the summary of Goldscheid's position in Fritz and Mikl-Horke,[45] the functioning of the state in the public interest could 'not be achieved by fiscal means'. For taxes

again benefit, through the conduit of the state, only the most power-ful owners of capital. Their power would increase further, while that of the state as guardian of social needs would be weakened. The powerful would have ways of passing on taxes, whereas the mass of the population would have to bear the entire tax burden. Even progressive income taxes would simply mean that the state devel-oped hidden interests in the maintenance of inequality and the concentration of profits.

Goldscheid was not alone in his pessimistic view of fiscal policy. The possibility of a 'crisis of the tax state' was widely discussed in the period immediately after the First World War, an especially influential

---

44 W. Fritz and G. Mikl-Horke, *Rudolf Goldscheid: Finanzsoziologie und ethische Sozialwissenschaft*, Vienna: Lit. Verlag, 2007; R. Goldscheid, 'Staat, öffentlicher Haushalt und Gesellschaft', in Wilhelm Gerloff and Franz Meisel (eds), *Handbuch der Finanzwissenschaft*, vol. 1, Tübingen: Mohr Siebeck, 1926, pp. 146–84; R. Goldscheid, 'Finanzwissenschaft und Soziologie', in Rudolf Hickel (ed.), *Die Finanzkrise des Steuerstaats. Beiträge zur politischen Ökonomie der Staatsfinanzen*, Frankfurt/Main: Campus, 1976 [1917], pp. 317–28.
45 Fritz and Mikl-Horke, *Rudolf Goldscheid*, p. 166.

contribution being the young Joseph Schumpeter's lecture of 1918 to the Austrian Gesellschaft der Soziologie.[46] His conclusion was that the historical institution of the tax state had not yet reached its limits, and that the war debts of Germany and Austria in particular could be settled without general socialization. Looking further ahead, however, he did not rule out the possibility – indeed, he expected it – that the tax state and the capitalist mode of production as a whole would one day cease to be viable.[47] This idea would subsequently be banished to the catacombs in the history of economic thought, especially after 1945, when a welfare-state capitalism domesticated along Keynesian lines appeared to usher in a new era. Here and there, however, it continued to make itself heard in more or less new formulations – not least in the fiscal crisis theory of the Marxist James O'Connor and, following on from it, Daniel Bell's pessimistic reflections on the future of capitalism in the 1970s.[48]

FROM TAX STATE TO DEBT STATE

If the fiscal crisis of the state predicted by O'Connor and Bell is situated on the revenue rather than the expenditure side – so that it is defined à la Goldscheid and Schumpeter as a crisis of the tax state – then we are struck by two trends of recent decades that no one foresaw in their actual significance. The first is the transformation of the *tax state* into a *debt state* – that is, a state which covers a large, possibly rising, part of its expenditure through borrowing rather than taxation, thereby accumulating a debt mountain that it has to finance with an ever greater share

---

46   J. Schumpeter, 'The Crisis of the Tax State' [1918]. In Richard Swedberg, ed., *The Economics and Sociology of Capitalism*, Princeton, NJ: Princeton University Press, 1991, pp. 99–141.

47   'By and by private enterprise will lose its social meaning through the development of the economy and the consequent expansion of the sphere of social sympathy. The signs of this are already with us and it was inherent in the tendencies of the second half of the nineteenth century, whose perhaps final aberration was all that which culminated in the world war. Society is growing beyond private enterprise and tax state, not because but in spite of the war. That too is certain' (Schumpeter, 'The Crisis of the Tax State', p. 131).

48   D. Bell, 'The Public Household: On "Fiscal Sociology" and the Liberal Society,' in *The Cultural Contradictions of Capitalism*, New York: Basic Books, 1976, pp. 220–82.

of its revenue. The minor role that *this* answer to the funding problem of modern states played in earlier discussions – it is only a marginal aspect in O'Connor, for instance[49] – is probably due in part to the fact that routine funding of public debt first required the construction of an efficient finance sector and the 'financialization' of capitalism through the deregulation of finance markets. Moreover, finance markets had to be integrated internationally in order to satisfy the huge credit needs of rich industrial countries, especially the United States. This process, as we said before, was under way globally by the 1980s at the latest.

The development of the debt state may be understood both as a retarding factor in the crisis of the tax state and as the rise of a new political formation with its own laws. In what follows, I shall mainly employ the second of these perspectives. But it should be noted in advance that the formation of the debt state was impeded by a countervailing force which, in the neoliberal reform movement of the 1990s and 2000s, sought to consolidate government finances by *privatizing* services that had accrued to the state in the course of the twentieth century. This was the other historical development that the crisis theories of the 1970s had not yet been able to foresee: the total or partial return of an increasing number of state functions – from retirement provision through health care and education to responsibility for the level of employment – to society and the market economy. As we have seen, the easiest way of achieving this was by simultaneously improving the access of private households to credit. In part, the privatization of a broad swath of public services was facilitated and justified by the higher level of prosperity and consumption. But the elimination of postwar social rights through marketization ran parallel to the development of a new form of democracy (what Crouch

---

49 'The growth of state debt normally does not exacerbate the fiscal crisis, but neither does state borrowing alleviate the crisis. State and local government debt has been partly "self-liquidating" . . . Federal government debt also has partly "paid for itself" during periods when actual output is less than potential output by expanding credit and increasing the level of aggregate demand, production, employment, income, and the tax base' (O'Connor, *The Fiscal Crisis of the State*, pp. 179f.). This was written in 1973, when Keynesianism was still alive and US government debt still low (42.6 per cent of GDP, compared with 89.6 per cent in 2010).

calls 'post-democracy'),[50] in which political participation was rede-
fined as popular entertainment and disconnected from policy,
especially in the sphere of the economy.[51] In this perspective, the
present efforts at national and international levels to secure lasting
fiscal consolidation by cutting expenditure are nothing other than the
continuation of the neoliberal reforms of the 1990s and 2000s with a
new, more sophisticated toolkit.

Before turning to the political anatomy of the contemporary
debt state, I should like to summarize the argument so far. What I
propose is to reverse, not discard, the 'common pool' account of
public debt and the explanation of government indebtedness in
terms of a failure of democracy. As far as the 'common pool' theory
is concerned, I argue that the fiscal crisis of the state is not due to an
excess of democracy having enabled the mass of the population to
extract too much from the public purse; rather, those who have profited most from the capitalist economy have been paying too little,
and increasingly little, into the public purse. If an 'explosion of
demands' has caused a structural deficit of public finances, then it
has occurred among the upper classes; it is their income and their
assets that have multiplied rapidly over the past twenty years, not
least thanks to tax cuts, while wages and social services at the bottom
end of society have stagnated or fallen – a development masked, and
for a time legitimated, by money illusions supported by inflation,
public debt and 'credit capitalism'.

This makes clearer the real *failure of democracy* in the neoliberal
decades. Democracy and democratic politics failed to recognize and
oppose the counter-revolution against postwar social capitalism for
what it was; when they neglected to regulate the mushrooming financial
sector amid the illusory boom of the 1990s; when they gave credence to
the talk of 'hard' government giving way to a 'soft' governance friendly
to democracy;[52] when they refrained from making the beneficiaries of

---

50   C. Crouch, *Post-Democracy*, Cambridge: John Wiley & Sons, 2004.
51   This disconnection is analysed below in terms of a transition from Keynesian to
Hayekian political economy.
52   Convincing on this is C. Offe, 'Governance: "Empty Signifier" oder

capitalist economic growth pay the social costs of their gains;[53] and when they not only accepted growing inequality between those at the top and those at the bottom of society, but promoted it by tax and welfare reforms to provide greater incentives for capitalist progress. Furthermore, democratic politics contributed to the formation of the debt state when they failed to secure the stable political participation of social groups that would have an interest in preventing tax cuts for the better-off. Instead, the ongoing upward shift in the composition of the electorate made it harder and harder to impose tax increases.

I shall leave it open whether and how, in an increasingly international economy, nationally organized democratic politics could have successfully brought such tendencies under control. Evidently, the greater international mobility of industrial and finance capital has raised its 'reservation profit',[54] and so has the dependence of states upon the confidence of international investors. The liberalization policies that all governments in the capitalist world (both conservative and social democratic) adopted by the 1990s at the latest were supposed to deliver prosperity for the long-term future, through the full-scale adaptation of society to the new conditions of production demanded by increasingly mobile capital. What they overlooked was the highly limited compatibility of capitalism with democracy, and the fact that it could be achieved at all only through strict and effective political regulation and intervention. The structural and the ideological failure of democracy thus went hand in hand. The results have been there for all to see since 2008.

---

sozialwissenschaftliches Forschungsprogramm?', in Gunnar Folke Schuppert et al. (eds), *Governance in einer sich wandelnden Welt*, vol. 41, special issue, *Politische Vierteljahresschrift*, 2008, pp. 61–76.

53 In Germany, discussion of higher top rates of income tax, inheritance tax and various capital levies began only in summer 2012, after the French presidential elections and under pressure from the Left party; see, for example, S. Bach, 'Vermögensabgaben – ein Beitrag zur Sanierung der Staatsfinanzen in Europa', *DIW Wochenbericht*, 2012, pp. 3–11. There is still no realistic prospect of higher taxation of the rich, however.

54 I use this term by analogy with the 'reservation wage', which in labour economics denotes the wage below which workers are not prepared to enter into employment. The reservation profit is thus the lowest rate of profit that an investor will tolerate in order to put his or her money to work.

DEBT STATE AND DISTRIBUTION

Another failure of democracy in the transition to the debt state is that public discussion has almost entirely ignored the impact of the latter on distribution. In everyday political debate, conservative middle-class parties are thought of as less inclined than social democratic ones to run up high levels of debt. Comparative statistical analyses do not always confirm this[55] – though, to be sure, their cognitive value is, for a number of reasons, rather slender. Rhetorically, it may indeed be the case that criticism of debt has played a greater role on the political Right than on the Left. But one reason for this may be that the social groups represented by conservative parties are concerned not so much with freedom from debt as with the ability of governments to service and repay the loans they have raised from their affluent citizens – a worry powerfully voiced by 'the markets' in the current debt crisis.

The political link between public debt and wealth distribution only reveals itself if the debt-financing of governments in the period of the neoliberal turn is understood as the result of low taxation of the property-owning classes of society. The less is taken for the collective from high-earners and their families,[56] the more unequal is the distri-

---

55   U. Wagschal, *Staatsverschuldung: Ursachen im internationalen Vergleich*, Opladen: Verlag für Sozialwissenschaften, 1996; U. Wagschal, 'Staatsverschuldung', in Dieter Nohlen et al. (eds), *Kleines Lexikon der Politik*, Munich: C. H. Beck, 2007, pp. 547–52.

56   There is no shortage of grotesque examples. The Greek Constitution contains a tax exemption clause for shipowning families such as the Onassis and Niarchos families. This was introduced in 1967 immediately after the military putsch, and in 1972, the dictator Papadopoulos was gratefully elected president-for-life of the shipowners' association. Today, Greeks account for roughly 15 per cent of the world's merchant navy: see 'Insecurity Touches the Tycoons of Greece', *New York Times*, 24 May 2012, which points out that attempts to end shipowners' tax exemption would simply lead them to transfer their wealth and business abroad. How much the richest families of Greece actually own cannot be precisely established, 'because much of the money exists off-shore, secreted away in Swiss bank accounts or invested in real estate in London and Monaco'. For this reason – and also because of their sizeable holdings in Greek banks – the Greek oligarchs have every motive to remain in the European currency union. Instead of paying taxes, some of the rich families set up US-style philanthropic foundations. Others are said to have 'bolstered their already tight security forces by hiring more bodyguards'. Cf. 'Greece's Super-rich Maintain Lavish Lifestyles and Low Profiles', *Guardian*, 13 June 2012. Even the good-willed must wonder

bution of wealth – which is expressed *inter alia* in a high savings-rate at the upper end of society. For those whom fiscal policy allows to form private surplus capital, this creates the problem of finding opportunities for investment; the Keynesian rentier, who was supposed to have been wiped out by political euthanasia,[57] thus makes a powerful comeback. Governments' reliance on credit – due not least to successful resistance to taxation – provides a perfect answer in the search for secure investments. Not only is state poverty the investors' wealth; it offers them a golden outlet to invest that wealth profitably.

The only economist I know who has drawn attention to this nexus is Carl Christian von Weizsäcker, even though – or perhaps because – he gives it a positive spin. Unlike nearly all other German economists, he argues for an *increase* in public debt, at least in states with a current account surplus.[58] His justification for this is the long-term capital surplus in rich countries such as Germany, which he attributes to the greater needs of an ageing population to provide for the future. If this is not to result in an investment emergency, the state must be prepared to borrow from their savings, especially as the purpose of their investments rules out riskier alternatives, and also because investment opportunities in a developing knowledge-based economy with relatively low capital requirements are inadequate. Weizsäcker does not consider two possibilities with egalitarian implications: that higher taxation could relieve the 'investment emergency' of the well-heeled by converting surplus savings into regular government revenue ('confiscation', in the literal sense); and that needs for provision could as well be met collectively on a pay-as-you-go basis, instead of individually out of private assets.[59]

---

why such reports are almost completely lacking in the German press.

57   J. Keynes, *The General Theory of Employment, Interest and Money*, London: Macmillan, 1967 [1936], ch. 24.

58   See, for example, his article 'Das Janusgesicht der Staatsschulden', *Frankfurter Allgemeine Zeitung*, 5 June 2010.

59   Higher taxes to bring down public debt would also put to rest the tawdry rhetoric according to which 'we' should not live at the expense of 'our children' – when the real problem is that the 'better-off' live at everyone else's expense by largely avoiding the

Indeed, Weizsäcker leaves no doubt that political rather than technical motives lie behind his favoured solution, since 'explicit and implicit private wealth is, for reasons to do with provision as well as inheritance . . . a kind of "structural parameter", which cannot be changed without massive encroachments on . . . the bourgeois social structure of our society'.[60]

Weizsäcker's analysis makes it clear that, *so long as the state's capacity to repay its creditors can be relied upon*, the long-term debt-financing of government activity is definitely in the interests of financial asset-holders. For their victory to be complete, the winners in the distribution struggle in the market and with the tax authorities must be able to invest safely and profitably the capital they have wrested from state and society. They need a state that will not only leave them their money as private property but borrow it and keep it safe, pay interest on it and, last but not least, let them pass it on to their children – by virtue of inheritance taxes that have long been inconsequential.[61] In this way, the state as debt state serves to perpetuate extant patterns of social stratification and the social inequality built into them. At the same time, it subjects itself and its activity to the control of creditors in the shape of 'markets'. That control appears alongside the democratic control of the state by its citizenry, with the possibility of overlaying it or even, as we see today, eliminating it altogether in the transition from the debt state to the consolidation state.

---

social costs involved in the upkeep of their hunting grounds. An appropriate minimum wage for private services would in the same way reduce savings rates among the middle and upper classes and therefore help to overcome their investment problem, with a positive effect (as Keynes showed) on both consumption and growth.

60   C. Weizsäcker, 'Das Janusgesicht der Staatsschulden', *Frankfurter Allgemeine Zeitung*, 5 June 2010.

61   On inheritance taxes, see the works of Jens Beckert (for example, 'Der Streit um die Erbschaftssteuer', *Leviathan*, vol. 32/4, 2004, pp. 543–57).

THE POLITICS OF THE DEBT STATE

The present fiscal crisis and the transition from the tax state to the debt state have inaugurated a new stage in the relationship between capitalism and democracy, one that was not foreseen in traditional theories of democracy. The post-2008 crisis has raised the indebtedness of the rich democracies to a level at which creditors can no longer be sure that governments will be able and willing in the future to meet their payment obligations. As a result lenders seek far more than in the past to protect their claims by exerting influence on government policies. In the debt state, therefore, a second category of stakeholders appears alongside the citizens who, in the democratic tax state and established political theory, constituted the only reference group of the modern state.

The rise of creditors to become the second 'constituency'[62] of the modern state is strikingly reminiscent of the emergence of activist shareholders in the corporate world under the 'shareholder value' doctrine of the 1980s and 1990s.[63] Like the boards of publicly listed companies in relation to the new 'markets for corporate control', the governments of today's debt states in their relationship with the 'financial markets' are forced to serve a further set of interests whose claims have suddenly increased because of their greater capacity to assert themselves in more liquid financial markets. Like capital markets in the transformation of corporate governance, credit markets in the transformation of democracy are eager to deploy their newly won power (especially the option they have to sell shares and pull out) in order to minimize the influence of competing claims on the relevant executive – that of the workforce on management or of citizens on the elected government. Both cases boil down to a distribution conflict: in companies, over whether surpluses should be allocated to shareholders rather than the workforce, or retained to

---

62 Constituency not only in the electoral sense, but as 'a body of customers, supporters, etc.' (*New Shorter Oxford Dictionary*). One might perhaps, with Hegel, describe the constituency of a state as its 'moral root'; the debt state would then have two such roots.
63 A. Rappaport, *Creating Shareholder Value*, New York: The Free Press, 1986.

strengthen the hand of management; in debt states, over the preservation of what might be called the 'bondholder value' of government securities. Much as an increase in shareholder value requires management to hold down the workforce or – better still – to lock it into common efforts to boost the share price, so does the trust of creditors require that governments persuade or compel their citizens to moderate their claims on the public purse in favour of the 'financial markets'.

In what follows, I would like to outline a stylized model of the contemporary debt state as addressee and mandatary of two differently constituted collectives, and as an intermediary system between two conflicting environments. While these function in accordance with logics that tend to be incompatible with each other, government policy must as far as possible satisfy them at one and the same time: the *Staatsvolk* (the general citizenry) and what I refer to as the *Marktvolk* (the people of the market) (Fig. 2.6).[64] A Staatsvolk is nationally organized and consists of citizens tied to a particular state, from which they can claim certain inalienable rights of citizenship. One of these is the expression of their will at periodic elections. Between elections citizens can influence the decisions of their constitutional representatives by speaking out and contributing to the formation of a 'public opinion'. For this they have a duty of loyalty to the democratic state, including the payment of taxes, whose use is in principle freely decided by the competent bodies of the state. The loyalty of citizens may be seen as being given in return for the state's role in safeguarding their livelihood, and especially in guaranteeing democratically founded social rights.

The democratic state, ruled and (qua *tax state*) resourced by its citizens, becomes a democratic *debt state* as soon as its subsistence depends not only on the financial contributions of its citizens but, to a

---

64 The model recalls the account of interest groups as social systems that must survive simultaneously in two environments with different action logics: a social base with its governing 'membership logic' and a political-institutional system with its 'logic of influence'. In each model, an organization has to rely on mobilizing resources from two environments that place contradictory demands on its behaviour (P. Schmitter and W. Streeck, *The Organization of Business Interests: Studying the Associative Action of Business in Advanced Industrial Societies*, MPIfG Discussion Paper No. 99/1, Cologne: Max-Planck-Institut für Gesellschaftsforschung, 1999).

significant degree, on the confidence of creditors. In contrast to the *Staatsvolk* of the tax state, the *Marktvolk* of the debt state is transnationally integrated. They are bound to national states purely by contractual ties, as investors rather than citizens. Their rights vis-à-vis the state are of a private rather than public character, deriving not from a constitution but from the civil law. Instead of diffuse and politically expandable civil rights, they have claims on the state that are in principle enforceable before a court of law and come to an end with the fulfilment of the relevant contract. As creditors, they cannot vote out a government that is not to their liking; they can, however, sell off their existing bonds or refrain from participating in a new auction of public debt. The interest rates that are determined at these sales – which correspond to the investors' assessment of the risk that they will not get back all or some of their money – are the 'public opinion' of the *Marktvolk*, expressed in quantitative terms and therefore much more precise and easy to read than the public opinion of the *Staatsvolk*. Whereas the debt state can expect a duty of loyalty from its citizens, it must in relation to its *Marktvolk* take care to gain and preserve its confidence, by conscientiously servicing the debt it owes them and making it appear credible that it can and will do so in the future as well.

FIGURE 2.6. *The democratic debt state and its two peoples*

Staatsvolk	Marktvolk
national	international
citizens	investors
civil rights	claims
voters	creditors
elections (periodic)	auctions (continual)
public opinion	interest rates
loyalty	'confidence'
public services	debt service

In trying to understand the functioning of the democratic debt state, one is at first surprised that no one seems to know who its all-important *Marktvolk* really are. Nor has much been written, at least in the sociological literature or the weekly and daily press, about how the prices that the states must pay for their credit are established.[65] What we know is that every government offers bonds for sale several times a year, mainly to refinance existing debt; this means that at virtually every moment a public sale is taking place somewhere in the world. Economic theory seems to take it for granted that there is a perfect market for government bonds, and does not like to see this doubted; that is probably not the least of the reasons why data about the market's demand structure are almost unobtainable – which is all the more surprising since, in most other sectors of the economy, at either national or global level, statistics about market share and concentration ratios tend to be readily available. We know the names of a few large funds that specialize in the government bond market, like Calpers and PIMCO (Public Investment Management Company),[66] but we do not know whether, as in other markets, there is a small group of large corporations that exercise something like market and price leadership. What we do know is that the finance ministers of many countries tend to request meetings with PIMCO's chairman to get his advice about their budgetary policy.[67] There is no international anti-trust legislation banning

---

65 For example, the high volatility of risk premiums for government loans, over short-term periods when the fundamental data remain the same, is an astonishing phenomenon in need of explanation. It is equally mysterious why high-debt countries such as Belgium, Japan or the United States can borrow on relatively favourable terms, whereas a country like Spain, whose debt ratio is rather on the low side, must pay high interest rates to obtain a loan.

66 PIMCO is probably the world's largest company managing investment funds that specialize in public loans; the size of its Total Return fund alone is US$263 billion. In 2011 the company's founder and president, William H. Gross, drew an income of $200 million, while his chief executive officer and designated successor, Mohamed A. El-Erian, had to be content with $100 million. In the five crisis years from 2007 to 2011, Total Return netted an average annual return of approximately 9.5 per cent ('The Bond Market Discovers a New Leading Man', *New York Times*, 29 July 2012).

67 An interview with Mohamed El-Erian in the English online edition of *Der Spiegel* (2 August 2011) contains the following passage:

agreements between market leaders or the public signalling of plans to buy or not to buy; unlike price-fixing among producers of cement or underwear, it would not be a punishable offence if the world's leading investment funds agreed in a teleconference to stay out of the next auction of, say, French government bonds.[68]

Democratic debt states must manoeuvre between their two categories of stakeholders, keeping them both at least sufficiently happy that they do not withdraw their loyalty or, as the case may be, their confidence. For this, states must not allow themselves to be monopolized by either side, since that might trigger a crisis in their relations with the other side. A democratic debt state can satisfy its creditors only if its citizens continue to cooperate with it; should they come to regard the state as an extended arm of its creditors, it will be in danger of losing their allegiance. At the same time, such a state can claim legitimacy in the eyes of its citizens – especially those who, despite internationalization, continue to pay taxes – only if its creditors are

SPIEGEL: Pimco is in regular contact with governments around the world. How would you advise, for example, a Spanish finance minister?

EL-ERIAN: I think it was my colleagues in London who met with him and his delegation, and they did so at the request of the Spanish authorities.

SPIEGEL: How many finance ministers have called you recently?

EL-ERIAN: Some do, as do some central bankers from around the world. The typical question we get asked is this: 'What does it take for Pimco to make long-term investments in our country.' The answer is always the same: an outlook of high and sustainable growth.

SPIEGEL: And your people then tell the Spanish finance minister: 'Sorry, but your bonds are too risky for us.'

EL-ERIAN: We are very cautious about exposures to Greece and Ireland. Spain is under more active discussion, with a lot depending on how they deal with the problem of the *cajas* [savings banks]. (From www.spiegel.de, last accessed 26 November 2012).

68   Little is known either about the role of the rating agencies in the public debt market. Unlike the securitization market, no one – or anyway no issuing government – pays for the rating of government bonds; whether the bond purchasers pay is not certain. For a time the ratings of the three large agencies (Standard and Poor's, Fitch and Moody's) were awaited impatiently – sometimes in a state of panic – by European governments and international organizations, and 'the markets' reacted to them as to a command. Recently this seems to have no longer been the case. Whether the rating agencies coordinate their behaviour with creditors on the international loan market, and if so how they do it, must remain for now an open question.

willing to finance and refinance its debt on terms that are tolerable. This willingness, however, will decline or disappear if a government pays too much heed to its citizens' wishes and in doing so ties up resources that might later be required for debt service. Which of the two sides commands greater attention from a debt state's government will depend on their relative strength. This in turn depends on how likely a threatened withdrawal of confidence or loyalty, respectively, appears to be, and on how much pain it would cause to the country and its government.

The conflict between the two stakeholder groups competing with each other for control of the democratic debt state is a new, developing and as yet hardly understood phenomenon. There is much to be said for the view that the emergence of finance capital as a second people – a *Marktvolk* rivalling the *Staatsvolk* – marks a new stage in the relationship between capitalism and democracy, in which capital exercises its political influence not only indirectly (by investing or not investing in national economies) but also directly (by financing or not financing the state itself). In the 1960s and 1970s critical crisis theory studied how postwar states more or less succeeded in securing their democratic legitimacy despite the special position occupied by citizens in command of the means of production and investment. The rapid, class-skewed decline of democratic organization and participation within the liberalization process, as well as the diminishing scope for political action in the crises of the past four decades, might signify that something similar may not be possible after the transition from the tax state to the debt state.

I would now like to bring together a few stylized observations on the politics of the debt state and the constellation of interests operating within it, even if the underdeveloped state of research in this area means that they can be no more than impressions gleaned from news reports.

1) The rising indebtedness of the rich democracies has for some time been curtailing their effective sovereignty, by subjecting the policies of their governments to the discipline of financial markets. As early as April 2000, the head of the Deutsche Bank, Rolf Breuer,

argued in a much-noted article in the weekly *Die Zeit* that politics would 'more than ever [have to be] formulated with an eye to the financial markets': 'If you like, they have taken on an important watchdog role alongside the media, almost as a kind of "fifth estate".' In Breuer's view, this was not to be regretted as it would 'perhaps not be such a bad thing if politics in the twenty-first century was taken in tow by the financial markets'. For, in the end:

> Politicians . . . themselves contributed to the restrictions on action . . . that have been causing them such pain. Governments and parliaments made excessive use of the instrument of public debt. This entails – as with other debtors – a certain accountability to creditors. The higher the public debt, the more are countries exposed to the judgement of the financial markets. If governments and parliaments are forced today to pay greater heed to the needs and preferences of international financial markets, this too is attributable to the mistakes of the past.[69]

Just a few years later it was possible to express the same idea more bluntly. In September 2007, in an interview with the Zurich daily *Tages-Anzeiger* (19 September 2007), the chairman of the US Federal Reserve, Alan Greenspan, gave the following reply to the question of which candidate he supported for the presidency of the United States: 'We are fortunate that, thanks to globalization, policy decisions in the US have been largely replaced by global market forces. National security aside, it hardly makes any difference who will be the next president. The world is governed by market forces.'[70]

The limitation of national sovereignty by 'market forces' amounts to a limitation of the freedom of the *Staatsvolk* to make democratic decisions and a corresponding empowerment of the *Marktvolk*, which becomes increasingly essential for financing government decisions.

---

69   Rolf-E. Breuer, 'Die fünfte Gewalt' (available at www.zeit.de, last accessed 26 November 2012).

70   Quoted in, and translated from, U. Thielemann, 'Das Ende der Demokratie', *Wirtschaftsdienst – Zeitschrift für Wirtschaftspolitik*, vol. 91/12, 2011, p. X.

Democracy at national level presupposes nation-state sovereignty, but this is less and less available to debt states because of their dependence on financial markets. The organizational advantage that globally integrated financial markets have over nationally organized societies, and the political power resulting from it, first became dramatically clear in September 1992, when the financier George Soros was able to assemble so much money that he could successfully speculate against the Bank of England and blow apart the European monetary system of the day. His profits from the operation have been estimated at $1 billion.

2) The main aim of lenders to governments in their conflict with a state's citizens must be to ensure that, in the event of a crisis, their claims take precedence over those of the *Staatsvolk* – in other words, that debt service gets priority over public services. They can best achieve this by means of institutions such as a 'debt ceiling', ideally enshrined in the constitution, which limit the sovereignty of voters and future governments over public finances. The creation of such institutions may be enforced through the threat of higher-risk premiums or rewarded with lower premiums. In principle, what is involved is a key issue in the legal implication of bankruptcy, projected onto government financial policy: that is, which claims have priority over other claims? As far as the creditors are concerned, they need to ensure that any future 'haircut' will affect not them but, for example, pensioners and clients of national health care systems – in other words, that governments exercise sovereignty only over their *Staatsvolk*, not their *Marktvolk*. If we think of the discussions of recent years, we can see that this principle is now already taken for granted: it is a commonplace across the political spectrum that 'the markets' must not be 'unsettled' at any cost,[71] whereas the unsettling

---

71 A quotation from Ulrich Thielemann, a student of business ethics, may serve to illustrate this point. In September 2011, the German economics minister Philipp Rösler wrote in an article for *Die Welt* that there should be no 'ban on thinking' and that 'the possibility of an orderly state insolvency' should be considered. According to Thielemann, 'Finance Minister Wolfgang Schäuble reacted at once. He was "strictly against any public discussion of insolvency", on the grounds that it might lead to "uncontrollable reactions in the financial markets". "The markets", Schäuble had said a few days earlier, "must be in no doubt about Europe's capacity to act" . . . The opposition took this opportunity to display

of citizens-as-pensioners or citizens-as-patients has to be accepted in the name of the public good.

3) In the struggle for 'market confidence', debt states must make visible efforts to show that they are always ready to fulfil their civil law contractual obligations. In times of crisis, confidence-building of this kind is most successful with resolute austerity measures against the national population, preferably involving the opposition parties and by legally enshrining permanent limits on spending. So long as voters are still able to remove a government serving the capital markets, the *Marktvolk* can never be entirely sure of its position. The mere possibility that a less market-friendly opposition might come to power may cost the state dearly in confidence and therefore in money. The best debt state, then, is one governed by a Grand Coalition, at least in financial and fiscal policy, with tried-and-tested techniques to exclude deviant positions from the common constitutional home. Already before the 2013 election, the Federal Republic of Germany came very close to meeting those conditions.

4) One difficult problem for 'the markets' is that, if spending cuts for the citizenry go too far, they may have a negative impact on economic growth. Growth lowers the debt ratio and makes it easier for governments to service their debts;[72] a stagnant or shrinking economy increases the likelihood of a default. To combine austerity with growth is like squaring the circle: no one really knows how it could be done.[73] This also lies behind the interminable dispute among schools of economics over how to solve the crisis of public finances.

---

what is commonly referred to as "economic competence". The leader of the Green group in the Bundestag, Jürgen Trittin, described Rösler's remarks as "amateurish" and said they demonstrated that a "novice was in charge in the economics ministry". The stock markets will react' (Thielemann, 'Das Ende der Demokratie', p. 820).

72 Presumably this is so only beneath a certain level of debt. An influential expert view is that 80 per cent of GDP is the threshold beyond which the public debt hinders future growth (C. Reinhart and K. Rogoff, *Growth in a Time of Debt*, NBER Working Paper No. 15639, Cambridge, MA: National Bureau of Economic Research, 2009). If this is true – like all econometric 'laws', it should be treated with utmost caution – many developed economies are already incapable of growth.

73 See a few thoughts on the subject in chapter 4 below.

While some concentrate on the supply side – that is, on tax cuts and a cutback on government activity to revive the private sector – others call for a boost to public and private demand as a precondition for new investment in the real economy.

5) Further complications result from the fact that an ever larger part of the *Marktvolk* also belongs to the *Staatsvolk*, so that their interests include not only the reliable servicing of public debt but also, and perhaps even more, the maintenance of intact public services. This group has grown considerably in recent years, with the privatization of areas of social security provision (supplementary pensions, for example) and the increase in middle-class savings. For them the question poses itself of which would harm them more: a government default vis-à-vis 'the markets' (which would reduce their invested savings) or cuts in social spending in order to forestall such a default? Politically, they could probably be won either to austerity (which would protect their capital) or to resistance to austerity (to protect the social welfare state). Sociologically, they may be seen as a new kind of intermediate group, under pressure from contradictory interests.

6) Little is known about the power relations between national peoples and the *Marktvolk*, and how they impact on the ongoing negotiations over the 'terms of trade' between the two. The power of investors feeds mainly on their advanced international integration and the presence of efficient global capital markets, both of which make it possible for them to switch quickly from one investment to another if 'confidence' is lost. Under certain circumstances, the rating agencies may also help them coordinate their activity as a single, unified *Marktvolk* ('the markets'), so that they can jointly exert pressure on countries whose citizens or governments are reluctant to comply with their wishes. On the other hand, owners of monetary assets appear to depend on safeguarding their portfolios by investing at least part of their capital in government bonds. Governments, for their part, can introduce regulatory measures that force 'the markets' to invest in public debt – for example, by raising the risk-cover requirement for banks and insurance

companies.[74] They may also at their discretion one-sidedly 'restructure' government debt, since as 'sovereign' debtors they are not subject to any legal bankruptcy procedure.[75] Governments can also apply a 'haircut' to their creditors or, in extreme cases, cease all servicing of their debt. That is a constant nightmare for lenders.[76] Since a suspension of payments is damaging to a country's future credit-worthiness, governments resort to it only if they can see no other way out. In principle, however, unilateral debt reduction can be a powerful weapon for governments defending their citizens' claims on public services. So long as they can threaten with some credibility to use it, creditors of a debt state may feel compelled to exercise restraint in enforcing their interests.[77]

7) 'The markets' may engage the services of the 'international community' and its organizations to back up their claims on a debt state. In doing this, they can take advantage of their organizational

---

74 In combination with low interest rates, capital controls and high inflation, this may add up to a public debt reduction strategy. The technical name for it is 'financial repression' (C. Reinhart and M. Sbrancia, *The Liquidation of Government Debt*, NBER Working Paper No. 16893, Cambridge, MA: National Bureau of Economic Research, 2011).

75 Systems to regulate state bankruptcies have often been proposed. For creditors, they would limit the freedom of debtor states in the event of a payment default, although they could never be sure that governments would agree to play by the rules. Moreover, a regulatory order might have the effect that state insolvency became a more normal and therefore more frequent phenomenon.

76 They try hard to find ways of guarding against this eventuality. In January 2012, the *New York Times* reported on a hedge fund which was looking for ways to institute proceedings against Greece – on the grounds of having forced its creditors to carry part of the burden in the country's 2011 debt restructuring (that had since proved insufficient) – for violation of property rights, in a case to be heard by the European Court of Human Rights. One investor was quoted as saying: 'What Europe is forgetting is that there needs to be respect for contract rights.' See 'Hedge Funds May Sue Greece if It Tries to Force Loss', *New York Times*, 19 January 2012.

77 Restraint, for example, in increasing risk premiums on government bonds. It seems generally agreed that, beyond an interest rate of approximately 7 per cent, governments are no longer able to service their debt. Of course, a country's debts are always financed or refinanced in tranches, so that it takes a while before an increase in interest rate applies to such a large part of its total debt that the possibility of a default becomes acute. It cannot be in the creditors' interest to see that situation arise, since it would kill the goose that lays their golden egg – unless, of course, they can count on another stepping into the breach. Obviously this would create a 'moral hazard' if ever there was one.

lead over a state system which, while embedded in global markets, continues to be nationally based. In today's interwoven financial markets, it is impossible to predict with any certainty the numerous external effects that the collapse of one debt state would have on the others. For example, foreign financial institutions may suffer such damage that they have to be rescued by their 'own' governments at a high fiscal cost;[78] or the privatized sector of the pension system may collapse; or 'the markets' may lose confidence in government bonds as such, with a knock-on effect for the interest rates paid by other countries on refinancing their debt. A state in danger therefore comes under pressure from other states and international organizations to meet its obligations in relation to its creditors, even at the price of not fulfilling its obligations to its citizens. At the same time, other states may come under pressure to stand by the affected country in the name of 'international solidarity', preventing a default by means of loans and transfers. Theoretically, of course, states may also unite against markets – for example, by jointly refusing to accept demands for austerity. But this raises classical problems of collective action, bound up with the different interests and structural positions of the countries in question. A country like Britain, which depends as none other on the health of its financial sector, can hardly enter into an international agreement demanding a 'haircut' from 'financial markets', unless it receives compensation payments from other states.

DEBT POLITICS AS INTERNATIONAL FINANCIAL DIPLOMACY

The politics of the modern debt state, particularly in Europe, has become both more complex and less democratic because it takes place largely as international politics, in the shape of intergovernmental financial diplomacy. Here the distribution conflict between national

---

78   To be sure, one does not know exactly how the financial institutions of various countries are intertwined with one another. So-called stress tests, precisely if administered by international organizations, may tell us nothing about this: first, because they can only use data collected and passed on by national supervisory bodies; and second, because they have to be organized in such a way that, even in the worst of cases, their results do not cause panic.

peoples and the international *Marktvolk*, itself a derivative of the conflict between wage-earners and profit-makers, is projected onto a new level where it appears distorted beyond recognition – a further ideal stage for the performances of post-democracy. There the public of European nation-states has for years now been breathlessly following a drama whose amazing turns have all the weirdness of Alice's adventures in wonderland.

Of course the stakes in the politics of debt are incomparably more serious. The charging of international 'governance' with the fiscal supervision and regulation of national governments threatens to end the conflict between capitalism and democracy for a long time to come, if not forever: that is, to settle it in favour of capitalism, by expropriating the means of political production from the citizenry of nation-states. If the plans adopted in 2012 to restructure the European state system with the help of a 'fiscal pact' come to fruition, member-states and their politics, under the pressure of financial markets and international organizations, will have tied themselves to market principles in international and constitutional law and will largely have forfeited the possibility of modifying them in the name of social justice.[79] At that point, the liberalization of modern capitalism will have achieved its objective by durably immunizing its markets from discretionary political interference.

The internationalization of fiscal crisis and debt policy conceals the political and economic actors of democratic capitalism behind the construct of a world of nations with internally homogeneous but externally different and opposing interests. Countries appear, like football teams, as participants in a tournament for the top places in a league table, with respect to economic performance, competitiveness, scale of corruption or political clientelism, and the like.[80] At the same

---

79   For more on this, see the discussion in Chapter 3 on the European Union as an international 'consolidation state'.

80   In the social sciences, this perspective is cultivated by comparative policy research that nearly always has agonistic undertones. Typically the question is which country or group of countries is 'better' at economic growth, environmental policy, health care, popular contentment, political participation, and so on.

time, they are portrayed as bearers of collective rights and duties towards one another – for example, with regard to claims for solidarity and support in an emergency. The upshot is an astonishingly popular reformulation of the politics of public debt in nationalist terms with high demagogic potential, as well as a rapid renationalization and nationalist moralization of international political discourse, while respect for claims to national sovereignty is made dependent on a country's good behaviour vis-à-vis the global financial markets and international organizations and its observance of the rules of conduct that they prescribe.

In the rhetoric of international debt politics, nations appear as homogeneous moral individuals with joint liability; no attention is paid to internal relations of class and domination. This clears the way for discursive distinctions between 'nations that keep their house in order' and others that, having neglected to do their homework, cannot complain if other countries take over as their government. 'Lazy' countries must earn the solidarity of upright nations by reforming themselves in their image, or at least trying as hard as they can to do so. Conversely, countries in dire straits expect their more fortunate, and therefore wealthier, neighbours to offer them solidarity out of a sense of moral obligation; if this is not forthcoming, or not on the hoped-for scale, they are considered collectively arrogant and callous. The new, or old, nationalist clichés may be found in Germany in Thilo Sarrazin's book *Europa braucht den Euro nicht* (2012), and in countries such as Italy and Greece in newspaper depictions of the German Chancellor as a spiritual heir of Adolf Hitler.[81]

---

81   See 'Antideutsche Stimmung kocht in Italien hoch', *Frankfurter Allgemeine Zeitung*, 7 August 2012: 'The tone in the Italian euro-debate is becoming more and more aggressive towards Germany. The nadir, at least for now, was last Friday's headline "The Fourth Reich" on the front page of *Il Giornale*, which is jointly owned by Silvio Berlusconi's brother Paolo and the exchange-listed Mondadori publishing corporation controlled by Silvio. After two world wars with millions of dead, writes the paper's chief editor Alessandro Sallusti, the Germans have supposedly not had enough: "Now they are returning, not with guns but with the euro. The Germans see it as their affair: we must swallow everything and bow to the new emperor called Angela Merkel, who now wants to give orders in our country too." The problem for Sallusti, writing on page one of Berlusconi's daily, is that Italy does not react, in the same way as the allied powers did not react towards Hitler in 1938 . . . Recently,

In a political-economic perspective, however, international debt politics appears as intergovernmental collaboration to protect financial investors from losses, with the aim of keeping down risk premiums on government borrowing and averting the danger that one's 'own' national banks will have to be compensated for losses or bailed out through recapitalization. In the process, governments also protect their better-off citizens who have invested in national debt and similar financial instruments. 'Markets' and governments are equally eager to keep debt states at risk of default from making use of their sovereignty and suspending payments. The first priority for the international community of debt states is that all members, including the weakest, maintain the fullest possible servicing of their existing debt.

Part of the conflict between national peoples and the *Marktvolk* is that the citizens of countries still in good repute with the financial markets are urged by their own and other governments, as well as by international organizations and financial investors, to exercise 'solidarity' with countries that threaten to become insolvent.[82] Since the real point is not to rescue countries but to save creditors' portfolios, thereby stabilizing the global market for national debt, it does not matter whether the per capita income of a donor country is lower than that of the recipient country.[83] For the same reason, it is no

---

in an interview with *Der Spiegel*, Italy's new premier Mario Monti had warned of anti-German resentment in Italy and downplayed the significance of national parliaments. This came in for much criticism in Germany. Against this background, Monday's internet edition of the right-populist *Libero* ratcheted up the Italian attacks still further: "The Nazi Germans want to give us lessons in democracy." '

82   As repeatedly done by the grand speculator George Soros with major public effect. According to the *Frankfurter Allgemeine Zeitung* (26 January 2012), Soros warned at the Davos world economic forum 'that the euro is undermining the political cohesion of the EU . . . Germany carries the main responsibility in this . . . To contain the danger, Soros recommended that the Europeans should exercise strict financial discipline and implement structural reforms . . . One means to this end are Eurobonds.' Soros happily has his appeals distributed by economists and social scientists he funds, in the form of academic policy advice on European unification. See 'Breaking the Deadlock: A Path Out of the Crisis', issued on 23 July 2012 by the Institute for New Economic Thinking founded by Soros in 2009 (available at ineteconomics.org, last accessed 26 November 2012).

83   Thus Slovakia was expected as a matter of course to participate in aid to Ireland, even though its per capita income was much lower than Ireland's (which before

contradiction if the financial support never arrives in the country that is allegedly supported but goes directly to its foreign creditors.[84] Countries 'rescued' by other countries are nevertheless required to impose deep cuts in their citizens' living standards, for the sake of long-term confidence-building in the financial markets, but also to pacify the citizens of donor states, who must themselves accept cuts in their public budgets and social services to finance the solidarity of the community of states with 'the markets'.[85] In this way, on both the

---

the crisis was even higher than Germany's). As to the calls for German 'solidarity' with Greece, the moral justification is supposed to be the higher per capita income in Germany. Public rhetoric, however, makes no reference to the fact that quite a few Greeks are far richer than nearly all Germans, and that the living standards of more and more Germans are below those of the Greek middle class. The contribution expected by them to the rescue of the Greek state, mainly in the form of reduced social budgets of every kind, allows the banks owned by the Greek upper classes to avoid losses and subsidizes the non-taxation of the large Greek fortunes. In 2005 Greece collected the equivalent of 4 per cent of GDP in income tax, compared with 10 per cent in the fifteen West European EU countries. All taxes together amounted to 29.7 per cent of the national product, whereas the figure was a third higher, at 39.7 per cent, in the EU fifteen (H. Grözinger, 'Griechenland: Von den Amerikas lernen, heißt siegen lernen', *Blätter für deutsche und internationale Politik*, vol. 9, 2012, pp. 35–9). In 2001, the year in which Greece joined the currency union and cheap loans began to feed high levels of government debt, Greece lowered the top rate of taxation on corporate profits from 40 to 20 per cent (M. Markantonatu, *The Uneasy Course of Democratic Capitalism in Greece: Regulation Modes and Crises from the Post-war Period to the Memoranda*, discussion paper, Cologne: Max-Planck-Institut für Gesellschaftsforschung, 2012).

84   'Its membership in the euro currency union hanging in the balance, Greece continues to receive billions of euros in emergency assistance from the so-called troika of lenders overseeing its bailout. But almost none of the money is going to the Greek government to pay for vital public services. Instead, it is flowing directly back into the troika's pockets. The European bailout of 130 billion euros that was supposed to buy time for Greece is mainly servicing only the interest on the country's debt – while the Greek economy continues to struggle . . . On the face of it, the situation seems absurd. The European authorities are effectively lending Greece money so Greece can repay the money it borrowed from them' ('Most Aid to Athens Circles Back to Europe', *New York Times*, 30 May 2012).

85   In the holistic–nationalist worldview of international financial diplomacy among debt states, Greek workers whose pensions are cut in the wake of a foreign bailout are supposed to be paying for 'their' banks. There is no place in the long-hegemonic *Sprachspiel* of a neoliberal national holism for the idea that the first to bail out the Greek banks should be their own shareholders and those who pocketed the profits, value increases, incomes and bonuses of recent years. No doubt this also reflects the lack of power vis-à-vis the financial markets that (only seemingly) sovereign states have experienced since the neoliberal turn.

'donor' and the 'recipient' side, a common tribute to the financial markets is made to appear as mutual blackmail among countries or peoples that are unequally 'rich' or deserving they be so.

International solidarity, which in practice amounts to a punitive austerity policy ordered from abroad and above, holds the citizens of an insolvent debt state jointly liable for their past governments. The justification is supposed to be that they democratically elected them. Democracy thus serves to construct an identity between citizens and government, between the electorate as principal and the government as agent, which is sufficiently deep to require that citizens repay out of their own pockets the loans contracted in their name – regardless of whom they voted for and whether any of the borrowed money ever found its way to them. Moreover, as state citizens they are denied what would be readily available to them as economic citizens: something like a bankruptcy seizure exemption threshold, as might be safeguarded by the European Convention on Human Rights.

Whereas neonationalist public discourse blames excessive national debt levels on the easy life that one country's citizens made for themselves at the expense of another country's citizens – which then justifies affording them solidarity-as-punishment – debt states actually incurred their debts to make up for taxes that they had failed to raise from their citizens (especially the richest) or that they had been unable or unwilling to impose for fear of breaking the social peace or of losing investment. This turns international support for a debt state into solidarity not only with its creditors but also with its low-taxed (and under neoliberalism ever lower-taxed) upper classes; solidarity ultimately subsidizes a skewed distribution of income, also because it spares the citizens of a bailed-out state from politically organizing to correct that distribution and taking on themselves the associated conflicts and risks. The fact that the well-to-do today can avoid taxation more easily than ever, forcing their home countries to pile up debt, is also a result of the liberalization of capital markets over the last few decades. Countries such as the USA, France, Britain and Germany profited greatly from the flight of capital out of countries with a weak taxation regime and an uneven distribution of income; and their richest citizens have profited most of all, in the form of rising prices in the luxury property market. The bill for this is now being presented to the citizens of countries whose governments happily granted free movement to capital (to the acclaim of the 'financial markets') or were pressured into doing so by the 'international community'.

In the topsy-turvy world of financial and fiscal diplomacy embedded in international financial markets, the surrender of national sovereignty to supranational institutions, like international assistance and cross-border regulation, becomes a tool not only for the protection of financial investment and the collection of debt but also for the insulation of 'the markets' from political interference in the name of corrective social justice. As a result capitalism is emptied of democracy. National sovereignty – a central prerequisite of national democracy – is de-legitimized in that it is made to seem a means of running up debt at the expense of other countries, with the result that, cheered on by the national peoples enlisted to provide Europeanized debt relief, it can then be eliminated in favour of supranational disciplining agencies deaf to democracy – not only in debt states with excessive levels of debt but also more generally, with reference to values such as international solidarity or the peaceful overcoming of nationalism through supranational integration.

CHAPTER THREE

The Politics of the Consolidation State: Neoliberalism in Europe

In the wake of the financial and fiscal crisis, the debt state that supplanted the tax state has to convert itself into a state dedicated to fiscal consolidation, completing the neoliberal farewell to the European state system and to the political economy of its Keynesian founding period. This *consolidation state* is being constituted, not accidentally, as an international regime operating at multiple levels of government. The possibility that internationalization and denationalization may be linked with liberalization has been present in the public mind at least since the discussions on the political consequences of 'globalization'. But no one spelled out this connection earlier or more clearly than Friedrich von Hayek, in his article 'The Economic Conditions of Interstate Federalism', which first appeared in the *New Commonwealth Quarterly* in September 1939, just as the Second World War was beginning.[1]

INTEGRATION AND LIBERALIZATION

In keeping with the times, Hayek's article begins with the question of the conditions under which a stable international peace would be possible. In his view, the key must be an interstate federation strong enough to settle disputes among its members and to guarantee their collective external security. An indispensable requirement for this would be a common defence and foreign policy operated by a central government. It cannot stop at that, however: 'there is no historical example of countries successfully combining in a common foreign

---

1 F. Hayek, 'The Economic Conditions of Interstate Federalism', in *Individualism and Economic Order*, Chicago: Chicago University Press, 1980 [1939], pp. 255–72.

policy and common defence without a common economic regime'.[2] If the federation had different economic regimes and policies, a 'solidarity of interests' would develop within each of its individual member states, with the result that their frontiers with one another would always represent lines of economic conflict among their citizens.[3] The same groups – rather than groups of changing composition – will then always confront one another. For the unity of the whole, it is therefore necessary that 'these groupings should not be permanent and, more particularly, that the various communities of interest should overlap territorially and never become lastingly identified with the inhabitants of a particular region'.[4] But if a single economic regime is essential to hold a federation together, so that solidarity does remain nationally bounded, what would such a regime look like? The following two steps form the core of Hayek's argument. First, Hayek shows that a common economic regime with free movement of people and capital and no customs barriers – a union with a 'single market'[5] – will greatly restrict the range and purchase of each member country's economic policy. Second, he explains that the kind of political intervention in the market that can no longer be operated at individual state level cannot be transferred to the level of the federation to be replaced there: 'certain economic powers, which are now generally wielded by the national states, could be exercised neither by the federation nor by the individual states', implying that 'there would have to be *less government* all round *if federation is to be practicable*'.[6]

On the first point, Hayek remarks that with free movement of 'goods, men and money'[7] national state intervention in the market – for example, to promote domestic products – would have more far-reaching effects on the federation as a whole than could be tolerated. Nor would it be possible for member-states to operate their own

---

2 Ibid., p. 256.
3 Ibid., p. 257.
4 Ibid., p. 258.
5 Ibid.
6 Ibid., p. 266 (emphases added).
7 Ibid., p. 260.

monetary policy: 'Indeed, it appears doubtful whether, in a Union with a universal monetary system, independent national central banks would continue to exist; they would probably have to be organized into a sort of Federal Reserve System.'[8] Furthermore, competition will ensure that no government can burden its economy with too many regulations: 'Even such legislation as the restriction of child labour or of working hours becomes difficult to carry out for the individual state.'[9] Free movement within the union will also make it difficult for individual states to tax their citizens: high direct taxation will drive people and capital abroad, and the absence of border controls will hinder the indirect taxation of many goods. National business associations and trade unions would be subject to similar constraints: 'Once frontiers cease to be closed and free movement is secured, all these national organizations, whether trade unions, cartels or professional associations, will lose their monopolistic position and thus, qua national organizations, their power to control the supply of their services or products.'[10]

But why should it be impossible to replace at international level that which must be given up at national level to maintain the cohesion of the federation? The reason is that, in a federation of national states, the variety of interests is greater while the sense of common identity will be weaker than it is in the individual countries. Tariffs to protect particular industries, for example, require the society as a whole to make sacrifices in the form of higher prices. This may be acceptable among fellow-countrymen, but things are different in a federation:

Is it likely that the French peasant will be willing to pay more for his fertilizer to help the British chemical industry? Will the Swedish workman be ready to pay more for his oranges to assist the Californian grower? Or the clerk in the city of London be ready to

---

8   Ibid., p. 259.
9   Ibid., p. 260.
10   Ibid., p. 261.

pay more for his shoes or his bicycle to help American or Belgian workmen? Or the South African miner prepared to pay more for his sardines to help the Norwegian fishermen?[11]

The same applies to many other kinds of political intervention in the economy: 'Even such legislation as the limitation of working hours or compulsory unemployment insurance, or the protection of amenities, will be viewed in a different light in poor and in rich regions and may in the former actually harm and rouse violent opposition from the kind of people who in the richer regions demand it and profit from it.'[12] Structural homogeneity resulting from small size, as well as common national traditions and identities, makes possible deep interventions in social and economic life that would not be accepted in larger (and therefore more heterogeneous) political entities. Thus, *federation inevitably entails liberalization.*

> That Englishmen or Frenchmen should entrust the safeguarding of their lives, liberty and property – in short, the functions of the liberal state – to a superstate organization is conceivable. But that they should be willing to give the government of a federation the power to regulate their economic life, to decide what they should produce and consume, seems neither probable nor desirable. Yet, at the same time, in a federation these powers could not be left to the national states; therefore, federation would appear to mean that neither government could have powers for socialist planning of economic life.[13]

Hayek's argument starts from the economic preconditions of international peace and ends by establishing why a cohesive federation of states must necessarily have a liberal economic policy.[14] Peace-seeking

---

11   Ibid., pp. 262f.

12   Ibid., p. 263.

13   Ibid., pp. 263f.

14   And why, conversely, 'the abrogation of national sovereignties and the creation of an effective international order of law is a necessary complement and the logical consummation of the liberal programme' (ibid., p. 269).

states must combine in a federation, but that requires them not only to liberalize their own economic order but also to shape that of the federation in a liberal manner. Socialism must be left behind together with nationalism, and so too must the nexus joining them that is so threatening to democracy and the rule of law.[15] The only kind of democracy achievable in this way, however, is a strictly liberal one that respects the freedom of the market, since that alone is capable of preserving internal and external peace within a federation of states.

> If, in the international sphere, democratic government should only prove to be possible if the tasks of the international government are limited to an essentially liberal programme, it would no more than confirm the experience in the national sphere, in which it is daily becoming more obvious that democracy will work only if we do not overload it and if the majorities do not abuse their power of interfering with individual freedom. Yet, if the price we have to pay for an international democratic government is the restriction of the power and scope of government, it is surely not too high a price.[16]

Hayek's article from 1939 reads like a blueprint for today's European Union – and not only in its rhetorical use of the theme of peace. It is true that the politics of integration of the postwar period initially conceived of European unification as the building of a transnational mixed economy,[17] and at the time Hayek's arguments for the unavoidable (and in his view welcome) liberalism of a supranationally integrated political economy probably seemed absurd to most.[18]

---

15   Ibid., p. 271.

16   Ibid., p. 271.

17   A. Shonfield and S. Shonfield, *In Defense of the Mixed Economy*, Oxford: Oxford University Press, 1984.

18   Apart, that is, from the ordo-liberals around West German economics minister Ludwig Erhard, who saw in the European Economic Community of the time an opportunity to introduce into Germany, via Brussels, an economic policy, in particular a competition regime, in line with their views. See D. Gerber, 'Constitutionalizing the Economy: German Neo-Liberalism, Competition Law and the "New Europe"', *American Journal of Comparative Law*, vol. 42, 1988, pp. 25–84; D. Gerber, 'The Transformation of European Community Competition Law', *Harvard International Law Journal*, vol. 35, 1994, pp. 97–147. If they had

With time, however, European integration grew out of its Keynesian illusions and its enthusiasm for planning, and the more integration progressed and advanced into the centre of the European political economy, the more it followed Hayek's intuitions of 1939: on the necessity within a federation to neutralize the effect of democratic institutions on the economy and to leave allocation decisions to free markets; on the need for a ban on market-distorting state intervention in the member-states, including the abolition of national currencies; and on the political obstacles which (in Hayek's view, fortunately) stand in the way of federal integration beyond the creation and liberalization of markets.

In fact, after the Second World War, the European interstate quasi-federation that initially came about to preserve the peace proved in the long term – by virtue of its inherent political and economic logic anticipated by Hayek – to be a reliable and ever more powerful engine for the liberal transformation of Europe's national economies and the curbing of national democratic projects to make social justice prevail against market justice. It was as if Hayek's article had worked out the lines of force along which the institutions of European unity, originally designed for something quite different, would eventually position themselves. This became especially clear once the neoliberal turn began in the early 1980s, and clearer still in the continuing process of the institutionalization of what I refer to as the consolidation state. Today, and more than ever since the democratic–capitalist distribution conflict shifted to the level of international financial diplomacy, the 'market forces' whose aim it is to free the capitalist accumulation process from political correctives support themselves on the institutional dynamic foreseen by Hayek in 1939. The conversion of the European Union into a vehicle for the liberalization of European capitalism did not suddenly begin in 2008; it is the essence and result of a continual metamorphosis that is the European variant of the global

not actually read Hayek's federalism article of 1939 – which seems unlikely, since he was in the 1950s a professor at the university of Freiburg – they had a complete grasp of the connections he analysed.

liberalization process under way since the 1980s. This dual process – the now rapidly advancing liberation of the economy from democracy and the separation of democracy from the governance of the economy, intended to enshrine the institutional hegemony of market justice over social justice – might be described as the *Hayekization* of European capitalism, in memory of its long-forgotten, but then all the more successfully revived, theoretical promoter.[19]

THE EUROPEAN UNION AS A LIBERALIZATION MACHINE

Already in its early years, the European Union was seen to suffer from a 'democratic deficit', as well as from the lack of a 'social dimension'.[20] It is true that the democratic deficit was also blamed on the limited powers of the European Parliament, which reflected the absence or

---

19   Hayek himself, having ripened into the global ideologue of the battle against democracy in democratic capitalism, developed clear views about how to institutionalize a political democracy which, unlike 'the form we are practising today', is not just a 'synonym for the process of vote-buying, for placating and remunerating those special interests' that used to be known as 'sinister interests', or 'a system of auction by which every few years we entrust the power of legislation to those who promise their supporters the greatest special benefits' (F. Hayek, *Law, Legislation and Liberty: A New Statement of the Liberal Principles of Justice and Political Economy*, Abingdon: Routledge, 2013 [1976], pp. 374f.). Democracy, according to Hayek, will be compatible with freedom (especially economic freedom) only when government activity (especially in the sphere of economic policy) is strictly bound by general rules and can never be 'arbitrary'. Above all, democracy must be prevented from yielding to the constant temptation to interfere to correct the results of free markets; this must be prevented by constitutional provisions (F. Hayek, *Die Verfassung der Freiheit*, Tübingen: J. C. B. Mohr, 1971). More specifically, Hayek proposes to transfer law-making powers to a 'legislative assembly' whose members are elected for fifteen years, for one term only. Each citizen would be able to vote only once in their life, at the age of 45, so that people born in a given year would occupy a fifteenth of the seats in the assembly. Representatives of political parties and interest groups (trade union officials!) should not be allowed to stand for election; the independence of deputies should be strengthened by generous provision for their old age. The means used today to immunize the capitalist economy against democratic–interventionist politics are of course different, although the European Commission and the management of the European Central Bank are even less elected than Hayek's proposed assembly.

20   Commission of the European Communities et al., *Social Europe. The Social Dimension of the Internal Market. Interim Report of the Interdepartmental Working Party*, Luxemburg: European Commission, 1988.

not-yet-presence of a European people. But probably more important was and still is the strengthening of national executives under a developing multilevel regime in which the governments of member-states equip themselves in Brussels with internationally binding mandates that they can use against domestic political opponents, especially workers and other organized interests.[21] This has made it possible again and again to circumvent the democratic interplay of forces in the individual states, for example with regard to the privatization of public enterprises.

In the 'social dimension' too, we find with hindsight that national institutions were weakened without being offset by corresponding international ones. In the 1980s, still mindful of the workers' unrest of 1968, the European Community's proclaimed goal was to build a supranational social welfare state more or less in line with the then West German model. As social democratic dominance came to an end in the member-states, however, and the Thatcher government lashed out at its programmatic remnants in the Brussels institutions, the integration process began to stagnate, not least because organized business, now attuned to liberalization, threatened to lose interest. It fell to the two commissions headed by Jacques Delors to reverse the trend. The way this was achieved was by means of the European single market project, which gave business its desired market expansion in the shape of the 'four freedoms', while workers were promised a social and political embedding of the market, as something that would inevitably follow. The latter did not materialize, however, because of stubborn resistance from employers and the British government[22] – regardless of the attempts of a new subdiscipline of political science, European integration studies, largely funded by the Brussels

---

21   A. Moravcsik, 'Warum die Europäische Union die Exekutive stärkt: Innenpolitik und internationale Kooperation', in Klaus Dieter Wolf (ed.), *Projekt Europa im Übergang?*, Baden-Baden: Nomos, 1997, pp. 211–70.

22   W. Streeck, 'From Market-Making to State-Building? Reflections on the Political Economy of European Social Policy', in Stephan Leibfried et al. (eds), *European Social Policy: Between Fragmentation and Integration*, Washington, DC: The Brookings Institution, 1995, pp. 389–431.

Commission, to make the world believe that the Emperor was wearing new clothes.

What emerged was today's stable pattern of 'negative' without 'positive' integration,[23] in which cross-border markets and market freedoms increasingly overlay and suspended the legal systems, political power structures and democratic processes of the national states. The main player in this *integration through supranational liberalization, or liberalization through international integration*, was the European Court of Justice, whose rulings became increasingly unassailable for member states and their citizens, especially as majorities for social protection measures could no longer be found following the accession of Eastern Europe.[24] Whereas in the 1990s it was mainly the Commission that successfully propelled the privatization of large parts of the public sector,[25] using the tool of competition law, in the following decade the European Court of Justice handed down judgments in the name of the free movement of services and capital that questioned the right of workers to strike and threatened to curtail workforce participation. The EU thus became a machine for the liberalization of European capitalism, enabling (and sometimes compelling) governments to impose any manner of pro-market reforms against the resistance of their citizens.

---

23 F. Scharpf, 'Negative and Positive Integration in the Political Economy of European Welfare States', in Gary Marks et al. (eds), *Governance in the European Union*, London: Sage, 1996, pp. 15–39.

24 M. Höpner and A. Schäfer, 'A New Phase of European Integration: Organized Capitalism in Post-Ricardian Europe', *West European Politics*, vol. 33, 2010, pp. 344–68.

25 The first to recognize the possibility of reshaping the political economies of European nation-states by means of European competition law were Ludwig Erhard's advisers, who were looking for ways to reverse their defeat in the battle over German antitrust legislation. Nearly fifty years later, the institutional machinery they erected was capable, under Mario Monti's leadership as EU commissioner, of deploying competition law to attack the German public banking system that had long been a thorn in the side of the private banks (D. Seikel, *Der Kampf um öffentlich-rechtliche Banken. Wie die Europäische Kommission Liberalisierung durchsetzt*, Doctoral thesis, Cologne, 2012). At the time of writing, the EU Commission's assault on the strong position of the government of Lower Saxony and the workforce at Volkswagen is still under way in the name of the free movement of capital (B. Werner, *Die Stärke der judikativen Integration. Wie Kommission und Europäischer Gerichtshof die Unternehmenskontrolle liberalisieren*, Economics and Social Science Faculty, Cologne University, 2012).

The European currency union marks the peak so far of the development of the emerging European federation into a mechanism for the freeing of the capitalist economy from democratic distortion of markets. It is useful to recall that the currency union was decided at a time when the rich democracies of the West were first attempting to consolidate their public finances. From the beginning, budgetary discipline at national level was part of the package: none of the member-states would be allowed to run an annual deficit above 3 per cent of GDP or accumulate a total debt greater than 60 per cent. At the same time, it would be impossible by definition for less 'competitive' economies to devalue their currency as a way of adjusting the 'level playing field' (the euphemistic name for the competition regime of the common market as a whole) so as to avoid or pacify domestic distribution conflicts. In this way, the claim of more productive, export-oriented countries for market justice was to be protected from any use of national sovereignty for purposes of national–particularistic social justice. The only option left to countries under Monetary Union that fell behind economically was a so-called internal devaluation: that is, wage cuts, 'incentive-compatible' cuts to social services and the 'flexibilization' of labour markets; in other words, the completion at the level of national politics of the liberalization programme associated with the common currency.

None of these objectives was achieved at the first attempt. Monetary union regulations were not sufficiently unambiguous and did not involve sufficient sanctions to enforce rule-bound budgetary policies; national states always retained enough leeway to bow to citizens' demands that did not comply with the justice of the market. French ideas to make European regulations more flexible by instituting a European 'economic government', so as to create new space at EU level for discretionary political intervention, failed mainly because they clashed with the interests and the domestic politics of France's German partner. As a result the rules of the treaty of Monetary Union were broken with impunity on a number of occasions, when France and Germany among others thought they had no other alternative. At the same time, some countries, struggling to cope with what for them was the novelty of a hard currency regime, were unable or unwilling to 'modernize' their societies and their demands for social justice. To avoid ruin, they gratefully drew on the abundant sources of credit that the international money industry gladly placed on tap after the currency changeover.[26] Time was bought once more – until the financial and fiscal crisis put a stop to it, at least for the time being.

Current arguments over a European stability pact are a continuation of the trends under way in Europe since the 1990s; they may be seen as an attempt to strengthen the newly built or reformed political and economic institutions, in such a way as to complete and perpetuate the liberalization of European capitalism. It is true that the crisis is the immediate reason for the fiscal pact, but the plan for one is much older and has long been a basic part of the neoliberal strategy in Europe. This is clear also from the fact that, although it is being marketed as a solution to the current financial and fiscal crisis, it is not suited for this purpose because its effects will at best make themselves felt only in the long term.

It is neither possible nor necessary to discuss here in detail the rush of new regulations, institutions and instruments that the European Council has negotiated and decided upon since the beginning of the crisis. Less than three months separated the coming into force on 13 December 2011 of the 'sixpack' – six European laws to reform the Maastricht stability and growth pact – and the signing of the European Fiscal Pact on 2 March 2012. Additional rule changes, going ever further beyond the powers assigned by the treaties to the bodies of the EU, were under active preparation in summer 2012. The tendency has for a long time been the same:

1) Guidelines for the fiscal policy of member-states are becoming more and more detailed. Their observance is required in return for any rescue measures by the European 'community of states', and particularly for its willingness, under the pressure of market threats, to mutualize public and private credit risks.

---

26   See more on this below.

2) National governments are under ever tighter obligations to press ahead with the market-conforming reconstruction of their economic, social and legal orders. For example, in line with the German model, they must incorporate debt ceilings into their constitution. They must also find ways of adapting their wage formation systems to macroeconomic stability goals defined by the EU, and must for this purpose be prepared to 'reform' their national institutions, if necessary against the resistance of their citizens and without regard for either national rights to free collective bargaining or the limits of the jurisdiction of European-level institutions.

3) Equally important are the areas in which the new EU statutes refrain from interfering in the autonomy of member-states. No provisions stipulate a minimum level of taxation, such as would limit fiscal competition within the single market.[27] This keeps up the tradition of the European Monetary Union, whose convergence and admission criteria contained nothing about a maximum tolerable level of unemployment or social inequality.

4) EU institutions, whether already existing or still to be built, get ever more far-reaching rights to oversee the economic, social and fiscal policies of member-states, even prospectively and in matters before national parliaments. The body with the greatest powers at European level is the Commission; the Council, representing the democratically legitimated member-states, takes only second place, with some kind of veto right, often on the condition of unanimity.

5) The penalties that the EU can impose on member-states for failing to observe its rules are growing larger. Enforcement

---

27   In this spirit, not the slightest consideration was given to making the 'rescue package' for Greece dependent on an end to tax exemption for its shipowners or a ban on the flight of capital practised by its wealthy families. As Grözinger suggests, Greece could adapt its citizenship and taxation laws to those of the United States, making its citizens around the world liable to pay taxes and levying an 'exit tax' on rich emigrants (H. Grözinger, 'Griechenland: Von den Amerikas lernen, heißt siegen lernen', *Blätter für deutsche und internationale Politik*, vol. 9, 2012, pp. 35–9). It could also 'cancel any dual taxation agreement that prevents this, obtaining access to the (probably considerable) assets and incomes its citizens are likely to have moved abroad in order to evade taxation'. But nothing of the kind has ever been demanded of Greece, even by the German 'opposition' parties (SPD and Greens) as a quid pro quo for their unswerving support for the Merkel government's European crisis policy.

procedures have an increasingly judicial form and are automatically started, with less and less scope for discretionary political decisions.

6) The national and European regulations that are supposed to determine the economic and fiscal policies of member-states are to be formulated in such a way as to be valid forever, protecting them from being changed by new political majorities.

7) Lastly, in the event of non-compliance by a member-state, it is increasingly demanded that Brussels, in particular the Commission or the Court of Justice, get the power to act on behalf of the respective national state and take decisions for it and in its place to ensure conformity with the requirements of the market.

The direction in which this is heading is clear from a speech that Jens Weidmann, the president of the Bundesbank (who before this had been the chancellor's closest economic policy adviser), gave in Mannheim on 14 June 2012. At a key point he remarked:

> In the event that a country does not keep to the budgetary rules, national sovereignty would automatically pass to the EU level to the extent necessary for the targets to be reached . . . One example might be the right to implement – and not simply demand – tax increases or proportionate spending cuts . . . Within such a framework, the EU level could secure the path to consolidation, even if no majority can be found in the national parliament concerned.[28]

By late summer 2012, the Fiscal Pact, until then the most important agreement in the negotiations to save the common currency, had not yet been ratified by all EU countries. In several member-states, moreover, there had been protests against a policy to win back the 'confidence' of 'the markets' by making balanced national budgets, to be achieved mainly through expenditure cuts, internationally binding. Neither in Greece nor in Italy had the Brussels-appointed heads of government, in both countries introduced as 'technocrats', been

---

28 The speech may be found on the Bundesbank website at www.bundesbank.de (last accessed 26 November 2012).

able to break the resistance of the population against their externally imposed austerity programmes. In Greece there was for a short time even the possibility that a new left-wing party would get into power, declare state bankruptcy and a return to a national currency – the last of which, like the exclusion of a member-state, had not been provided for in the treaty establishing the European Monetary Union. When Hollande replaced Sarkozy in France, an EU-wide discussion got under way on programmes to stimulate economic 'growth', especially in the heavily indebted countries but also more generally. It was not clear how these were meant to work, however. In view of the vagueness and financial paltriness of the proposals on offer, one is tempted to regard the fast-spreading rhetorical commitment to a new growth policy as the invocation of a *deus ex machina* able to make everybody equally happy – from a financial industry eager for its loans to be serviced, through the Greek and Spanish middle classes, to the citizens in the creditor states fearful for their living standards. But it is also conceivable that the new growth programmes, if they ever get beyond mere talk, will translate into transfers to the Southern European member-states who may increasingly demand compensation for remaining available, in the capacity of permanent losers, to the winners from market expansion. This would turn them into side payments for the imposition of a Hayekian economic regime, payable to those who can get nothing else out of it.

INSTITUTIONAL CHANGE: FROM KEYNES TO HAYEK

The historical significance of the transition from a Keynesian to a Hayekian political economy, which has been taking place since the 1970s, becomes clearer if we recall the situation at the beginning of the neoliberal turn. Whereas today, with open borders, formerly sovereign states with independent central banks must pursue a rule-bound economic policy in accordance with the prescriptions of efficiency theory, the Keynesian mixed economy of the postwar decades had at its disposal a wide range of instruments for discretionary government intervention, especially in the distribution of the national product and the life chances of national citizens. In the internationally 'embedded liberalism'[29] of the 1950s and 1960s, the nation-states of the capitalist West had their own currencies and were able, within certain limits, to devalue them to compensate for a loss of external 'competitiveness' resulting from concessions to powerful trade unions and Communist parties. In this way, states and governments could distort markets and yield to domestic political demands for social justice, without being punished in their external economy. Capital flight could be prevented, or at least restricted, by means of capital controls, and this weakened the bargaining power of investors with respect to the minimum profit level they could demand from society in return for investing their, more or less captive, capital.

Central to the Keynesian political economy were the corporatist interest associations of labour and capital, together with the negotiating system established between them.[30] Supporting itself on these, government policy aimed to ensure full employment and a distribution acceptable to the working class, by means of negotiated tripartite incomes and, if possible, also price policy. Wage moderation was achieved through 'political exchange', in which an efficient tax state, pursuing an active social policy in return for macroeconomic trade union cooperation, helped to protect wage-earners from market uncertainties (that is, translated into crisis theory, from the volatile moods of the class of profit-dependants) and thereby to stabilize effective demand. For this, the Keynesian state needed strong unions that encompassed the whole workforce, and it provided many different kinds of assistance to help them organize. Solid employers' and business associations were equally desirable; firms and entrepreneurs were therefore under pressure from both unions and government to form organizations capable of representing their members and acting

---

29 J. Ruggie, 'International Regimes, Transactions and Change: Embedded Liberalism in the Postwar Economic Order', *International Organization*, vol. 36/2, 1982, pp. 379–99.

30 P. Schmitter and G. Lehmbruch (eds), *Trends Towards Corporatist Intermediation*, London: Sage, 1979.

on their behalf, so that they could play a role in steering the capitalist economy within the limits set by democratic politics.[31]

The neoliberal revolution left almost nothing of this. Its objective was to trim the states of postwar capitalism as much as possible, reducing them to providing for the functioning and expansion of markets and making them institutionally incapable of corrective intervention in the self-regulating enforcement of market justice. Its full triumph, however, came only with the internationalization of the European political economy and the conversion of the European system of states into a multilevel regime with nationally confined democracy and multinationally organized financial markets and supervisory authorities – a configuration that has long proved an ideal vehicle for the neutralization of political pressure from below while expanding the realm of private contractual freedom vis-à-vis the state. The latest phase of this development is the ongoing transition from the national debt state to the international consolidation state. With it the Hayekian blueprint of a liberalized capitalist market economy immune from political pressure finally comes close to full realization.[32]

THE CONSOLIDATION STATE AS A EUROPEAN MULTILEVEL REGIME

The politics surrounding the consolidation of public finance is meant to reassure the new, second constituency of the modern state, the financial markets, that in case of doubt their claims can and will have priority over those of citizens. From the viewpoint of 'the markets', a structurally sound budget is one that has sufficient reserves and institutional flexibility for this purpose. The precise point at which this is attained remains open; much as 'the markets'

31   For a summary account of the functioning of the neocorporatist political economy, see Streeck, 'The Study of Interest Groups: Before "The Century" and After'.

32   For a concrete utopia from the point of view of German Ordnungspolitik, see J. Matthes and B. Busch, 'Governance-Reformen im Euroraum: Eine Regelunion gegen Politikversagen', *IW-Positionen. Beiträge zur Ordnungspolitik aus dem Institut der deutschen Wirtschaft*, No. 56, Cologne: Institut der deutschen Wirtschaft, 2012.

want clarity from governments, they are not prepared to give it themselves. It is part of the consolidation ritual that governments have to subject themselves and their voters to harsh fiscal discipline solely in the hope that at some point they will be rewarded with lower interest rates on their remaining debt or on new loans for new projects. They cannot demand this as their right, as such rights do not exist in a 'free market'.[33]

The main competitors of the *rentiers,* united as the people of the market, are *pensioners* and public employees as members of the people of the state. To be credible from the market perspective, consolidation policy must limit their number and scale down their claims. Above all, it must redress what has been called the 'policy legacies' of the 1960s and 1970s: that is, historical claims to social rights that exceed the level still financially viable after the collapse of the tax state.[34] Pruning the public sector also means continuing the privatization of public services, with as a rule anti-egalitarian effects on distribution. The main effect of social spending cuts is to reduce pensions and lengthen the working life; to the extent that lower pensions are offset by additional private insurance, such cuts – together with the privatization of public services – lead to a politically desirable expansion of capitalist corporations' field of activities.

'Reforms' of this kind are politically delicate operations, partly because, as we have seen, some of the public provision scheduled for cuts actually consist of deferred wages from the time when workers and unions yielded to pressure from social democratic governments and agreed to wage moderation for the sake of macroeconomic

---

33 Governments discover – or markets inform them – only *post factum* whether the confidence-building measures negotiated and imposed with such difficulty have actually built market confidence. The success or failure of political operations to calm and mollify the markets can be gauged solely from their effect on stock prices or on the risk premiums on government bonds. All too often it turns out, after initial successes and despite positive 'signals' from analysts and fund managers, that the hunger of the markets for money and fine words may suddenly return at any moment.

34 R. Rose, 'Inheritance Before Choice in Public Policy', *Journal of Theoretical Politics,* vol. 2/3, 1990, pp. 263–91; R. Rose and P. Davies, *Inheritance in Public Policy: Change Without Choice in Britain,* New Haven, CT: Yale University Press, 1994.

stability. A breach of such implicit contracts was for a long time thought too risky for a democratically elected government; even Reagan and Thatcher experienced the social programmes of their predecessors as 'immovable objects'.[35] One reason for the widespread admiration of Gerhard Schröder among today's consolidation strategists is that, ultimately at the price of his office, he faced down all resistance, stuck to his 'reform policies' and partly succeeded in carrying them through.

Nevertheless, from the point of view of the markets, examples like this notwithstanding, the domestic policies of democratic states can never be fully relied upon to deliver structural consolidation. Since in Europe it is not yet possible, in the name of economic rationality, to do away with the remnants of national democracy, especially the accountability of governments to their voters, the method of choice is to integrate national governments into a non-democratic supranational regime – a kind of international superstate without democracy – and have their activities regulated by it. Since the 1990s, the European Union has been converted into such a regime. Today the integration of member-states into a supranational system of institutions insulated from electoral pressure, and above all the binding force of a common currency, serve to eliminate national sovereignty as one of the last bastions of discretionary politics in an internationally integrated market society. In particular, the removal of devaluation ensures that investors, and in particular financial investors, need no longer fear that struggling governments will use sudden exchange-rate adjustments as a weapon of self-defence; in this way the single currency too serves the ends of market justice.[36]

Multilevel politics in the international consolidation state brings about the mediatization and neutralization of domestic

---

35   P. Pierson, *Dismantling the Welfare State? Reagan, Thatcher, and the Politics of Retrenchment*, Cambridge: Cambridge University Press, 1994; P. Pierson, 'The New Politics of the Welfare State', *World Politics*, vol. 48/1, 1996, pp. 143–79; P. Pierson, 'Irresistible Forces, Immovable Objects: Post-Industrial Welfare States Confront Permanent Austerity', *Journal of European Public Policy*, vol. 5/4, 1998, pp. 539–60.

36   For more on devaluation, see the concluding chapter.

policies by locking nation-states into supranational agreements and regulatory regimes that limit their sovereignty. A tried and tested means to this end are the regular summit meetings of heads of government, which, after much to-ing and fro-ing, produce agreements and announce decisions that each is expected to enforce against any opposition in their own country. Governments that are unable to do this lose international respect. Since national executives can refer to this at home and easily claim that any renegotiation would be fruitless, institutionalized summitry strengthens their hand vis-à-vis their parliaments and national interest groups – an effect that made itself felt early on in the history of the European Union. Crisis meetings held under pressure from the markets further reinforce this, since any resistance that makes the swift implementation of summit decisions seem less likely might trigger dangerous 'reactions'; at least governments and 'the markets' can maintain this.

Still, national parliaments and opposition parties are not totally defenceless in the face of summit agreements. Recent attempts within member-states to involve national parliaments, as distinct from the so-called European Parliament, in Europen-level decisions have not been completely without success, at either EU or national level. Especially since the onset of the crisis, as member-state parliaments are required to rubber-stamp in the space of a few days extensive legislation agreed between European executives, resistance has been growing in a number of countries, including Germany. The German Constitutional Court, for example, is working hard to reject the doctrine – propagated by the Brussels technocracy along with 'the markets' and the supporters of a European federal state – that national democratic institutions have no choice but to fall into line with international summit diplomacy. Governments may also improve their international bargaining position by arguing that policies they do not like could not be pushed through in their own country.[37] When Italian

---

37   A formal analysis of the complex logic of multilevel diplomacy may be found in R. Putnam, 'Diplomacy and Domestic Politics: The Logic of Two-Level Games', in Peter

premier Mario Monti reminded the German chancellor in August 2012 that governments had a duty to tell their parliaments that inter-governmental agreements have to be respected,[38] this showed that displays of parliamentary and judicial resistance to the pretensions of EU policy over domestic policy are taken seriously.[39] In the long run, of course, it is another question whether such resistance can lastingly slow down or prevent the march towards the international consolidation state.

The European consolidation state of the early twenty-first century is not a national but an international structure – a supra-state regime that regulates its participating nation-states, without a democratically accountable government but with a set of binding rules: through 'governance' rather than government, so that democracy is tamed by markets instead of markets by democracy. This is a historically novel construct, designed to ensure the market conformity of formerly sovereign nation-states: a market strait-jacket for democratic politics, with powers formally resembling various other innovations in international law, except that in this case what they involve are not a 'duty to protect' but a duty to pay. The purpose of the whole edifice, whose completion is drawing ever closer, is to depoliticize the economy while at the same time de-democratizing politics.

B. Evans (ed.), *Double-Edged Diplomacy*, Berkeley: University of California Press, 1993, pp. 431–86.

38 'Every government also has a duty to educate parliament. If I had just mechanically adhered to the guidelines laid down by my parliament, I would have been unable to agree to the decisions of the recent Brussels summit.' Interview with Mario Monti in *Der Spiegel*, 6 August 2012, p. 46.

39 As a former Brussels commissioner, Monti knows the logic of strengthening the executive through international diplomacy, but he is also aware that resistance at home can improve a government's bargaining position abroad. Within limits, governments can decide how they want to make use of their intermediary position within an international multilevel system. Since Italy is even in stable times normally governed by presidential decrees bypassing the country's parliament, Monti may have viewed references to resistance in the Bundestag against certain European crisis policies as tactical in nature.

FISCAL CONSOLIDATION AS A REMODELLING OF THE STATE

The consolidation of government finances as an answer to the fiscal crisis comes down to a remodelling of the European state system coordinated by financial investors and the European Union – a reconstitution of capitalist democracy in Europe, with the purpose of enshrining the results of three decades of economic liberalization. The goal is a dual binding of national politics to market principles of economic reason, effected both by the countries themselves, through constitutional 'debt ceilings', and by international treaties or obligations under European law. The underlying vision is of a state reduced to the safeguarding of market relations and a self-sufficient society that wants nothing from the state other than guarantees for property and freedom.

The future of Europe today is one of a secular implosion of the social contract of capitalist democracy, in the transition to an international consolidation state committed to fiscal discipline. The latter development involves the insertion of a Chinese wall between the economy and politics – in the jargon of the financial industry: a 'firewall' – which will permit the markets to assert their version of justice undisturbed by discretionary political intervention. The society needed for this must have a high tolerance of economic inequality. Its surplus population must have learned to regard politics as middle-class entertainment from which it has nothing to expect. Its worldviews and identifications it must derive not from politics but from the dream factories of a global culture industry, whose massive profits must also serve to legitimate the rapidly increasing extraction of surplus value by the stars of other sectors, especially the money industry. Another mass base for the progressive freeing of capitalism from democratic intervention is a neo-Protestant middle class of owners of 'human capital', keen on competition and performance, willing to invest privately in its advancement and that of its children, and imbued with standards of consumption so demanding that collective goods are almost by definition unable to satisfy them.[40]

---

40   Streeck, 'Citizens as Customers'.

Internationally coordinated attempts to consolidate the public finances of the rich democracies have been undertaken since the 1990s, and they give us some idea of how the future consolidation policies now being roped into national and EU law will look and function. An important difference is that in many countries the first wave of fiscal consolidation went together with a liberalization of capital markets, which enabled broad layers of the population to borrow money in various ways to compensate for stagnant or declining incomes and cutbacks in social assistance and public services. These possibilities no longer exist in the financial crisis, and tighter regulation of the finance industry is anyway supposed to limit them even more. The impending transition to an international consolidation state will therefore take place not only under greater pressure from 'the markets' and international organizations but must also do, as it were, without a local anaesthetic.

There are three main ways in which the impending processes of consolidation will reshape the European system of states and its relation to the capitalist economy:

1) If the experiences before 2008 tell us anything, it is that only a small part, if any, of the budgetary consolidation will come from higher revenues, while most or all of it will come from spending cuts.[41] In public discourse, consolidation is anyway almost invariably equated with cuts as if this were self-evident. Global liberalization, especially of capital markets, makes tax increases on high incomes and internationally mobile corporate profits appear so unrealistic that

---

41 This is also what economic theory advises: 'While expenditure-based adjustments are not recessionary, tax-based ones create deep and long-lasting recessions. The aggregate demand component which reflects more closely the difference in the response of output to [expenditure and revenue-based] adjustments is private investment. The confidence of investors . . . recovers much sooner after a spending-based adjustment than after a tax-based one' (A. Alesina et al., *The Output Effect of Fiscal Consolidations*, unpublished manuscript, 2012, p. 26). The authors further conclude 'that the fiscal stabilizations which have the mildest effect on output are those that are accompanied by a set of structural reforms which signal a "decisive" policy change'. Between the two consolidation policies there are no differences 'in the monetary policy stance . . . but mostly differences in the policy packages regarding supply side reforms and liberalizations'.

they are not even discussed.[42] Tax increases would have to be pushed through against the trend of the last decade and a half (Fig. 3.1). If they were in fact achieved, they would in all likelihood be limited to immobile sources – mainly in the form of social security contributions and sales taxes. The implication is that they would hardly be sufficient to finance the historically grown expenditure levels of modern states as they are at present constituted. At the same time, they would make national tax systems even more regressive than they already are.

2) The spending cuts in prospect will mainly affect people whose low incomes make them the most reliant on public services. They will further reduce employment and squeeze pay in the public sector, which will be accompanied by fresh waves of privatization and wider pay differentials. Access to previously unitary public services – for example, in health care and education – will increasingly be differentiated depending on the purchasing power of diverse clienteles. All in all, spending cuts and reduced levels of government activity will reinforce the market as the chief mechanism for the distribution of life chances, extending and completing the neoliberal programme for the recasting and dismantling of the postwar welfare state.

3) Smaller budgets will mean that a growing part of public expenditure will have to be used on existing commitments, at the expense of discretionary spending and new programmes responding to newly arising social problems.[43] This holds true even though fiscal

---

42 An exception is the above-mentioned study of the German Institute for Economic Research (S. Bach, 'Vermögensabgaben – ein Beitrag zur Sanierung der Staatsfinanzen in Europa', *DIW Wochenbericht*, 2012, pp. 3–11). According to press reports, the higher taxes on the rich announced by the newly elected French president in 2012 soon triggered extensive preparations for capital flight. See *New York Times*, 7 April 2012: 'Indigestion for "les Riches" in a Plan for Higher Taxes': 'Many companies are studying contingency plans to move high-paid executives outside of France, according to consultants, lawyers, accountants and real estate agents – who are highly protective of their clients and decline to identify them by name. They say some executives and wealthy people have already packed up for destinations like Britain, Belgium, Switzerland and the United States, taking their taxable income with them.'

43 W. Streeck and D. Mertens, *An Index of Fiscal Democracy*, MPIfG Working

austerity usually goes hand in hand with reduced entitlements to social benefits. Since the number of potential claimants increases as the economy worsens or the population ages, benefit cuts may not reduce the total volume of expenditure by a corresponding amount, however painful they may be to individual recipients.

Disproportionately affected by public spending cuts is public investment, including investment in the physical infrastructure as well as spending on family, education, research and labour market policy, all of which are discretionary.[44] As could be shown for the United States, Sweden and Germany, public investment declined in the first phase of fiscal consolidation in the 1990s not only as a share of public expenditure but also in relation to the national product (Fig. 3.2). Among the countries where public investment *increased* was Britain under New Labour; there, however, public debt did not fall but grew continually year by year. The positive relationship between government deficits, or public debt, and public investment remains if spending on physical expenditure is disregarded and only 'social' investment – i.e., government spending on the human, social and knowledge capital of society – is taken into consideration. This applies not only to a country like Germany, where social investment expenditure has fallen since 1981 from a little under 8 per cent to 6.5 per cent (Fig. 3.3), but also to Sweden, traditionally the leader in social investment, where it fell from 13 to 10 per cent (Fig. 3.4).[45]

The relationship presented here is not logically necessary; governments might attempt, in the second phase of fiscal consolidation that is now under way, to avoid the mechanism of structural

---

Paper, No. 10/3, Cologne: Max-Planck-Institut für Gesellschaftsforschung, 2010. Public spending counts as obligatory if, for political or legal reasons, it cannot easily be cut. This includes personnel costs, public retirement pensions and the servicing of old debt. In the long term, of course, all public spending, even if legally protected, is at the disposition of the legislature.

44   W. Streeck and D. Mertens, *Fiscal Austerity and Public Investment: Is the Possible the Enemy of the Necessary?*, MPIfG Discussion Paper No. 11/12, Cologne: Max-Planck-Institut für Gesellschaftsforschung, 2011.

45   Ibid.

sclerosis of public expenditure in the consolidation state[46] and to protect, or even expand, their social investment in spite of deficit reduction. Experiences from before 2008 indicate, however, how challenging such a project would be. They suggest that fiscal consolidation will very likely involve further privatization of social provision, maintaining the trend of the neoliberal turn, in parallel with a progressive reduction of public spending to the historical claims of ageing cohorts of citizens and voters, until the traditional welfare state eventually loses its constituency through natural wastage.[47] A shrinking scope for political choice, combined with declining possibilities for government to address new problems and provide for the future of society and its citizens, will then cause public expectations to decline as well, which will negatively affect political participation.

Consolidation does not necessarily entail greater freedom from the pressure of financial markets. In the consolidation state too, borrowing must take place even if there is an annual budgetary surplus, since the government can only gradually pay off its debt and must meanwhile find ways of refinancing it. True, it is often promised that consolidation will enable a country to regain its sovereignty vis-à-vis 'the markets';[48] but the time when that might happen, if at all,

---

46 A mechanism that may be summarily described as follows: 'Public deficits generate accumulating public debt, which in turn gives rise to pressures for fiscal consolidation. In the absence of an increase in taxation, consolidation must be achieved by cuts in expenditure. Inevitably, these will affect discretionary more than mandatory spending. Since public investment is discretionary, it is highly likely to be cut if public expenditure is cut. Apparently, this applies not just to traditional public investment in physical infrastructure, but also to what we have called "soft" investment, even though its magnitude may seem small in absolute terms. If governments want or need to pursue fiscal consolidation, protecting or, as arguably needed, increasing soft investment appears to be impossible without higher taxes' (ibid., p. 23).

47 The meltdown of obligatory public spending can be accelerated to a degree if welfare benefits are linked to 'grandfather clauses', putting them out of reach or scaling them down for future generations. This also makes it easier to discredit them politically as a privilege secured by old people for themselves.

48 This was a strong motive behind the consolidation of Sweden's public finances during its second financial crisis in the 1990s. The finance minister of the time, Göran Perrson, later described the connection as follows: 'It was about democracy itself! Why

FIGURE 3.1. *Tax revenue, selected OECD countries (% of national product)*

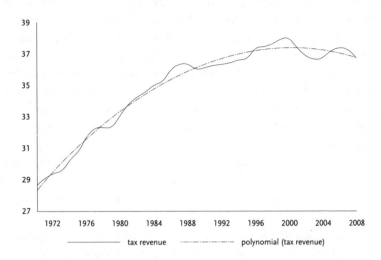

Countries in unweighted average: Australia, Austria, Belgium, Canada, Denmark, Finland, France, Germany, Greece, Ireland, Italy, Japan, Netherlands, Norway, Portugal, Spain, Sweden, Switzerland, UK, USA.

Source: Comparative tables, OECD Tax Statistics Database

lies in a far-distant future. Freedom from debt would require decades of budget surpluses, which could probably be achieved only through high growth combined with some measure of inflation. Until then, government policy must keep offering 'bondholder value' to the *Marktvolk*, who have the power to punish any deviation from the path of fiscal virtue with higher interest rates.[49]

---

elect parliamentarians if in the end it is after all the IMF that will take the decisions? Why go for an election campaign if you don't have the full capacity to take decisions? That was humiliating . . . When I went to Wall Street for the first time trying to borrow money to finance the deficit I met a crowd of young boys, 27, 28 years old, and they were all sneering, looking at me as an alien. Many of them – if not all – had never been in Sweden. They didn't know anything about the country!' (P. Mehrtens, *Staatsentschuldung und Staatstätigkeit: Zur Transformation der schwedischen politischen Ökonomie*, Cologne: Universität Köln und Max-Planck-Institut für Gesellschaftsforschung, 2013).

  49 In practice, governments that have committed themselves to a 'debt ceiling' are forced to find and use new types of advance financing that will not appear in their budgets,

FIGURE 3.2. *Public investment, three countries (% of national product)*

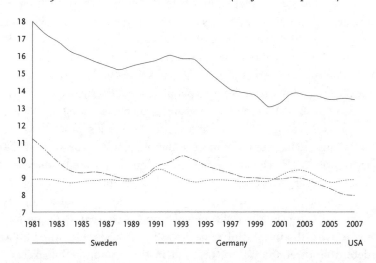

Source: OECD *Education at a Glance*; OECD R&D Database; OECD Social Expenditure Database; OECD Database on Labour Market Programmes; OECD *Public Educational Expenditure, Costs and Financing: An Analysis of Trends 1970–1988*; National Accounts Statistics

One precondition for long-term balanced budgets is that the level of taxation does not fall. This, however, is not to be expected even in the consolidation state. As the US presidential changeover from Clinton to Bush Jr demonstrated, budget surpluses can serve as a pretext for tax cuts that generate new deficits, which then

---

especially for public investment projects. Thus, in consolidation states one can expect there to be a wide market for public–private partnerships (PPPs), whereby private firms instead of the government take on loans for public construction projects which the state or its citizens have to pay off as users over years or decades. Early experiences with arrangements of this kind give reason to fear that governments and parliaments, especially at subnational level, only seldom have the competence to understand thousand-page partnership agreements drawn up by international law firms, or to grasp the true costs and risks attached to them. Consultants and lawyers are likely to find lucrative work here that will cost public authorities dear. A good introduction to the subject may be found in the Wikipedia entry on 'Public–private partnership'.

require further spending cuts to restore the surpluses.[50] The interplay between tax and spending cuts shows that the balancing of budgets in the consolidation state is not pursued for its own sake but, as part of a programme of privatization and liberalization, is intended to bring about a general rollback of the state and its intervention in the market. Under the auspices of austerity, budget surpluses give occasion 'to give people back what belongs to them' (George W. Bush). In this way, consolidation becomes self-sustaining – especially as citizens who can expect less and less from the state and therefore have to make more and more private provision will be correspondingly reluctant to pay taxes. Thus lower public spending leads to lower government revenues which in turn requires further spending cuts if the debt state is to continue consolidating its finances. A constantly declining government share in the economy fits in with the interest of those investing in the remaining public debt: the lower the rate of taxation in the economy, the easier it should be for the government, in case of need, to service its creditors' claims by a short-term tax increase.[51]

---

50   P. Pierson, 'From Expansion to Austerity: The New Politics of Taxing and Spending', in Martin A. Levin et al. (eds), *Seeking the Center: Politics and Policymaking at the New Century*, Washington, DC: Georgetown University Press, 2001, pp. 54–80. Today this justification is no longer necessary. In the record deficit year of 2012, the US presidential candidate Mitt Romney promised to leave the Bush tax cuts in place and in addition to lower taxes by a further $456 billion beginning in 2015. See 'A Tax Plan That Defies the Rules of Math', *New York Times*, 11 August 2012.

51   A similar mechanism is at work in a formerly arch-social democratic country such as Sweden. As Philip Mehrtens has shown in his Cologne dissertation, Sweden has posted budget surpluses ever since the successful overcoming of its last financial crisis in the mid-1990s. The conservative government re-elected in 2011 uses these to reduce the public debt, despite the country's good economic situation. Since it also constantly lowers the level of taxation, it can, and indeed has to, maintain the austerity policy of the years immediately following the crisis (Mehrtens, *Staatsentschuldung und Staatstätigkeit*). The proclaimed objective of making the Swedish state free from public debt, which is widely accepted by voters, is thus being used, despite a long-term structural surplus in the government budget, silently to press on with the dismantling of the Swedish welfare state.

FIGURE 3.3. *Germany: public social investment as percentage of national product, deficit, public debt and public expenditure*

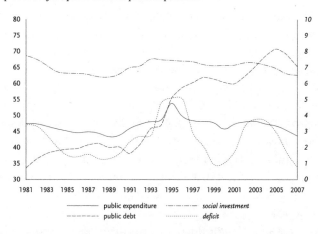

public expenditure   ————·—— social investment
———— public debt   ·············· deficit

Sources: OECD *Education at a Glance*; OECD *R&D Database*; OECD *Social Expenditure Database*; OECD *Database on Labour Market Programmes*; OECD *Public Educational Expenditure, Costs and Financing: An Analysis of Trends 1970–1988*; OECD *Economic Outlook: Statistics and Projections*

FIGURE 3.4. *Sweden: public social investment as percentage of national product, deficit, public debt and public expenditure*

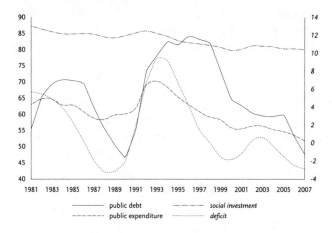

public debt   ————·—— social investment
———— public expenditure   ·············· deficit

Source: OECD *Education at a Glance*; OECD R&D Database; OECD Social Expenditure Database; OECD Database on Labour Market Programmes; OECD *Public Educational Expenditure, Costs and Financing: An Analysis of Trends 1970–1988*; OECD *Economic Outlook: Statistics and Projections*

GROWTH: BACK TO THE FUTURE

Since the onset of the crisis in 2008, events have come thick and fast in European politics. Some of them – for example, the replacement of elected government leaders such as Papandreou or Berlusconi with representatives of the financial sector by the European 'community of states' – had been simply unimaginable until then. The public, to the extent that there still is one, is less and less able to follow what is happening and forgets it ever more rapidly. This must be good news for governments. It explains why, after the Greek and French elections of 2012, they could suddenly speak again of European 'growth programmes' and claim that austerity, if it is to lead to consolidation, must be supplemented with a so-called growth component funded by public or private loans.

The reasons for the turn to growth, however short-term, in European crisis politics included the end of the Sarkozy presidency in France, a temporary strengthening of the radical Left in the Greek elections, and resistance in Italy to the policies of the Monti government. Even in Germany discontent began to spread as the contours of the emerging consolidation state became increasingly visible. A renewal of the promises of growth, as in the golden age of postwar capitalism, was hoped to offer some immediate relief. The decisive factor, however, was probably that in June 2012 it seemed possible for the first time that one of the debtor countries on the European periphery, Greece, might soon have a government that felt under no obligation to the West European centre and might resolve to cancel its debt unilaterally. In such a case France especially, but to a lesser extent Germany as well, would have had to make further injections of taxpayers' money to rescue their private banking system from collapse as a result of exposure to Greek debt. The announcement of a so-called 'growth package' was therefore also intended to make the Greeks give up a strategy which, from a West European point of view, inevitably appeared as a kind of financial suicide bombing.[52]

---

52   The new growth rhetoric not only answered the need to legitimize austerity

By making a Greek exit from the euro seem a real possibility, the country's turn to the left raised the price that the West Europeans were prepared to pay to keep it in the monetary union. Yet whether anything will grow as a result of the spending programme agreed on 28 June 2012 is more than doubtful. In fact the promised new growth policy looks as unrealistic as the one that preceded it, and the question of why it should be any more successful has never been discussed. EU growth programmes, not only for Greece but also for Spain and Portugal, were not at all in short supply over previous decades, after the three countries had overthrown their fascist regimes in the 1970s and embraced Western European–style parliamentary democracy. Well into the 1990s, the EU's various structural and cohesion funds contributed the lion's share to public infrastructural investment in the three Mediterranean countries, partly as a quid pro quo for their renunciation of a Eurocommunist path of development (not entirely unrealistic in the 1970s), and in the shared hope of rapid social and economic convergence with Germany, France and Northern Italy. The latter was still a long way off in the 1990s, however, when financial assistance from Western Europe became increasingly sparse (Fig. 3.5)[53] – not only because it had to be shared with the young East European democracies (Fig. 3.6) and Germany was busy with rebuilding its new Eastern *Länder*, but also because by then the rich countries had embarked on their first phase of fiscal consolidation.

What happened then may be best described as a foreign-policy equivalent of the 'privatized Keynesianism'[54] that the member-states adopted as a domestic pacification strategy in the 1990s: a replacement

policies – by holding out the prospect of growth as a reward for the imposed 'saving' – but also responded to hopes on the part of governments in the debtor countries that they would receive some sort of support payments from Brussels. The expectation of growth as a proven cure for democratic-capitalist distribution conflicts was cultivated especially by the new French president, who otherwise was at a loss to explain how his domestic policy could possibly be compatible with the binding consolidation objectives agreed at EU level.

53   Italy, as a founding member of the European Economic Community, had in its early years received by far the largest share from the Brussels regional fund as structural aid to the South. As a result of its improved economic performance, from the 1980s on Italy was in balance with the EU.

54   Crouch, 'Privatised Keynesianism: An Unacknowledged Policy Regime'.

of government transfer payments with improved facilities for borrowing, this time between states rather than within them. As early as 1990, when Germany agreed to the euro in return for French acceptance of reunification, it had been decided that the three structurally weak Mediterranean countries would join the monetary union as a kind of growth and convergence programme, whereby ensured access to West European markets and the elimination of currency risks for foreign investors would cause a swift blossoming of their economies. First, however, the interest rates to be paid by the Mediterranean states to finance their public deficits and refinance their growing public debt fell rapidly, already in the period leading up to monetary union, and by the time of its official launch they stood more or less at the same level as in Germany (Fig. 3.7). The only explanation for this is that 'the markets' thought there was reason to expect that, in the event of a default, the states of the monetary union would as a whole step in and so justify the convergence of interest rates that had run ahead of the expected, or somehow hoped-for, convergence in economic performance.[55]

Greece – a member of the European Community since 1981 and of the European Monetary Union since 2001 – may serve as an ideal-typical example of the privatization of the EU's international welfare state (Fig. 3.8). In the mid-1990s, after it became known that the West European countries intended to include Greece in the EMU, the interest rate that it had to pay on its debts fell within five years from 17 per cent to just under 6 per cent. At the same time, the EU's net payments to Greece were reduced from 4 to 2 per cent of Greek GDP, obviously

---

55 The convergence of interest rates at a low level, which enabled countries like Greece and Portugal to run up large debts, was actively encouraged by the European Commission. In the late 1900s, the Commission allowed European banks to use bonds issued by any member state of the currency union as collateral in so-called repo (repurchase) operations, including across national borders (D. Gabor, *Fiscal Policy in (European) Hard Times. Financialization and Varieties of Capitalism. Rethinking Financial Markets*, World Economics Association, November 2012, pp. 1–30). This made it possible for economically weak countries to contract loans on advantageous terms. The EU commissioner responsible for the regulation was the one responsible for the single market and for 'financial services' – none other than Mario Monti.

FIGURE 3.5. *Net EU payments as percentage of national income*

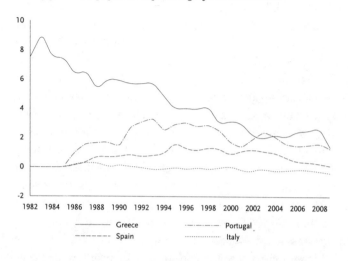

Source: European Commission, *EU Budget Finance Report*; OECD National Accounts Statistics; author's own calculations

FIGURE 3.6. *Gross EU payments to South and East European countries (billion euros)*

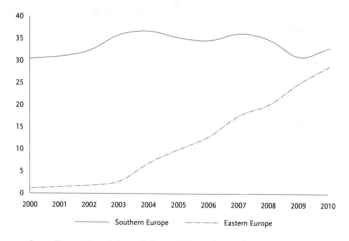

Source: European Commission, *EU budget 2010 – Finance Report*

in the expectation that the country would now be in a position to fill the gap by having recourse to the capital market. In the run-up to the monetary union, Greece managed to shrink its budget deficit in a very short space of time from 9 to 3 per cent of GDP, which meant that it fulfilled at least one of the entry criteria. But once its membership had made it cheaper to finance its public expenditure with credit, its deficit shot up again and by 2008 it was higher than it had been in 1995. Because of the extremely low rate of interest, however, debt service as a percentage of total public spending (the interest quota) continued to move downward, and the level of government debt, which had been just over 100 per cent at the EMU launch, increased only gradually at first. This ended in 2008 when both the deficit and the interest rate began to climb steeply, and with them the interest quota and the total government debt. Today, the only thing that Greece has definitely acquired from EMU membership is a public debt higher than where it stood in 1995 by nearly 60 per cent of its annual economic output.

In the brief heyday of the euro, Greece and Portugal in particular were able to use cheap loans almost at will to make up for the decline in transfer payments from Brussels.[56] Yet, as became painfully clear after 2008, the huge inflow of money during those years served mainly to create bubbles that may have looked like growth but were not so in reality; the rude awakening came when the cheap loans dried up amid the crisis of the world financial system and governments, like households and enterprises, were no longer able to service their debt.

Surprisingly, public discussion of the financial and fiscal crisis hardly touches on the question of why nobody in the vast supervisory machineries of the large nation-states and the EU, ECB, OECD or IMF noticed what was going on before their eyes. When Greece had to mask its debt burden in order to gain admission to the

---

56 In Spain it was not the state but the private sector that ran up large debts, thanks to a wholesale relaxation of controls enabling Spanish banks to supply themselves with credit as cheaply as the Greek government.

FIGURE 3.7. *Interest rates on government bonds of selected European countries*

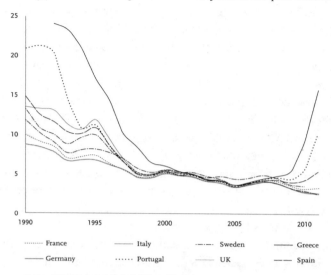

Source: OECD *Economic Outlook: Statistics and Projections*

FIGURE 3.8. *Greece: monetary union and government finances*

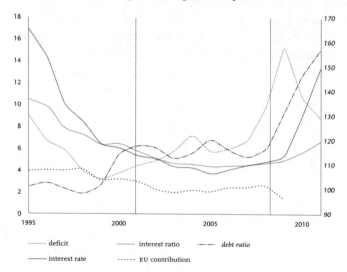

Sources: European Commission, *EU Budget Finance Report*; OECD *National Accounts Statistics*; OECD *Economic Outlook: Statistics and Projections*

European Monetary Union, and then set about running up huge debts at the new low interest rates, it is now public knowledge that the infamous American investment bank Goldman Sachs helped it – for its usual exorbitant fees – to brighten up its accounts.[57] It seems scarcely credible that none of this was suspected in the highly 'networked' international 'financial community'. The president of the Greek central bank at the time was the economist Lukas Papademos; his job done, he rose to become vice-president of the European Central Bank (and in 2011 was made Greek prime minister by EU governments, as an apolitical 'expert' from the outside, assigned to carry out 'reforms' that would ensure his country could repay its creditors). Are we supposed to believe that, after his promotion to Frankfurt, his contacts back home were so completely broken that he could no longer get reliable information on the real state of Greece's public finances? At roughly the time when Papademos moved to the ECB, Mario Draghi, vice-chairman of Goldman Sachs with special responsibility for its European business, was appointed governor of the Bank of Italy, with a seat on the ECB executive. Rather than this move, too, involving an attack of amnesia, it likely signifies that the worlds of politics and high finance were both more than happy with the replacement, facilitated by the monetary union, of international fiscal subsidies with national borrowing: governments, because their room for fiscal manoeuvre was exhausted; and the money industry, because new markets were opened up for it and because it felt encouraged to believe that, if all else failed, the richer member-states would pay the debts of the poorer ones, so that the financial institutions of Europe and America would come out undamaged, whatever happened.

---

57   See *Bloomberg*, 6 March 2012: 'Goldman Secret Greece Loan Shows Two Sinners as Client Unravels'. The article begins: 'Greece's secret loan from Goldman Sachs Group Inc. (GS) was a costly mistake from the start. On the day the 2001 deal was struck, the government owed the bank about 600 million euros ($793 million) more than the 2.8 billion euros it borrowed, said Spyros Papanikolaou, who took over the country's debt-management agency in 2005. By then, the price of the transaction, a derivative that disguised the loan and that Goldman Sachs persuaded Greece not to test with competitors, had almost doubled to 5.1 billion euros.' And so it goes on.

In the light of the experience before the crisis, the growth programmes introduced on short order into the European arena after the Greek and French elections of 2012 may seem no more than symbolic politics.[58] Everyone who took part in the decisions knew, or could have known, that the fiscal scope for European core countries to finance 'growth impulses' is today incomparably narrower than in the 1990s, *and* that borrowing on the capital markets is no longer possible on anything like the scale or the conditions of the period immediately after the turn of the century. If the available funds were not enough then to start more than pseudo-growth in the European periphery, how could they be today? All that the growth measures envisaged in summer of 2012 could do, in addition to helping the new French president save face, was to fuel hopes among peripheral governments for some fresh money, however little, with which to keep their state machineries going and award one contract or another to their clientele.[59]

Apart from this, as united Europe remains in thrall to neoliberal doctrine, the only 'growth policy' considered worthy of the name consists in eliminating organizations or institutions of any kind that are regarded as obstructing markets and competition, be they cartels,

---

58   I leave aside the crucial question of whether renewed growth can have a realistic political-economic perspective at all. See, for example, M. Miegel, *Exit. Wohlstand ohne Wachstum*, Berlin: Propyläen, 2010.

59   On the decisions taken in summer 2012, see Carsten Volkery, 'Window Dressing for Hollande: The EU's New Growth Pact', *Spiegel Online*, 27 June 2012. 'Officially, of course, EU rhetoric would suggest that Hollande's "growth pact", . . . aimed at creating "jobs and growth", . . . is on a par with Merkel's "fiscal pact". But the article points out that, unlike the fiscal pact, the 'growth pact' is not a legally binding agreement, only an appendix to the summit declaration of twenty-seven heads of government. It claims to provide a package worth 130 billion euros, but this figure includes 55 billion euros already earmarked for the structural fund in 2013 (which will go to *all* EU countries in need of support), as well as an unspecified residue from the same fund not disbursed in 2012; no explanation is given as to how these sums will stimulate growth. The European Investment Bank will then supposedly allocate a further 60 billion euros over a four-year period to public-private partnerships in the debtor countries. However, partly because of the high risk involved for private partners, no projects are actually under way. Finally, guarantees up to a total of 18 billion euros are meant to come from the current EU budget to cover loans to the private sector for infrastructural projects – although there is no sign of such projects either. In none of these cases will any new money be allocated.

chambers of commerce and industry, trade unions and taxi guilds,[60] or minimum wages and employment protection. This is all that is meant when today's creditors expect debtor states to implement 'structural reforms' – which actually does bear out the claim that growth measures were from the beginning part of European modernization policies. Deregulation as a programme for growth has the considerable political advantage that no one can seriously expect it to work miracles in the short term – and that, if miracles do not appear in the long term either, it can always be argued in a less than perfect world that the dose was not large enough. In between, to quieten the patient while the bitter medicine is administered, democracy has to be suspended as much as possible, for example by the installation of 'governments of experts'. If necessary, deregulation can also be given a human face through symbolic gifts of money on the model of the growth programmes considered in 2012. Since deregulation itself costs nothing – except, perhaps, for occasional police deployments – it fits in well with the present financial and fiscal crisis. Besides, even without growth effects, its demonstrative enforcement in a debt state on the margin of insolvency is per se valuable today since it contributes to confidence-building on the part of 'the markets' by showing that the government has sufficient capacity to control its people.

EXCURSUS ON REGIONAL GROWTH PROGRAMMES

Until the late 1990s, the EU directed considerable sums of financial aid into the Mediterranean countries that would go on to become today's debtor states. Why did these flows not bring about sustainable economic growth? Technocratic talk of 'cranking up' economies

---

60 At least rhetorically, taxi guilds were a favourite target for deregulation as nominated by the expert liquidators hired by Brussels, Papademos and Monti. High taxi fares irritate the middle class hurrying to their office or their family; if deregulation makes them cheaper, it cannot be altogether wrong. Of course it remains to be seen whether lower fares in Rome or Athens can promote lasting economic growth in the Mediterranean.

that for one reason or another are lagging behind leaves out of account that growth requires not only institutional but also social–structural and cultural conditions, which are by no means universal and certainly cannot be generated by ministerial fiat. States and governments eager to promote growth in backward regions have repeatedly wagered on instruments such as help with start-up costs, wage subsidies, investment grants, special capital allowances, tax relief and public investment in local infrastructure. Such intervention always proved to be extremely expensive while its declared objectives were achieved only in the long run, if at all. Two telling examples are the Italian Mezzogiorno and the Neue Länder – the former German Democratic Republic – that acceded to West Germany in 1990.

As regards Italy, the central state and the European Community spent large sums during the postwar years on the economic development of the South, but failed to narrow the gap with the North in a sustainable way. Whereas per capita income in the Mezzogiorno[61] was less than half the average for Italy at the beginning of the 1950s, the gap had closed to approximately 33 per cent (Fig. 3.9) by the time that postwar growth came to an end around 1970. It then rose again to just under 45 per cent by the mid-1990s, before declining slightly to 41 per cent around 2010.[62]

In the sociological literature, the seemingly ineradicable economic backwardness of the Italian South is usually put down to its traditional social structure, including the power of local elites afraid of losing control in the wake of capitalist modernization. Following Jens Beckert, capitalist economies presuppose a social order that permits and rewards orientation of everyday behaviour to the basic principles of competition, creativity, commodification and credit (the

---

61   The Mezzogiorno comprises the islands of Sicily and Sardinia, as well as the regions of Abruzzo, Basilicata, Campania, Calabria, Molise and Puglia.

62   It is of course common knowledge that Southern Italy has an extensive underground economy – which one can expect to be accompanied by poor governability, in terms of both tax collection and control over the use of central government subsidies.

'four Cs').[63] Mainstream economic theory differs from sociological theory by virtue of a kind of anthropological act of faith, which assumes that such behavioural orientations are universally human.[64] This makes it hard for them to understand why, despite all the 'incentives', capitalist rationalization does not much appeal to societies such as that of the Mezzogiorno, or why the introduction of modern institutions like capitalist private property may not as such be sufficient to get capitalist modernization under way.

FIGURE 3.9. *Italy: income gap and net transfers to Mezzogiorno, as percentage of national product, 1951–2008*

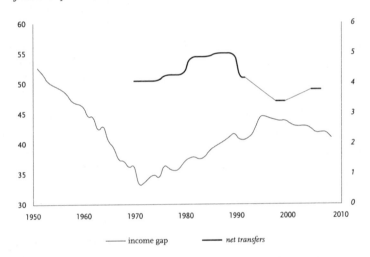

Source: Vittorio Daniele and Paolo Malanima, 'Il prodotto delle regioni e il divario Nord-Sud in Italia (1861–2004)', *Rivista de Politica Economica*, 2007, pp. 267–316

---

63   J. Beckert, *Capitalism as a System of Contingent Expectations. On the Microfoundations of Economic Dynamics*, Cologne: Max-Planck-Institut für Gesellschaftsforschung, 2012.

64   From this perspective, *Homo oeconomicus* sits at the heart of every society and individual, waiting only to be released. That a society may be locked into a low-productivity equilibrium escapes standard economic comprehension, which inevitably concludes that the solution is a forced 'reformation' to create a new way of life.

In part because calculation methods have kept changing and the relevant institutions have repeatedly been reformed, even specialists cannot say just how much the Italian state and the European Community have spent on promoting regional development in the Mezzogiorno and national convergence in Italy.[65] The best available estimate puts the current net transfer to the Mezzogiorno at roughly 4 per cent of Italian GDP, with a peak of 5 per cent in the late 1980s; subsequently, during the first phase of public financial consolidation, this fell to 3.4 per cent at the end of the century (Fig. 3.9).[66] Despite this considerable resource input, Southern Italy serves as an example of how regional development programmes can fail because of political and social circumstances. Today there is broad agreement that Italian government aid was absorbed by local power structures and used to bolster traditional local relations of clientelist domination. At the same time, the parties running the central state – especially Democrazia Cristiana – learned how to use regional development funds to buy political support, which could take the form of guaranteed votes at elections. The tolerance long shown in the North for the major transfer payments to the South was possible only because the Left especially saw the creation of roughly equal living conditions in the South as a national cause and an expression of national solidarity – and because the EU massively backed Italian regional policy from the beginning.[67] That this support ended in the 1980s drew public

---

65   Thus, in 1992 the Cassa per il Mezzogiorno – a special fund for the development of the South – was abolished and replaced with a system of tax rebates. Government infrastructural investment, subsidies for particular sectors, investment grants and tax exemptions for private businesses kept alternating with one another, while new European support programmes were continually added.

66   The calculations of Italian net transfers were made available to the author by Prof. Carlo Trigilia of the University of Florence.

67   In the negotiations leading to the formation of the European Economic Community, Italy insisted that the EEC should take on some of the costs of supporting the Mezzogiorno. Without massive transfer payments to the South, exceeding what the Italian state could afford at the time, the Christian Democrat government did not feel able to maintain the country's cohesion, as well as its own parliamentary majority in Rome. The case can serve as an illustration of the fact that, far from phasing out the constituent nation-states, European integration often served to stabilize them (A. Milward, *The European Rescue of the Nation State*, London: Taylor and Francis, 1992).

attention to the fact that the vast resources spent on regional 'development' in the South had not even been able to prevent the gap between the two halves of the country from widening again for more than a decade. Since then, resistance to further aid programmes has been growing; one of its most visible expressions is the rise in Northern Italy of a secessionist regional party, the Lega Nord.

The Italian example shows that regional growth and development policies, as rhetorically envisaged also for monetary union, must solve two problems that are closely associated with each other. The *first* is how to deploy within a traditional social structure funds dedicated to the promotion of economic development in such a way that they give rise to self-sustaining growth and eventually make themselves redundant. In other words, the task is to ensure that aid is used for investment rather than consumption, difficult though the distinction may be in individual cases. Whether there is a prospect that it will at some point be possible to solve the *efficiency problem* of regional aid will determine whether the regions that have to come up with the funding are actually willing to do so. *Second*, it must be established who has control over the use of growth funds, or how control is to be divided between central donors and local recipients (or, more generally, between centre and periphery). Too much local control may lead to funds being used for consumption rather than investment; too much central control raises the danger that local conditions will not be sufficiently taken into account. The problem to be solved *here* is one of *governability*. The relevant factors include the political and legal constitution of the regional government institutions, their linkage to the centre, the regional social structure, and the political dependence of the centre on support by the periphery.

As far as Germany is concerned, it was often feared after reunification that the 'new states' that had been the GDR would become a German Mezzogiorno. Over the next two decades the federal government devoted considerable sums to the equalization of living conditions and economic competitiveness in the two parts of the country. Here too there was a suspicion that the aid went more on consumption than on investment. By 1994 the income gap between

FIGURE 3.10. *Germany: income gap and net transfers to Neue Länder, as percentage of national product, 1991–2010*

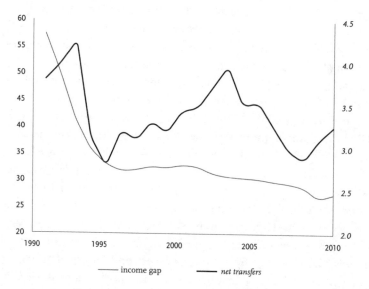

—— income gap   —— *net transfers*

Sources: VGR der Länder: Bruttoinlandsprodukt, Bruttowertschöpfung in den Ländern und Ost-West-Großraumregionen Deutschlands, 1991–2010, ifo Dresden Institut (2012): Studie 63

East and West had fallen from just under 60 per cent to 33 per cent of the national per capita income (Fig. 3.10). Afterwards, however, it took another one and a half decades for the gap to decline by a further 6 per cent. This went together with annual net transfers which, between 1995 and 2003, rose from 2.8 per cent of GDP to roughly 4 per cent and then fell back to under 3 per cent; in 2012 they amounted to approximately 3.3 per cent, around half a percentage point below the Italian level. Since the 'new states' account only for little more than 20 per cent of the total population of Germany, whereas in Italy the share of the Mezzogiorno has for decades been roughly 35 per cent, the sums transferred in Germany were not only easier to raise but had relatively fewer beneficiaries. A crude estimate suggests that in Italy some 6 to 7 per cent of GDP would have been needed to reach an effective transfer level comparable to that in Germany.

Although in Germany, unlike in Italy, the gap between the rich and poor parts of the country clearly narrowed (in Italy, at 41 per cent, it was roughly the same at the outbreak of the crisis as it had been in 1990, one and a half times larger than in Germany), it is still not possible to say that the gap has closed. So, even though the distribution of the population is more favourable than in Italy, the German federal government will have to retain for the foreseeable future the 'solidarity surcharge' on top of income tax that was introduced in the wake of reunification.[68] The stubborn economic lag of the former GDR[69] is all the more remarkable since, at the time of reunification, there was no established power structure to stand in the way of capitalist modernization or to demand bribes from the central government. Not only was the Communist leadership completely discredited; the older manorial domains of the East of Germany – structurally akin in many ways to the large landholdings in Sicily and Calabria – had been destroyed first by the Nazis (after the attempted Wehrmacht coup of 20 July 1944) and then by the Soviet occupation regime and the ruling Socialist Unity Party, so that there could be no talk of a feudal legacy impeding economic progress.[70]

It is still a matter of dispute how much the slow speed of the convergence of the two parts of Germany since 1995 should be

68   Another factor in this, of course, is the electoral influence of the *Neue Länder* on the composition of the Upper House (the Bundesrat) and the federal government. Debates over the continuation of the 'solidarity pact', due to expire in 2019, were going on already in 2012. In a commentary on demands by a regional economics minister in East Germany for further support, the *Süddeutsche Zeitung* of 5 September 2012 conceded that, 'despite trillions spent on building up the East', a 'self-sustaining economic and funding structure has still not been established in the new *Länder* . . . Less than 10 per cent of Germany's total business taxes are raised there; and the figure is between 5 and 7 per cent for corporate taxes.'

69   According to the federal government report of 2012 on the 'State of German Unity' (*Bundesministerium des Innern 2012*), the economy in East Germany grew by 2.5 per cent in 2011, compared with 3 per cent in Germany as a whole. Per capita GDP had fallen from 73 per cent of the West German level in 2010 to 71 per cent in 2011, while productivity was at 79 per cent. The unemployment rate was 11.3 per cent, compared with 6 per cent in West Germany.

70   A. Hirschman, 'Rival Interpretations of Market Society: Civilizing, Destructive, or Feeble?', *Journal of Economic Literature*, vol. 20/4, 1982, pp. 1463–84.

attributed to the monetary union, the conversion of the GDR currency into the West German mark at a rate of 1:1, and the wholesale extension of the West German social welfare state to the East. All these measures were and are seen by some as vote-buying in the East by the Kohl government of the time, and would in this respect be comparable to Italian practices in the Mezzogiorno. Indeed, there is much to suggest that the large scale of transfer payments in the 1990s and later is in part explicable in terms of the shock that resulted from monetary and social union. What seems certain is that, despite the constitutional requirement to equalize living conditions in all parts of the country, the high cost of support for the *Neue Länder*, which came as a surprise to voters,[71] was politically sustainable only because of an unexpectedly strong sense of shared identity and national duty.

The lessons of the two cases are not encouraging for the EU 'growth programme' adopted in summer 2012 for the Southern debtor countries. Greece, Portugal, Spain and other European countries that might be in need of aid are nation-states, not federal *Länder* or provinces. Their governments and parties are even less easy to bypass for the European Commission or the European Council than are regional powerholders for national governments.[72] The Commission has repeatedly tried to steer regional policy measures past national governments, but it has never actually succeeded.

---

71   One thinks of Helmut Kohl's promise of 'blossoming landscapes' in a short time, without tax increases in the West.

72   In East Germany, many of the key positions in the post-unification *Länder* were filled by West German politicians and officials, who had internalized the political culture of the old Bundesrepublik. There was never a comparable changeover of elites in the Mezzogiorno. Mario Monti, the EU-appointed prime minister of Italy, revealed in summer 2012 to great public effect that the president of the Sicilian region, Raffaele Lombardo, earned more than Angela Merkel, and that Sicily employed 24,000 foresters and 20,000 administrative personnel, at an annual cost of 349 euros per citizen (compared with 21 euros in Lombardy). Monti forced the president to resign when he also discovered, no doubt to his surprise, that he had collaborated with the Mafia (despite having been elected as a pro-reform candidate, whose predecessor had to serve time in jail). As for the Sicilian budget deficit, Monti's hands were tied by the regional autonomy statute.

Everything that is true of Italy is therefore applicable, at a higher level and a *fortiori*, to the EU. Moreover, unlike in Italy or Germany, the bond of a historically developed sense of community is lacking between payers and receivers of economic aid in the Europe of the EU. National identities can, however, be mobilized at any moment to delegitimize solidarity payments as undeserved, or attack the strings attached to regional assistance programmes as imperialist interference.

To gauge the Herculean task of helping Mediterranean crisis countries not to fall ever further behind in a currency union with Germany, it will be useful to keep in mind their relative size and the extent of economic differences within the Eurozone (Fig. 3.11). Spain, Greece and Portugal – the three poorest countries in the Mediterranean arc of crisis – have a combined population of 68.1 million. The three largest countries in the European monetary union, and the only ones really able to pay sizeable sums of regional aid, are Germany, France and the Netherlands, which together have a population of 163.5 million. This amounts to a ratio of 41 to 100. The corresponding ratio of East to West Germany is 27 to 100. In 2011 the weighted per capita income of the three Mediterranean countries was roughly 21,000 euros, whereas that of the three potential supporting countries was 31,700 euros – an income gap amounting to no less than 34 per cent. That is 7 percentage points more than within Germany, where, for a still unspecified time, some 4 per cent of national income will have to be used to prevent the East from falling behind the level it has currently reached. If Italy is included in the Mediterranean, the income gap with the North is smaller but the population ratio is worse, at just under 80 to 100. Even together with France, and even if its own economy continued to perform as well as in 2011 and 2012, Germany would obviously be hard put to finance a regional policy for the Mediterranean that offered any real prospects for the future.[73]

---

73   See, in connection with the demand for Eurobonds, the article 'Merkel Stresses Limits to Germany's Strength', *New York Times*, 15 June 2012.

In addition to their high cost, interventions from outside or above in regional policy would be difficult to manage. If the Italian central government was unable to control the use of its funds in Sicily, or the general fiscal conduct of Italian regional authorities, one can only wonder how the Brussels Commission, or indeed the German government, is supposed to control the Greek, Spanish, Portuguese or, for that matter, Italian government. And if, twenty years after reunification, despite the existence of a federal state and huge financial resources, there is still no end in sight to Germany's regional aid to the Neue Länder, how much longer is it likely to take for regional subsidies to become superfluous in a currency union of sovereign states – especially considering the effect of cumulative advantage in conditions of capitalist competition? The patience of voters would be stretched to the limit in the countries that provided the funds, at a time of shrinking public budgets and cutbacks in social services and benefits. Why should the Finns and the Dutch have greater patience with the Greeks and the Spanish than the citizens of Piedmont, Lombardy or the Veneto have with those of Palermo or Naples?

Everything indicates that the limited funds which Western Europe can transfer to the South under conditions of fiscal crisis will at most be sufficient to buy the loyalty of state apparatuses and centrist parties there – an arrangement remarkably similar to the multilevel national clientelism of Italy's postwar democracy, and one that would anyway be nothing new for the EU. When Portugal, Spain and Greece turned their back on fascism and military dictatorship in the 1970s, all three might have chosen a Eurocommunist option – especially with the Historic Compromise (the *compromesso storico*) already looming in Italy. This, of course, would have included a settling of accounts with the traditional upper classes discredited by collaboration with the dictatorships, and hence at least the possibility of a revolutionary modernization of the social structure. But such a course of events was not in the interest of Western Europe and the United States, which for geopolitical reasons needed reliable allies and calm conditions in their Mediterranean periphery.

FIGURE 3.11. *Relative size and income of selected EMU member-states, 2011*

	population	% of G + F + NL	income	income gap
Italy	60.1	36.8	26,000	18.0
Spain	46.2	28.3	23,300	26.5
Greece	11.3	6.9	19,000	40.1
Portugal	10.6	6.5	16,000	49.5
I + SP + GR + P	128.2	78.4	23,594	25.6
G + F + NL	163.5	100.0	31,711	-

The entry of the three countries into the EU – and almost simultaneously into NATO – ensued for political rather than economic
reasons: it was to reward their pro-Western, 'European' option with a
share in the prosperity of the West European core. Growth and prosperity, it was suggested, would result not from social revolutions but
from subsidies out of the EU's structural funds, together with the
Brussels-sponsored construction of modern state apparatuses on the
West European model. The aim was a Eurocapitalism with social
democratic cushioning, which would facilitate national reconciliation
in the newly democratic countries by means of growing prosperity:
modernization without bloodshed. New middle classes oriented to
Western Europe hoped that gradual economic-structural change
would allow them to establish themselves peacefully as a lasting
hegemonic force in their respective polities – despite initially unavoidable compromises with the old oligarchies, symbolized in Spain by
the monarchy and constitutionally enshrined in Greece by the prerog-
atives of the Orthodox church, including far-reaching tax exemptions
for its extensive landholdings and commercial activities.[74]

---

74 None of the 'rescuers' of the country has yet called for annulment of these privileges.
In Greece the Western powers, especially after the British had crushed the Communist popular
uprising that followed the German occupation, restored the monarchy and ensured that the
forces allied with it remained firmly in the saddle. The years up to the regime of the colonels
were marked by political instability and constant battles between the court and elected governments (see Markantonatu, *The Uneasy Course of Democratic Capitalism in Greece*).

Certainly the financial and fiscal crisis – and probably already the collapse of the Eastern bloc after 1989 and the resulting need to absorb another European periphery – put an end to the project of subsidized economic and social convergence. In none of the three new Mediterranean member countries – nor even in Italy, as it turned out – was the catching-up process so advanced by 2008 that it could withstand the onset of crisis. Today it is clear that, as early as the 1980s, the EU took on too much in its attempt to pacify the Mediterranean through Eurocapitalist modernization, and that the promise of social and political convergence by means of economic growth, contained in the programme of simultaneous widening and deepening of the European Union, was beyond the bounds of the possible. With the entry of new member-states, the pressures for austerity even in the West European core and an increased risk awareness of capital markets, no prospect remained of appreciable subsidies from outside – not even at the level of the structural fund of the 1980s and 1990s. A German 'Marshall Plan'[75] for Europe of

---

75   As demanded, among others, by the American historian Charles S. Maier in the *New York Times* in June 2012 (C. Maier, 'Europe Needs a German Marshall Plan', *New York Times*, 9 June 2012). One of the many things he overlooked was the political asymmetry among the parties to the original Marshall Plan – an asymmetry so profound that today's problems of funding or governance never arose. In the United States, the Marshall Plan could be advocated as a means of *containment* at the beginning of the Cold War. In Europe, an end to American aid could always be threatened if the wrong kind of government was elected. 'In the South . . . De Gasperi required the support of the Allies . . . The intensification of the Cold War was helpful . . . The United States sided with the Christian Democrats. Washington began to flood the peninsula with Western aid. Special propaganda festivals were staged for every ship with relief material as it neared an Italian port. Marshall warned that all American aid would immediately be frozen if the Communists won the election. Especially in the South, the Christian Democrats used Western aid to tie voters to them. The distribution of the goods in question was a prototype for the clientelist party machine that took shape in Southern Italy in the following years' (J. Hien, *The Black International: Catholics or the Spirit of Capitalism – The Evolution of the Political Economies of Italy and Germany and Their Religious Foundations*, doctoral dissertation, Florence: European University Institute, 2012, p. 279). In Greece, the Marshall Plan made it easier for the victors of the British-led civil war against the Communists to serve their clientele – for example, by providing jobs in the public sector. Postwar clientelism in Greece stems directly from the monetary rewards that the Allies made available as a reward for the outcome of the civil war (Markantonatu, *The Uneasy Course of Democratic Capitalism in Greece*).

more than symbolic significance would be unthinkable already because of the relative size of the countries involved – quite apart from the question of whether it could actually bring about growth. Besides, any benefits received by Greece would immediately be demanded by Portugal, Spain and perhaps even Italy, not to speak of Hungary (even though it is not yet part of the Monetary Union) and such countries as Serbia, Kosovo, Bosnia and Albania – in fact, the whole of the Balkans, which since 1989 has become another unstable *glacis* of the West European prosperity zone.

In the language of international relations, the fiscal crisis of the European state system may also be described as resulting from an overextension of the European Union as a 'civilian power' turned into an expanding empire of market economics. With funding now in short supply, the only hope for the continued cohesion of the Brussels bloc of states is neoliberal 'structural reforms' combined with the neutralization of national democracies through supranational institutions, and with the cultivation of local support from 'modern' middle classes and state apparatuses, which see their future in the West European economy and way of life. Structural, cyclical and growth-promoting programmes instituted by the centre are then mainly of symbolic value – as themes for public conversations and for well-rehearsed summit decisions, and as a means of absorbing residual social democratic memories into the world of political rhetoric.[76] Such programmes, however paltry in financial terms, can also be used to distribute loyalty bonuses and subsistence allowances to local supporters – as instruments of elite co-optation in the Hayekization of European capitalism and its state system.

---

76   See the 'Pact for Sustainable Growth and Employment', agreed on 21 June 2012 between the German government and the Social Democrat and Green opposition. It anticipated a corresponding Cabinet decision and the later European 'Pact' (see fn. 59 above), making it easier for the Greens and the SPD to go along once more with the Merkel government's policy on Europe. Published as Press Release 212/12 by the Press and Information Bureau of the Federal Government, 21 June 2012.

ON THE STRATEGIC CAPACITY OF THE
EUROPEAN CONSOLIDATION STATE

Only the innermost circles of the consolidation state can know whether the continual round of summit conferences and intergovernmental consultations has a strategic centre in which some kind of common objectives are agreed upon and pursued with prudence and expertise. Anyone who has tried to make sense of the confusing performances staged for years now in public will doubt that this is so. Those who watch the TV news see one enactment after another of decision-making power and capability, offered by virtuosi in the art of confidence-building and accompanied by a cacophony of 'expert' opinions and patent recipes with an ever shorter expiry date. Is that all? Or does something like continuity or even strategic capacity lie hidden behind the noisy pastiche, in the ECB, the EU Commission, the IMF, the national government apparatuses, or perhaps 'the markets' with their back rooms in New York and Frankfurt?

If we look for constants amid the jumble of crises and crisis policies, we find that everyone in a position of responsibility accepted from the start that, once introduced, the euro had to be defended by all means necessary, regardless of what it had or had not achieved so far. The coalition that wants to keep the euro naturally includes 'the markets', to the extent that they have invested in it and want to be sure that their euro-denominated loans will be repaid in full. However, they could also make money from a collapse of the common currency, if they were to adjust in time and, in so doing, make it happen faster. The governments of the Euroland countries, both strong and weak, are anxious to talk the markets out of this, and they have the EU on their side. In its eyes, monetary union is the final completion of the single market, supposedly 'completed' in 1992, which was to ensure a free play of market forces within Europe, unhindered by national boundaries, restrictive tariffs or the intervention of individual governments. The possibility of devaluation to defend the competitiveness of national economies conflicted with the spirit of the neoliberal single market project. If the market was to

come fully into its own, there could be no arbitrary political intervention to correct its distributive outcomes. The elimination of
national currencies, in favour of a common currency for, ideally, the
entire common market, was in the logic of the neoliberal turn
designed to free the economy from political encroachment; it was
the true crowning of the single market project.[77]

A stylized political economy of the pro-euro coalition that has
until the present day scripted European crisis policies begins with
the export industries of the surplus countries – above all those of
Germany, which in this respect are in complete agreement with the
unions that organize their workers. For them, the euro guarantees
that protective measures by foreign governments cannot make
their goods artificially more expensive in other European countries. A further reason why they defend the euro is that in the
current crisis the economic problems of the deficit countries lower
the exchange rate of the euro against other currencies, thereby
improving market opportunities for the competitive section of
European industry outside Europe as well. In Germany, therefore,
neither Christian Democracy, the party close to industry, nor the
SPD, which is close to the unions, questions the policy of sticking
with the euro at any price, both regarding it as a cornerstone of the
national interest and as the most important common ground of
German national policy.

It is remarkable how successful the pro-euro coalition has been,
in Germany, in equating monetary union with 'the European idea' or
even with 'Europe', regardless of its character as a market-expanding
rationalization project, and even though ten of the twenty-seven
countries that belong to the EU and the single market have not

---

77   To see the euro as an element in the neoliberal market expansion, and therefore
in late twentieth-century capitalist development, does not mean that other political motives
associated with monetary union should be disregarded. Important historical decisions are
always driven by several factors and often come about precisely because they fit into more
than one strategic context. In the case of the monetary union, one could think of the French
attempt to replace the European hegemony of the Bundesbank with a common currency
and monetary policy in which France would enjoy equal rights.

adopted the euro. Among these are indisputably 'European' countries such as Britain, Denmark and Sweden, which have insisted on special rights that allow them – contrary to the EMU treaty provisions – to remain outside the eurozone even if they fulfil the conditions for entry. Until the outbreak of the crisis, this was seen in Germany at least as a blemish that would soon be made good. Today it is clear that, whatever the treaties may say, an expansion of the EMU will at best be on the agenda in a distant future, if the present crisis has somehow been resolved and the Monetary Union, or even the EU itself, has not foundered in the meantime. In any event, Angela Merkel's cryptic 'If the euro fails, Europe too will fail' is still regarded by everyone except the Left Party as a formula for national consensus deserving enthusiastic support. Since it is beyond debate in Germany that German policy must be 'European', whatever that may mean, this makes defence of the euro at any price a matter not only of economic expediency but also of German political and moral *raison d'état*. Anyone who does not subscribe to it, or who even thinks it possible that 'Europe' could still exist without the euro, is sternly made aware that they are placing themselves outside what the Italians have long called the 'constitutional arc'.[78]

At first sight, it is more difficult to explain why the governments of countries that have got nothing but debts out of the euro remain so firmly attached to it.[79] The point is that the politics of these countries is dominated by an alliance between their state apparatuses and

---

78 In terms of the politics of sentiment, 'Europe' is to monetary union what the 'social dimension' was to the single market, with a few revealing differences. When Jacques Delors proposed the single market project to the European Left, he famously stated that one cannot 'love' a market. One could love only a socially just society – hence it was inevitable that the single market would be complemented at some point with a common social policy. Today there is no longer any talk of that in relation to the currency union. The rhetorical function of the 'social dimension' has now fallen to 'Europe' *tout court*, by which everyone may understand what they will: anything from holidays without passports and foreign exchange to the Christian Occident.

79 Apart from the then new Greek party of the Left, Syriza, on which silence soon descended again, no major political force in the Mediterranean has so far called for its country to leave the euro – and even Syriza left open how seriously it took the prospect in reality.

an urban middle class oriented to Western Europe. The latter values the greater mobility opened up for them and their savings by membership in the European Union, and associates with it lively hopes of future prosperity and regular access to imported goods without currency devaluations that would make them prohibitively expensive. On their side are assorted modernizers in the state and business, often acting out of nationalist motives, who seek to overcome what they consider their country's 'backwardness' through the 'internal devaluation' compelled by the monetary union – that is, through neoliberal 'reforms' wearing down the inertia of labour unions and traditional ways of life – as the only way of avoiding national impoverishment.

In the four Mediterranean countries currently in difficulty, the alliance between modernizing elites and urban middle classes has not been enough to eradicate the premodern feudal legacy that still blocks the path to Eurocapitalism. Their main hope has been, and still is, to find in Brussels the necessary allies and supporters for 'structural reforms' that they cannot push through alone. In this, political obligations imposed from outside can be as useful as financial subsidies. Nor does it seem unrealistic to hope that intergovernmental negotiations will deliver redistributive benefits within the EMU, since these may also correspond to the interest of core countries in stabilizing demand in the periphery. North–South transfers may be used by receiving countries either to strengthen their national economy (in the sense of a rationalization and modernization drive to make it more competitive internationally) or to bolster consumption and purchase support for the national political class, as in the Southern Italian model.[80] It suits the recipients well that, because of the long lead time of catch-up capitalist development, the two uses cannot be easily kept apart in practice.

Nevertheless, the North–South alliance to preserve monetary union harbours major conflicts, both within and between the

---

80   If such support is sufficiently 'European-oriented', it may appear from Brussels or, for that matter, Berlin as a desirable contribution to political stability.

countries involved. For those in the North, there is the question of how much money they have to (and are willing to) pay to those in the South, as compensation or as development aid, to make it easier for them and motivate them to remain in the EMU. In the domestic political arena, they must work out who will bear the costs of the currency union. In Germany, export sectors are keen to spread them among as many others as possible, including those that derive little or no advantage from the country's export surpluses. For the government this presents the difficult task of shifting onto the backs of ordinary taxpayers, consumers and welfare recipients what should in principle be a levy on the competitiveness of German export industries – and to do so as inconspicuously as possible. For this it has of course many means at its disposal, one of which is to call on the European Central Bank.

As to the Southern countries, their aim must be not only to set a high price for continued EMU membership, but also to keep to a minimum the sovereignty sacrifices, in terms of institutionalized powers of supervision and intervention, that the Northern countries will demand in return for their financial support. Internally, the front-line runs between resistance to a potential 'Euroimperialism', on the one hand, and readiness to collaborate with the surplus countries on the other, in the hope of large equalization payments or of gradual convergence with the prosperous West European core ('Europeanization'). Intergovernmental clashes can easily fuel nationalist sentiment on both sides, while domestic resistance must be held in check through the neutralization of democratic institutions: in the North by technical tricks or calculated silence to camouflage actual transfer payments; in the South by pointing to binding international obligations or by clientelist vote-buying.

Over and above the basic structure of interests in the political economy of the EU, here presented in a simplified account, many turbulent processes play themselves out in a climate of multiple uncertainties. What will happen if, as the treaty envisages, EU member-states such as Bulgaria, the Czech Republic, Hungary, Poland and Romania join the EMU? How should EU and EMU relate to each other in general in the years ahead? How does the fiscal pact agreed under international law fit into the system of European law? What should be done about the Balkan countries[81] and the idea of their joining the EU? Should they too receive 'growth aid', and who would pay for it? Everyone suspects that in a few years the EU (if it still exists) and the European state system as a whole will look completely different from how people imagined just a short time ago. But none of those in a position of 'responsibility' ever finds the right occasion to express themselves on the matter. Longer time periods are invoked only with respect to the return of growth, with everyone keeping their fingers crossed that this would finally bring the situation back under control.

Still, at the level of tactics and notwithstanding the general disarray, four lines of continuity have been observable in the actions of the EU and its leading states since the onset of the crisis.

1) The 'markets', whatever they may be, must as far as possible be spared the costs of 'rescuing' insolvent states. Only other countries, hence their citizens, must foot the bill. Today everyone agrees that, when the German chancellor insisted during the first Greek debt-relief operation that private creditors should take a modest 'haircut', she made a mistake that should never be repeated; anything it may have brought Merkel in terms of support from her national population could not remotely outweigh the loss of confidence among the financial *Marktvolk*. In any case, central banks and some state-owned banks seem to have had enough time before the event to buy most of the Greek government securities from private banks and other loan merchants on terms acceptable to their owners, so that most of the damage was inflicted on the public purse, and the same is true for a second bailout that will probably soon be necessary.

2) Ailing banks should not be nationalized but rescued with public funds, as discreetly as possible to avoid angering the national

---

81   Albania, Bosnia and Herzegovina, Kosovo, Macedonia, Montenegro and Serbia.

population. The task of financial engineers in the machine room of the consolidation state is to organize the necessary transactions in such a way that they do not appear in the government accounts. A comparatively transparent example of this was one of Mario Draghi's first official acts as head of the ECB, when he handed out a total of 1,000 billion euros to the banks at an interest rate of 1 per cent, later of 0.75 per cent, over three years. In return, with no binding under-taking and on a scale at their discretion, the banks appear to have agreed to buy the securities of ailing states in the eurozone, to help reduce their risk premiums. One can assume that the ECB will know how to protect the banks from losses in such deals done to do it a favour – to help it circumvent the prohibition on central bank state funding written into the Maastricht Treaty.[82]

3) As far as possible, insolvent states must be prevented from adopting the solution of bankruptcy or unilateral debt rescheduling. In critical cases, non-recoverable fiscal subsidies should enable them to meet their obligations to creditors, so that these remain prepared to supply the consolidated debt state in future with affordable loans. Technical safeguards should shield such transfers too from the scrutiny of national populations. An example of successful camouflage of major intergovernmental transfers, or potential transfers, is the handling of the so-called TARGET2 balances of national central banks with the ECB.[83]

4) Insofar as the financial and fiscal crisis can be dealt with only through a general devaluation of public debt – mainly, though not only, in the absence of growth – this should be done gently and over as long a period as possible, so that large investors with a capacity to retaliate are able to adjust their portfolios in time to protect themselves against losses. Here too the technical expertise

---

82 As we know, the effects of this operation fell flat after just a few weeks. In September 2012, the ECB took the next step and decided to buy in unlimited quantities, at a fixed price, the bonds of crisis-stricken states – at first only in secondary markets, that is, from banks rather than directly from governments.

83 Hans-Werner Sinn, 'Das unsichtbare Bail-Out der EZB', *Ökonomenstimme*, 11 June 2011.

in the central banks and international organizations is in demand. It would be incumbent on the experts to devise ways for governments to liquidate debt they cannot clear through economic growth alone: that is, measures of 'financial repression' at the expense of savers (preferably small asset holders outside the financial sector), involving a combination of high inflation with low interest rates and pressure on banks and insurance companies to invest in government bonds.[84] There are signs that preparations are nearly complete to launch this sort of policy as soon as the present crises are under control and the interests of the financial sector have been taken care of.

Continuities such as the above four do not necessarily point to shadowy decision-making centres with a high capacity for long-term strategy. In fact the scale of the confusion is remarkable in relation to such things as the temporal horizon for crisis management and state reorganization. For example, a 'banking union' is being agreed upon as a short-term measure to solve the crisis by cleaning up ailing banks in the South, but if it is to be more than cosmetic it will take years to become operational. Or to prevent state bankruptcy in Greece or Italy, the ECB subsidizes the two countries' refinancing costs, even though this may lead in the long term to American-style bubbles or could even halt the intended neoliberal rationalization of the countries in question.[85] What for all the chaos at the front of the stage may sometime appear to be a consistent neoliberal plot is in reality probably no more than a chain of short-term common-sense responses to the 'restrictive conditions' operative under capitalism,[86] as embodied

---

84 C. Reinhart and M. Sbrancia, *The Liquidation of Government Debt*, NBER Working Paper No. 16893, Cambridge, MA: National Bureau of Economic Research, 2011.

85 It should not be forgotten that increased refinancing costs raise the share of interest payments in government expenditure only in the long run since the accumulated debt does not have to be refinanced all at once.

86 J. Bergmann et al., 'Herrschaft, Klassenverhältnisse und Schichtung. Referat auf dem Soziologentag 1968', *Verhandlungen des Deutschen Soziologentags*, Stuttgart: Enke, 1969, pp. 67–87; C. Offe, 'Politische Herrschaft und Klassenstrukturen', in Gisela Kress et al. (eds), *Politikwissenschaft*, Frankfurt/Main: Europäische Verlagsanstalt, 1972, pp. 135–64.

in the threat potential of private investors. Of course, this requires that the common sense crystallized in relevant institutions is the right one, one that is elaborated and practised in the epistemic community of organizations such as Goldman Sachs and their ilk. Since for it there are no alternatives to satisfying the demands of the Marktvolk, it knows no strategic but only tactical problems, especially in dealing with national peoples made presumptuous by extravagant promises of democracy.

A fixed part of the worldview of economic policymakers, and the Ariadne's thread of their behaviour, is an unshakeable faith in the governability of Europe from above – or at least an unshakeable resolve to profess such a faith on a current basis in order to confirm themselves and others in it. This includes everybody: in Germany, not only the government and opposition, but also the integration-minded intellectual Left;[87] in Europe, the Brussels Commission and the ECB; and worldwide, the majority of economic 'experts'. Democrats see nothing wrong in the fact that a strong central state is needed for governability from above, since they hope to democratize it one day; and it is all the same to liberals, so long as the aim is a Hayekian liberation of markets from political correction – a use of the strength of the strong state to eliminate itself as an interventionist state.

Top-down governability must be believed in – and it is. Only that explains how the German Council of Expert Advisers (*Sachverständigenrat*) could propose, in its annual report for 2011–12, the setting up of a special debt repayment fund, which would require a country like Italy to secure in its public finance a 'constant primary surplus' of 4.2 per cent per annum, for a period of no less than twenty-five years;[88] or how Bofinger et al. can demand future 'strict budgetary discipline' in exchange for the present 'communitization' of debts in Europe; or how the ECB can make bond purchases in

87   P. Bofinger et al., 'Einspruch gegen die Fassadendemokratie', *Frankfurter Allgemeine Zeitung*, 3 August 2012, p. 33.

88   Sachverständigenrat zur Begutachtung der gesamtwirtschaftlichen Entwicklung, *Jahresgutachten 2011/12: Verantwortung für Europa wahrnehmen*, Wiesbaden: Statistisches Bundesamt, 2011.

ailing states dependent on promises of future 'reforms', such as cuts in pension benefits or the selling off of public enterprises. In all this, the idea of technocratic control of politics and whole societies functions as a working hypothesis amazingly impervious to disappointment, or even as an ideology in the sense of a necessary illusion. Repeated references to the experience of Bremen – a *Land* which, after a debt relief pact with the federal government in the early 1990s, saw its total debt *shoot up* rather than fall[89] – do no more to change thinking than does the experience of the European Central Bank's first programme to purchase Italian government bonds in 2011.[90]

Are the control fantasies of the would-be saviours of the Monetary Union realistic? Perhaps they merely express a resolve to use all available means to make the fantasies come true – plus a confidence that deception, intimidation and the moral marginalization of emerging opposition, together with robust measures of every kind to override parliamentary democracy and institutionalize oligarchy and expertocracy at national and European level, will eventually achieve their aims if they are pursued for long enough.

RESISTANCE WITHIN THE INTERNATIONAL
CONSOLIDATION STATE

The international consolidation state is in the course of degrading the political resources of the citizens of the democratic national state. These count for less and less in the new arena of the

---

89   K. Konrad and H. Zschäpitz, *Schulden ohne Sühne? Warum der Absturz der Staatsfinanzen uns alle trifft*, Munich: C. H. Beck, 2010.

90   According to the *Frankfurter Allgemeine Zeitung* of 6 September 2012, the ECB in 2011 imposed 'several conditions on the Italian government for the purchase of government bonds. So far only one of the seven conditions has been met . . . On 5 August 2011, Trichet and his designated successor Draghi wrote a letter to the then prime minister Silvio Berlusconi, setting out their detailed demands, and then began a programme for the purchase of government securities. The demands of Trichet and Draghi were the last straw that revealed the weakness of the Berlusconi government and led to its downfall . . . One year on, the new prime minister, Mario Monti, has largely fulfilled only one of the demands, while no results are discernible in relation to the other six.' Draghi had been governor of the Bank of Italy under Berlusconi – a detail that could have come straight out of Machiavelli.

capitalist-democratic distribution conflict that towers over national politics – that is, in the global finance markets and the meeting rooms of intergovernmental financial diplomacy. Opposition to supranational dictates of austerity is difficult when one is wedged within the boundaries of a national democracy that has been mediatized by an international association of states. But it is not impossible. The Greek case shows that, for all the attempts of the associated states to exert influence through threats and propaganda, if demands are going too far they can then still produce results that are sufficiently troublesome to drive up the price creditor states must pay for keeping their debtors in the game.

The events of summer 2012 in Greece and Italy, as well as in Germany, are rich in lessons. In Germany, the opposition supported the government line of sticking firmly to the euro, and together they called for strict budgetary discipline overseen by Brussels in the debtor countries.[91] The only difference is that the opposition shows itself willing to pay a higher price for the sake of European peace – for example, the 'mutualization' (*Vergemeinschaftung*) of old and new debts, or further 'growth programmes' – probably on the assumption that this cannot be avoided anyway, and in the hope of profiting electorally from concern among sections of the population over the growing European hostility towards Germany. Government attempts, with the tacit agreement of the opposition, to foreclose basic issues of European integration and German statehood in the daily round of international business, have run up against resistance in parliament, even from members of the governing parties who, facing

---

91 Even Bofinger et al. – who demand, on behalf of the SPD leadership and in agreement with the Council of Expert Advisers, *gemeinschaftliche Haftung* ('shared responsibility') for the European public debt, or at least for part of it – insist that this must be accompanied by 'strict community control over national budgets'. Elsewhere they argue: 'A transfer of sovereignty to European institutions is . . . unavoidable to effectively enforce fiscal discipline and, in addition, to guarantee a stable financial system' (Bofinger et al., 'Einspruch gegen die Fassadendemokratie'). 'Discipline' and 'control', combined with adjectives such as 'strict', and notions of 'top-to-bottom governability' (*Durchregieren*) have astonishingly become the stuff of consensus in German discourse on Europe – from the Christian Democrats to the Greens, from the Right to the Left.

disempowerment by their leaders, sought and found help in the Constitutional Court and its previous rulings on the relationship between democracy and national sovereignty.

In Greece and Italy too, parties, elections and parliaments have been delaying the march to the international consolidation state. In the former, after the failure of the 'technocrat' Papademos, the return of the political parties into government induced the Brussels community of states to ease the austerity pressure on the Greek people and increase the reward promised for the implementation of the imposed consolidation measures. In Italy, soon after taking office, the Monti government found itself driven to make concessions to the Left parties and trade unions that went beyond what was considered necessary in Brussels. Monti also began early on to cultivate nationalist sentiments, as a way of strengthening his hand vis-à-vis Germany, in order to soften the austerity measures demanded of him; it was another case of a return to 'politics as usual', resulting in a delay in the execution of consolidation policies.

On the other hand, as the American example shows, there is no guarantee that the resistance to a Hayekian 'transformation of democracy'[92] will be successful. Today the financial giants of Wall Street have almost total control of the US government apparatus, despite the election in 2008 of a Democratic president given to populist gestures. Following two decades in which social and economic inequality had risen to obscene levels[93] and unemployment had remained high, no more than one-half of citizens are taking part in national elections. In autumn 2012 they were allowed to choose between a billionaire hedge-fund manager and an incumbent president who, after a uniquely costly rescue of the economy from the 'finance markets' and of the finance markets from themselves, could do nothing to regulate their activities or to limit their power to suck the economy dry.[94]

---

92 Agnoli, *Die Transformation der Demokratie*.

93 Hacker and Pierson, *Winner-Take-All Politics: How Washington Made the Rich Richer – and Turned Its Back on the Middle Class*.

94 On finance market regulation after 2008, see R. Mayntz (ed.), *Crisis and Control: Institutional Change in Financial Market Regulation*, Frankfurt/Main: Campus, 2012.

It was also noticeable how a deeply divided and disorganized society, weakened by state repression and stupefied by the products of a culture industry that Adorno could not have imagined in his most pessimistic moments, was held in check by a corporate plutocracy spanning the globe, which seems to have no difficulty in buying not only politicians, parties and parliaments but also public opinion.

What is to be done in a Hayekian unified Europe, when intergovernmental obligations and the laws of the financial markets have closed the traditional democratic channels of interest articulation? The social democratic model of responsible opposition consisted of imposing on capital reform projects which, while benefiting workers and their organizations, also helped capitalism to tackle problems of production and reproduction that it could not solve with its own institutions alone. The classic reference here is Marx's chapter on the struggle to limit the working day,[95] and the most powerful historical example is that of Fordism, where wage increases obtained by labour unions provided the purchasing-power necessary for mass production to be profitable. Today, however, there no longer appears to be anything that the broad mass of ordinary people could offer capital, or wrest from it, while deriving benefit for itself. All capital still wants from people is that they give back to the market – perhaps not all at once, but certainly step by step and not too slowly either – the social and civil rights they fought for and won in historic struggles. In the early twenty-first century, capital is confident of being able to organize itself as it pleases in a deregulated finance industry.[96] The only thing it expects of politics is its capitulation to the market by eliminating social democracy as an economic force.

If constructive opposition is impossible, those who are not content to spend their life paying off debts incurred by others have no other option than destructive opposition. This is needed to strengthen the delaying effect of what is left of democracy in national societies. If

---

95 Marx, *Capital, Volume One*, ch. 8.
96 J. McMurtry, *The Cancer Stage of Capitalism*, London: Pluto, 1999.

democratically organized populations can behave responsibly only by giving up use of their national sovereignty, and by limiting themselves for generations to keeping their creditors happy, then it might seem more responsible to try behaving irresponsibly. If being rational means accepting as self-evident that the demands of 'the markets' on society must be met, at the expense of a majority who have nothing to show but losses after decades of neoliberal market expansion, then indeed irrationality may be the only remaining form of rationality. Of course, it may take a long time for this conclusion to impose itself. Its denunciation as 'populist' is a tried-and-tested technique of rule, which in Germany goes together with largely successful attempts to equate criticism of monetary union and of the general course European integration has taken in the past two decades with opposition to 'Europe' in general, a longing for parochial *Kleinstaaterei*, or even the imperialist nationalism of the interwar period.

For all the propaganda, there seems to be a growing feeling among the citizens of Europe that their governments are not taking them seriously – for example, when they are told again and again that further liberalization of the capitalist world order, including budget cuts, dismantling of the welfare state, higher unemployment and job insecurity, serves the general interests in terms of growth, while incomes soar for 'experts' on the executive floor but fall for those lower down who are dependent on wages and social benefits. Critical intellectuals should see it as their task to reinforce this feeling as best they can, and stop worrying about their reputation with those whose hegemony requires everyone to accept that 'there is no alternative'. The demand to believe in the absurd, when it comes from other mortals, soon affects human dignity. Significantly, protesters against the master narrative of austerity in Spain and Portugal refer to themselves as the *indignados*: 'the angry or indignant ones', certainly, but etymologically also 'those treated with contempt and made to feel unworthy'.[97]

---

97 Compare the now classical appeal of Stéphane Hessel in France: S. Hessel, *Indignez-vous*, Paris: Indigène, 2010.

In the language of sociological theory, outbursts of rage are expressive, not, as approprate in economic matters, instrumental. Rather than risk being trapped by 'rational', constructive proposals in the fulfilment logic of international financial diplomacy, for which the *Staatsvolk* must first render unto the *Marktvolk* that which is their due, a social movement against the consolidation state should take time to display in public its anger at the demands made on them by post-democratic capitalism. It will be recalled from the 1960s and 1970s that perceptions of political and cultural 'one-dimensionality' may generate an outbreak of 'irrational', 'unrealistic' or 'merely emotional' protests, which then – precisely because they are what they are – do not fail to have an effect; the immediate trigger in Germany was the passing of the so-called state of emergency legislation (*Notstandsgesetze*) and the formation of a Grand Coalition government, as well as the fear that they were about to close politics and society to alternatives to the ideology of technocratic modernization.[98] Perhaps the diagnosis was exaggerated, perhaps only premature. In any case, what was at stake then was nothing in comparison with what is taking place today, more than forty years later, in the Europe-wide transition to an economically disempowered post-democracy.

The first and most important point to be made by a movement against the annexation of democracy by the finance markets is that legitimacy is not on the side of the money factories: after all, why should the promissory notes they produce be allowed to eat up the lives of ordinary people? Here David Graeber's *Debt: The First 5,000 Years* has done invaluable preliminary work. The idea that it is only right and proper for all debtors to pay off what they owe is a myth that serves to moralize global finance markets under cover of the morality of everyday life – and to make opposition to their demands appear immoral. The fact is that, unlike private individuals,

---

98   Habermas, *Technik und Wissenschaft als Ideologie*; H. Marcuse, *One-Dimensional Man: Studies in the Ideology of Advanced Industrial Society*, London: Routledge & Kegan Paul, 1964.

governments are able unilaterally to impose debt rescheduling on their creditors or even to suspend payments altogether: this flows directly from their sovereignty. Nowhere is it written that they can use their sovereign powers only to meet their obligations to finance markets, by increasing taxes or decreasing benefits for their citizens. The first obligation of democracies is to their own citizens; they can make laws that dissolve contracts; anyone who lends them money can and must know that. Besides, it has long been the case under civil law that not everyone must pay back all their debts. Debtors can file for bankruptcy and get the opportunity to make a fresh start. That in the United States in particular no shame allegedly attaches to a businessman who goes bankrupt at one time or another is something that friends of capitalism never cease to note with admiration.

With regard to a country like Greece, or any other representative democracy, there must be considerable doubt whether its citizens really can be enlisted to repay the loans contracted by previous governments as agents and in the name of their people, especially if the money was mainly used to fill gaps in the public accounts resulting from a refusal by the rich, tolerated for power-political reasons, to meet their tax obligations. It may also be doubted whether the Greek political class informed its voters about the risks and side effects of the loans contracted in their name, as any financial adviser is legally obliged to do in dealings with his clients; applying the categories of civil law, what actually took place, on a huge scale and with the active involvement of the big international money factories, was nothing other than trading under false pretences. Today, ordinary Greek citizens must stand up for their health care and their pensions against transactions that were more or less secretly foisted on them by a closely knit community of national politicians, foreign governments, international organizations and global financial institutions, the scale and implications of which were never explained to them. Presumably an international civil court – if there were such a thing – would not take long to discharge the Greek people of their alleged repayment obligations to the 'finance markets'; and those who now threaten to punish them with decades of austerity would have to reckon with being found guilty of duress.

Professionalized political science tends to underestimate the impact of moral outrage. With its penchant for studied indifference, which it regards as value-free science, it strives to develop theories in which there can be nothing new under the sun, and has nothing but elitist contempt for what it calls 'populism', sharing this with the power elites to which it would like to be close. Consequently, it has no use for the observation that the old and new regents of the consolidation state fear nothing as much as the rage of those who feel duped by the expert skimmers working for global financial markets. In unclear situations – contrary to what is repeatedly claimed – fear can be a good counsellor. That the crisis might lead to 'social unrest' is a constant nightmare for the men and women at the helm, even though what has been seen on the streets up to now bears little relation to it. Apparently the ruling class has not yet totally forgotten the events of 1968 in Paris or Turin, and in this respect the occasional street battles in Athens or the global 'Occupy' movement of the '99 per cent' marked a good beginning. A lot can be learned from the excessive reaction of banks and governments, or from the sense of horror aroused by movements such as Occupy, tiny as they are.

The idea that 'the markets' should adapt to the people, not vice versa, is nowadays thought of as outright crazy – and indeed it is so if the world is taken as it is. It might, however, become more realistic perhaps if it were argued more often, with dogged persistence, bypassing the blocked channels of institutionalized democracy, so that the calculators have to build it into their calculations and to reckon with the incorrigibly romantic view of ordinary people that they should not have to spend the rest of their lives in thrall to the spreadsheets of some IOU buffs and their trained collectors. At present, opposition to the consolidation state cannot be much more than sand in the machinery of capitalist austerity and its associated discourse. But greater agitation and unpredictability among the people – a spreading sense of the profound absurdity of the market and money culture and its grotesque claims on the human lifeworld – would at least be a social fact; it could come to be seen as the 'psychology' of citizens, alongside the psychology of markets and demanding as much attention. Citizens, too, can 'panic' and react 'irrationally', just like financial investors, provided that they do not feel obliged to be more 'rational' than these, even though they have no banknotes as arguments but only words and (who knows?) paving stones.

CHAPTER FOUR

Looking Ahead

The present financial, fiscal and economic crisis is the end point so far of the long neoliberal transformation of postwar capitalism. Inflation, public debt and private debt were makeshifts allowing democratic politics to sustain the appearance of a capitalism that delivered growth, with equal material advances for all, or even a gradual redistribution from top to bottom of market and life chances. Each, however, exhausted itself after roughly a decade, once the beneficiaries and administrators of capital began to find them too costly, making it necessary to replace them.

WHAT NOW?

Can the buying of time with the magic of modern money – the periodic extension of the old promises of a socially pacified capitalism, long after they have lost their foundation in reality – continue in and after the great crisis of the early twenty-first century? Half a decade on from 2008, that is precisely what is being tested in a worldwide field experiment. The only money still available for it is the fiat money of the central banks; and the main authority left for the governance of once-democratic capitalism, now moving into its Hayekian phase, is the authority of the central bank presidents. The private money factories have been lying idle since their borrowers took on too much debt and they no longer know which of their outstanding loans can be repaid. Governments are blocked by their parliaments and what remains of their democratic constitutions: in the United States by a polarized Congress, which uses public debt as a pretext for abolishing public government; and in Europe by the growing resistance of voters to the demand that they pay the bill for a neoliberal growth regime from which the great majority have gained nothing.

So, for the immediate future at least, power is migrating to the Draghis and Bernankes and their technocracies, who have it in their hands to pamper the banks (and the profit-dependent classes) with never-ending injections of self-printed money and to refinance governments at low rates regardless of their debt. New tricks keep being found to buy a second spring, however brief, for the debt capitalism that failed so spectacularly in 2008. In Europe, a former Goldman Sachs director elevated to the position of Central Bank president has been searching since his arrival in office for ways to enable buyers and sellers of government bonds to continue their brisk trade with each other. In autumn 2012 connoisseurs clicked their tongues over a state-of-the-art plan for the ECB to purchase unlimited bonds in high-debt countries, at a fixed price and with freshly minted money, although only from banks that had previously (perhaps half an hour previously) bought them from the government concerned, with money from the central bank. While this maintains, without actually respecting, the ban on direct ECB funding of governments, 'the markets' are able to buy from the respective governments unlimited promissory notes for, let us say, 96 per cent of their nominal value, and then to sell them on immediately afterwards to the ECB for a guaranteed 96.5 per cent.

Of course, whether this can postpone the legitimation crisis of contemporary capitalism for another decade or more may well be doubted. There is much to suggest that the time to be bought in this way will be all too brief. By pouring in ECB money as a final confidence-building measure in relation to the – rising – debt mountains, the state runs the risk that this too will fail, that state self-financing will be seen as *internal trading* – an attempt worthy of Baron Münchhausen to pull itself up by its own bootstraps – and that the ECB will become one huge 'bad bank' with an electronic printing press attached. The enlistment of the ECB in the role of government of last resort may suit leaders such as Angela Merkel, who are hindered by contradictions and resistance in their national democracies from taking what the finance markets consider 'responsible' action; transferring government business to the ECB can save them much of the drudgery of securing political legitimacy. But the trust and reputation for professionalism normally enjoyed by central banks, and hence their actual political usefulness, must suffer if their policies degenerate into improvised and unprincipled crisis management, pettifogging circumvention of the law, and clientelist rewarding of ailing banks for the purchase of government securities at a guaranteed profit.[1]

All the greater is the ECB's fear that, if it openly switches from monetary policy to the funding of governments, it will lose its non-political aura. Were the Central Bank recognized as what it has become – a government – it might find itself having to justify its decisions politically, rather than simply on technical grounds, and to mobilize consensus behind them.[2] This would overstretch it in a democracy, not only because it is an institution standing outside the democratic process, but also because even the immense funds at its disposal would not suffice to buy the appearance of social justice for a neoliberal economic order. On the other hand, central banks really can become de facto governments in periods of political crisis. One interesting example occurred in Italy in the 1990s, when the governors of the Bank of Italy, Guido Carli and Carlo Azeglio Ciampi, temporarily served as prime minister, finance minister and state president, after the party system collapsed in 1993 under the weight of corruption scandals during the 'years of sludge'. Italy has a tradition of

---

1 See the ECB's Byzantine explanation of why the unlimited purchase of government bonds on the secondary market does not constitute a (forbidden) funding of governments but is only a form of monetary policy. Building confidence by bending the law is not a strategy with good long-term prospects.

2 Very likely the professional *deformations* of its governors would stand in the way of this. On 17 February 2012 one could read the following on the *currentmoment* blog: ' "In a democracy you have to push people to do things by scaring them." This past Tuesday, at a roundtable on "the future of the euro" at Harvard University, we heard Lorenzo Bini-Smaghi utter these exact words. His Royal Smaghiness was a member of the ECB executive board until last November, and was advising his audience on more than his personal views. He was giving us a glimpse deep into the technocratic vision that predominates in Europe at the moment, and the particular techniques in play to manage the situation. What stood out in the banker's comments was, first, an extraordinary ideological commitment to the euro and, second, a somewhat delusional vision of social control.' See the currentmoment. wordpress.com (last accessed 26 November 2012).

government by a strong central bank – one which Mario Draghi, governor of the Bank of Italy from 2006, after his time at Goldman Sachs, until his appointment as president of the ECB, continues today at EU level.[3] In the 1990s, it should be noted, the extensive transfer of government powers from the discredited party system to a central bank independent of it was possible in part because fulfilment of the entry conditions for the European Monetary Union was seen as an overarching national interest.

In Europe as in the United States, crisis therapy based on artificial money could be successful in the short run: that is, bankers' bonuses and shareholders' dividends might recover, and the risk premiums required by 'the markets' for the purchase of government securities might again be affordable after the central bank takes over the risk. But it is far from certain that this would help to ensure long-term growth – especially growth able to sustain a democratic-capitalist peace formula by narrowing, or at least concealing, the gap in Europe between rich and poor or North and South, and somehow reconciling market justice with social justice. One is struck by the ECB president's insistence that, for all the help beyond its legal mandate that the bank is ready to give in a crisis, it cannot spare governments the task of 'structural reforms'. Nor do neoliberal politicians offer anything different, in fact, when attempts are made to find a new growth regime that will prevent an expansion of money and debt (this time by the Central Bank itself) from once more leading to overheating and collapse in the financial markets or a repetition of the worldwide inflation of the 1970s.

If crisis management is not to be the prelude to the next crisis, if post-crisis is not to mean pre-crisis, there will have to be another growth spurt – and one, as things stand politically, that can take place only under the aegis of neoliberalism, as a result of 'reforms' aligned to the remodelling of the state in the last few decades. This

---

3   As Italian prime minister, former EU commissioner Mario Monti also fitted into the scheme of a 'government by experts' that took the place of government by parties. In any case, given the way the Italian parliament works, or does not work, most laws in Italy are first passed as governmental or presidential decrees.

is why the governing central bank combines its beneficence with strict political conditions. Whether it can impose them is another matter, of course; governments, in particular, may also be tempted to speculate that they are 'too big to fail'.[4] Nor can anyone guarantee that supply-side policies will actually work: witness the four-year stagnation in the United States, the country where a combination of looser central bank money and neoliberal 'flexibilization' – like that now taking shape in Europe – had for decades brought only a pseudo-growth liable to implode in periods of crisis. And even if growth were to pick up again, it has long ceased to be the case, as in the Keynesian welfare state of old, that 'a rising tide lifts all boats'.[5] After the market-induced self-elimination of redistributive politics – however deceptive its methods may have been in the end – and after the forced self-limitation of governments to the protection of market freedom and property rights (especially in government bonds), even growth would ultimately not be capable of calming the distributive conflict inherent in a capitalist market society; rather there would be a growing danger that the long-term losers in the regime of cumulative advantage would finally realize they were being taken for a ride.

If growth did nevertheless pick up again, to have its old calming effect it would have to be quantitatively and qualitatively different from that of the previous two or three decades. The moving average of growth-rates in the industrial countries fell constantly from the second half of the 1980s on. At the high point of the cycle, in 1988, growth still stood above 4 per cent, but by the year 2000 it had dipped to 3.4 per cent and by 2007, the year of the crisis, it was down to 2.7 per cent. In the three years from 2009 to 2011, the average

---

4   As we noted earlier, the European shadow government replaced Berlusconi with Monti because his government had not fulfilled a number of conditions for financial aid that Draghi and his predecessor at the ECB, Trichet, had set in an unpublished letter. Yet in his first year of government, Monti too proved either unable or unwilling to do what was expected of him.

5   An expression that seems to have originated among the yachting clubs of the northeastern coast of the United States, and which has been commonly used in US economic policy since the days of John F. Kennedy.

FIGURE 4.1. *Annual growth-rates of developed countries*

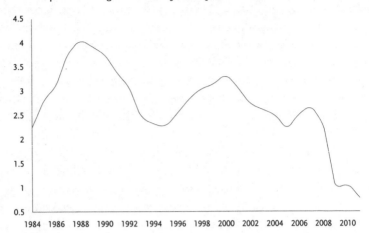

Rolling five-year averages. The following 34 countries are included in the calculation: Australia, Austria, Belgium, Canada, Cyprus, Czech Republic, Denmark, Estonia, Finland, France, Germany, Greece, Hong Kong, Iceland, Ireland, Israel, Italy, Japan, Korea, Luxemburg, Malta, Netherlands, New Zealand, Norway, Portugal, Singapore, Slovakia, Slovenia, Spain, Sweden, Switzerland, Taiwan, UK, USA.

Source: International Monetary Fund, World Economic Outlook Database, April 2012

growth-rate remained stalled at 1 per cent (Fig. 4.1). New growth capable of ensuring the stability of democratic capitalism would require a fundamental reversal of this trend, and there is no sign of how that might come about.[6] Since the 1990s, ever higher debt ratios have been necessary to produce even the levels of growth seen before the crisis period. Thus, total debt in the USA – private households,

---

6   See the left-wing *thecurrentmoment* blog on the occasion of Hollande's election as president on 7 May 2012: 'The socialist campaign in France was focused on Sarkozy's record as president. Its own economic programme was far weaker. The main thrust was to halt reform at the domestic level, bringing things back to the status quo ante, and to kickstart growth at the European level by using the creditworthiness of Germany to fund a new round of government borrowing... New governments in Europe, including the French Socialists, are relying on yet more borrowing to promote growth. This is not the end of austerity in Europe so much as a continuation of the underlying trends that brought about the crisis in the first place.' See thecurrentmoment.wordpress.com (last accessed 26 November 2012).

FIGURE 4.2. *Total liabilities relative to GDP, 1970–2010*

Sources: OECD *National Accounts Statistics;* OECD *Economic Outlook: Statistics and Projections*

private and public enterprises, finance industry and government – stood in 1980 at less than five times GDP, then kept increasing until it stood at nine and a half times in 2008. The development in Germany was astonishingly similar – partly driven, to be sure, by reunification (Fig. 4.2). This suggests that even more debt will have to be injected than previously if the desired effect is to materialize. It seems questionable whether, without help from already heavily indebted public and private households, the central banks of the USA and EMU will manage to pile up the debt mountains necessary for late twentieth-century capitalism to gain another temporary lease of life at a higher level. But even if they achieved this, the result would probably be no more than a move from the frying pan of economic stagnation to the fire of boom-and-bust, with the danger of ever more frequent and dramatic losses of political confidence and corresponding economic downturns.

The other possibility is a return of inflation – either by accident or as a debt reduction strategy, gradual at first, then gathering speed and perhaps even turning into an uncontrollable gallop. At first sight, this might look like a return to the beginning of the crisis cycle that started at the end of the postwar period. But in the social world one never steps into the same river twice. Unlike in the 1970s, inflation today would be driven not by the labour market but by central bank efforts to rescue lenders by bailing out debtors; it could therefore not as easily be ended as in the 1980s. And it would not mainly affect the owners of monetary assets – who, in a world without capital controls, can jump much more easily from one currency to another – but rather the, today, much larger numbers of pensioners and social assistance claimants. Workers too would suffer, since unlike in the 1970s trade unions are too weak now to ensure that wages keep pace with inflation. As an instrument for the taming of mass democracy, inflation would thus probably be used up much more quickly than in the past. The risk of it fuelling discontent and political instability would be immense.

CAPITALISM OR DEMOCRACY

If the capitalism of the consolidation state can no longer produce even the illusion of equitable growth, the time will come when the paths of capitalism and democracy must part. The likeliest outcome would then be the completion of a Hayekian social dictatorship, in which the capitalist market economy was protected from democratic correction. Its legitimacy would depend on whether those who once were its citizens would have learned to equate market justice with social justice and to think of themselves as members of a unified *Marktvolk*. Its stability would further require instruments for the ideological marginalization, political disorganization and physical restraint of anyone unwilling to accept this lesson. Those who refused to bow to market justice, in a situation where political institutions were economically neutralized, would then be left with what used to be described in the 1970s as extra-parliamentary protest: emotional, irrational, fragmented and irresponsible. And that is precisely what we should expect if the democratic channels for the articulation of interests and the formation of preferences are blocked, either because only the same outcomes can ever emerge or because what emerges no longer makes any difference to 'the markets'.

The alternative to capitalism without democracy is democracy without capitalism, or at least the capitalism we know. It would be the other, competing utopia. Unlike its Hayekian rival, however, it would not be going with the historical flow, but would require the latter to be reversed. For this and other reasons – because the neoliberal solution has a huge lead in both organization and implementation, and because of the fear of uncertainty that is inevitably associated with any abrupt change – today it appears completely unrealistic.[7] It too would start from the experience that democratic capitalism has proved unable to keep its promises – although for this it would blame capitalism, not democracy.[8] For democracy and capitalism, the issue would be not to achieve social peace through economic growth, and certainly not social peace in the face of growing inequality, but to improve the lot of those excluded from neoliberal growth, if necessary *at the expense* of social peace and growth.

If democracy means that social justice must not be reduced to market justice, then the main task of democratic politics should be to reverse the institutional devastation wrought by four decades of

7   Of course, throughout the long Keynesian era this was true also of the Hayekian utopia.

8   This view is already surprisingly widespread, even in circles where one would least expect to find it. See a report in *Die Welt* (26 January 2012) on the opening of the world economic forum in Davos: 'Ben Verwaayen, chairman of the telecommunications giant Alcatel-Lucent, spoke of the unfulfilled promises of capitalism . . . "The task is to learn from the excesses," said Brian Moynihan, chairman of Bank of America. But the banker did not seem too confident. "Will we get it right next time?" he asked the meeting. And he immediately gave the answer himself: "The Lord only knows." . . . In fact, according to the widely held view in Davos, capitalism simply has not delivered . . . For David Rubinstein, founder and boss of the American private equity firm Carlyle Group, the problems lie deeper. Business cycles were thought to be under control, said the financial investor. But it has turned out that capitalism "lacks the ability to manage the cyclical twists and turns". More, "capitalism has not solved the problem of inequality." And "no one in the world seems to have the answer".'

neoliberal progress, and as far as possible to defend and repair what is left of the institutions with whose help social justice might be able to modify or even replace market justice. It is only in this context that it seems meaningful to speak of democracy today, since it alone makes it possible to escape being fobbed off with the 'democratization' of institutions that have no power to decide anything. Today democratization should mean building institutions through which markets can be brought back under the control of society: labour markets that leave scope for social life, product markets that do not destroy nature, credit markets that do not mass-produce unsustainable promises. But before something like that can really come onto the agenda, at the least there will have to be years of political mobilization and lasting disruption of the social order that is today taking shape before our eyes.

THE EURO AS A FRIVOLOUS EXPERIMENT

In completing the single market, the euro established Euroland as a political jurisdiction close to the ideal of a market economy freed from politics by politics itself: a political economy with no parliament or government, composed of still formally independent nation-states, except that these had now renounced forever a currency of their own and with it any possibility of using devaluation as a means to defend or improve their citizens' economic situation. In accordance with the neoliberal programme, the euro thus eliminated a major element of political discretion from the constitution of the common market; member-state governments concerned for the employment, prosperity and social security of their citizens would now have to turn to the instrument of *internal devaluation*: that is, the raising of productivity and competitiveness through more flexible labour markets, lower wages, longer working hours, higher labour market participation, and a welfare state geared to recommodification.

Today the introduction of the euro may serve to illustrate how, with a political-economic ideology having turned into a religion, a 'frivolous experiment' (Polanyi) following the prescriptions of standard economics is to reshape a highly heterogeneous transnational society into a market society, with no regard for its diverse structures, institutions and traditions. The exclusion of devaluation as an instrument of national economic policy means nothing other than the grafting of a uniform economic and social model onto all countries subject to the single currency; it assumes as possible, and drives forward, the rapid convergence of their social systems and ways of life. At the same time, it acts as a further engine for that worldwide expansion of markets and market relations which has been described as capitalist land-grabbing, as it seeks more or less forcibly to replace governments and their policies with self-regulating markets, in the mode of what Polanyi called 'planned laissez-faire'.[9] In this respect, the exclusion of devaluation is akin to the nineteenth-century gold standard, whose devastating impact on the capacity of the then-emerging nation-states to defend their peoples from the unpredictability of free markets, together with its ramifications for the stability of international relations, was analysed so impressively in Polanyi's *The Great Transformation*.

In retrospect, it is not difficult to see the outward forms of Europe's economic, financial and fiscal crisis as manifestations of a political countermovement[10] against the market fanaticism institutionalized in the common currency. A short time ago – until the appointment of the *Kommissare* Papademos and Monti in autumn 2011 – the European Monetary Union still consisted of democratic countries, whose governments could not or would not declare war on their actually existing national populations (still quite different from the imaginary model populations of pure market theory) and put them through the mangle of 'reforms' prescribed by Brussels technocrats and rootless global economists. Like earlier countermovements, those of the nation-states yoked together by the euro did not always abide by the canon of political correctness or economic rationality; as Polanyi knew, social resistance to the

9 Polanyi, *The Great Transformation*, ch. 12.
10 Ibid., ch. 11.

market develops in a spontaneous and uncoordinated fashion, unlike the way laissez-faire developed. The result was budget deficits, public debt and credit and price bubbles in countries unable or unwilling to keep up with the timetable imposed on them for the capitalist rationalization of their lifestyles and lifeworlds, and whose reduced toolbox of protective policies allowed them nothing other than gradually to accumulate those systemic dysfunctions which, for some years now, have been threatening to tear apart the European state system and to undermine the long postwar peace among European nations.

What is happening now looks like something out of a Polanyi picture book. As peoples, represented by their states, resist the subordination of their lives to the laws of the international market, the *ecclesia militans* of neoliberal reform sees this as a governability problem that can and must be overcome by *more of the same* – by new institutions that will squeeze out the last remnants of national political discretion, replacing them with rational incentives (including negative ones such as fines) to fall in silently behind the destiny mapped out for them by the market. In this way, the austerity imposed for decades on ordinary people in countries that the market has left behind as uncompetitive will become a lasting reality, and the frivolous experiment of a single currency for a heterogeneous multinational society will have finally succeeded. In the end, once the reforms are over, the nations will acquiesce in their political expropriation, either because they have no other choice or because they will at some point have seen the light of neoliberal reason.

Of course, one has to believe in this, because it is not yet possible to see it. What can be seen is growing conflicts among and within the peoples of Europe over how much each owes the others (how many 'reforms' on the one side, how many transfer payments on the other) and who of the big and the small will have to cover the costs and get the benefits. The truly steadfast can hope that the really existing nations of Europe will sometime – and in standard economic models, where no allowance is made for time, that always means right now – grow into a model people adapted to the free market and united in market justice. But those who do not belong to the church will never cease to wonder at the power of illusion, or to fear what a theory can do that is not of this world.

DEMOCRACY IN EUROLAND?

Could democratization calm the conflicts that are today tearing Europe apart? Could it stem the centrifugal forces that have arisen from the straitjacketing of diverse societies in a common market and a common currency and the stripping of their capacity to act? Could it neutralize the national lines of conflict within Euroland by activating social and economic conflicts that cut across them? Many of those who look to democratization as the answer to the problems of the European political and economic system appear to imagine that it will sweep away overnight the particularist obstacles that have so far stood in the way of a cross-border wage policy, a European social policy, a common labour law and workforce participation regime, and a common regional development policy.[11]

Speculation about what is possible can easily end in a spiralling void, especially if combined with hope, or with self-imposed commitments to creative optimism. But perhaps it can be agreed that a project of democracy for Europe that is worthy of the name must sharply differentiate itself from the kind of 'political union' pursued by authoritarian neoliberal strategists like Wolfgang Schäuble, for whom the aim is to smooth the path to Hayekian governability. The question of whether the presidents of the European Commission and the Council are elected 'by the people' or not has nothing to do with democracy, so long as they have no say in comparison with the president of the ECB or the European Court of Justice, not to speak of the chairman of Goldman Sachs. The term 'façade democracy'[12] fits nothing better than a political system whose legal and actual constitution obliges it to stay out of self-propelling 'markets'. A democracy

---

11   Bofinger et al., 'Einspruch gegen die Fassadendemokratie', p. 33.
12   Ibid.

project consisting of the appointment of a 'European finance minister', who would then guarantee that 'the markets' are serviced and
kept 'confident' – in short, a democracy project that fails to link the
question of democracy to the question of neoliberalism or even capitalism – does not need democrats to toil and sweat on its behalf. It
runs under its own steam, close as it is to the neoliberal heart.

A project of democracy for Europe must also be less utopian than
the market project that has been hanging in the balance since 2008.
This means that it must avoid mirroring the latter's treatment of economy and society, of economic practices and ways of life, as if they were
independent of each other. In fact they are tightly interwoven. Just as a
single economic way of life cannot impose itself without violence on
different social practices, so different economic cultures cannot be
forced into a common political order.[13] Democracy in Europe cannot
be a project for institutional homogenization; unlike neoliberalism, it
cannot avoid taking into account the manifold historically rooted
differences between and within the peoples of Europe.[14] In Belgium, a
long-established nation-state consisting of two societies that threatens
to break apart because of the same contamination of identity and
distribution conflicts that is at the bottom of the Euroland version of
the financial and fiscal crisis, it recently took a year and a half for a
national government to be formed after a general election. A European
constitutional legislator would have to cope with the same sort of
conflicts, although on a much larger scale and greater degree of
complexity – and to do so all at the same time, not within an existing
democratic polity but as a preliminary to its coming into being.

---

13   See the repeated failure to sell the German form of industrial democracy –
participation at plant and company level – as a European model for strong workplace
representation.

14   Höpner and Schäfer (M. Höpner and A. Schäfer, *Integration Among Unequals:
How the Heterogeneity of European Varieties of Capitalism Shapes the Social and Democratic
Potential of the EU*, Cologne: Max-Planck-Institut für Gesellschaftsforschung, 2012) offer a
survey of the problems that social heterogeneity poses for European integration and for the
democratization of a unified Europe. See also M. Höpner, A. Schäfer and H. Zimmermann,
'Erweiterung, Vertiefung und Demokratie: Trilemma der europäischen Integration',
Frankfurter Allgemeine Zeitung, 27 April 2012.

In the real world, a unitary-Jacobin constitution for a democratic European state is unimaginable. No European democracy can develop without federal subdivision and extensive rights of local autonomy, without group rights protecting Europe's many identities and spatially based communities – not only in Belgium but also in Spain and Italy, as well as in the relations between Finland and Greece or Denmark and Germany.[15] A European constituent assembly, the would-be author of a European constitution, would have to find ways of allowing for the very different interests of countries such as Bulgaria and the Netherlands, as well as addressing the unsolved problems of incomplete nation-states like Spain or Italy whose internal diversity of identity and interests would have to be accommodated in any conceivable European constitution.[16] Constitutionalizing Europe would truly be a labour of Hercules, requiring a creative optimism not a whit less than that of the neoliberal market technocrats.[17]

The redemocratization of Europe would also take time, just as it took decades for the neoliberal market project to near completion, before it landed in the great crisis from which it is hoping to escape

15 For example, to be acceptable to small or economically weak countries, a postnational European constitution would have to contain so many safeguards against German supremacy that, for that very reason, it would be hard for Germans to accept.

16 For example, a European convention would immediately have to decide whether the delegates from Catalonia should be seated behind a Spanish or a Catalan flag. Then the discussion would turn to the Basques, Corsicans, Flemish, South Tyroleans and Sicilians, perhaps even to the Bavarians.

17 Not that such optimism would be lacking. Bofinger, Habermas and Nida-Rümelin think that in the course of a solution to the present crisis – in other words, in the foreseeable future – a treaty change approved by all twenty-seven EU member-states might 'establish a politically unified core currency area'. They add: 'That requires clear constitutional ideas regarding a supranational democracy, which allow for common government without taking the form of a federal state. A European federal state is a false model and overstretches the capacity for solidarity of the historically independent European nations. The overdue deepening of EU institutions could be guided by the idea that a democratic core-Europe should represent the collectivity of all citizens of EMU member-states, but each individual in his or her dual capacity as a directly involved citizen of the reformed Union and an indirectly involved member of one of the participating European nations' (Bofinger et al., 'Einspruch gegen die Fassadendemokratie'). It is unclear why such 'clear constitutional ideas' are supposed to be clear. Which issues would be handled and decided in which of the two identity frameworks?

through a new push forward. The institutions of a supranational European democracy could not come into being as a voluntarist concoction; there is no historical precedent for them, and they would have to be put together with the material passed down by history. A convention to draft the constitution of a democratic Europe could only consist of familiar political figures alive today. It would be attended by representatives of all EU countries, not only from member-states of the monetary union. And it would have to work amid the present conflicts over budgetary consolidation, debt relief, supervision and 'reforms', which would all the time be raising the temperature, sowing mutual distrust and prejudicing the outcome of discussions. Years would pass before a constitution to unify Europe – and, perhaps, to democratize Euroland by taming market capitalism once again – was on the table. It would come much too late to head off a neoliberal solution to the present threefold crisis.

For the foreseeable future, social heterogeneity in Europe will also mean a diversity of local, regional and national ways of living with capitalism. A democratic European constitution can come about only if these differences are recognized in the form of autonomy rights; a refusal of such rights cannot but result in separatism, which would have to be either bought off or violently suppressed. The more heterogeneous a national population is, the bloodier is the history of (successful or failed) attempts to unify it: witness France, Spain under Franco, and certainly the USA. Central to any heterogeneous polity are its constitutional rules governing public finances: that is, which part-society qua community should have a claim on the collective solidarity of other part-societies, and under what circumstances. This is also an issue within countries: the more regional autonomy, the smaller the claim on, and the smaller the obligation to provide, collective solidarity. There are always conflicts over what this means in practice, even in such a homogeneous national society as Germany, with its never-ending disputes over financial equalization between the *Länder*. In Euroland, whose extreme heterogeneity means that such conflicts have become ubiquitous after just a few years, they run too deep to be settled by majority decisions – especially when, secession not being an option, the institutional levelling of neoliberal utopianism provokes demands for the social correction of market justice through equalization payments among the part-societies. There would be no reason to expect that regional and national particularism, or the conflicts of identity and interest caused by it, to disappear if Euroland society, too heterogeneous for a single currency, were suddenly to acquire a single democratic constitution.[18]

Hayek's error of reasoning, in his plan for an international federation wedded to neoliberalism, was to think that all participating national societies would happily adapt to – and could therefore be induced to merge their particular interests and identities into – the free market that central government would have to seek to establish for the sake of international peace. What escaped him was that people would try to defend their way of life and their economic practices by building on their cultural traditions and using whatever political institutions they had left to them. Perhaps the reason was that he considered such peculiarities to be no more than tattoos on the skin of a universal *Homo oeconomicus*; or that the democratic possibility of collective action against the justice of the market simply did not exist in his world.

IN PRAISE OF DEVALUATION

Instead of watching neoliberal politics completing monetary union with 'reforms' that forever immunize the market from political correction and finally turn the European state system into an international consolidation state, we might remind ourselves and others of the institution of national currency devaluation. Indeed, the right of devaluation is nothing other than an institutional expression of respect for nations (represented by their states) as special

---

18   It is hard to imagine that German taxpayers would willingly pay off the Italian public or Spanish private banking debts if this was decided by majority vote in a European parliament, instead of through the machinations of (for example) the European Central Bank. Indeed, the problem would be all the greater as redistribution through parliamentary decisions would be much harder to conceal.

communities involving a shared life and destiny. It serves as a brake on the pressure for capitalist expansion and rationalization spreading outward from core to periphery. And for the interests and identities confronted with that pressure, which in the free trade world of the Great Single Market would otherwise be driven towards populism and nationalism, it offers a realistic collective alternative to the obedient self-commodification demanded of them by the market. Countries able to devalue can decide for themselves whether, and at what speed, they wish to discard their pre-capitalist or anti-capitalist heritage, and in which direction they want to transform it. For this reason, more than anything else, the option of devaluation is a thorn in the flesh of single-market totalitarianism.

Devaluation of a national currency corrects – roughly and for a limited time – the distributive relations within an asymmetrical system of international economic exchange, which, like every system under capitalism, operates according to the principle of cumulative advantage. Devaluation is a crude instrument – 'rough justice' – but it is better than nothing. If a country that is no longer keeping up, or does not yet wish to keep up, devalues its currency, the export opportunities of foreign producers diminish and those of domestic producers increase; this improves the job opportunities for people in the devaluing country, at the expense of other countries with a higher level of employment. Moreover, by making its imports more expensive, the devaluing country makes it more difficult for its better-off citizens to buy foreign goods while at the same time it helps its wage-earning population to secure higher pay, without necessarily making what they produce more expensive abroad and thereby putting their jobs in danger. To put it another way: the option of devaluation prevents 'competitive' countries from forcing 'less competitive' ones to cut the income of their less well-to-do citizens so that their more well-to-do can buy their BMWs at a fixed price from producers in 'competitive' countries.

Devaluation in an international economic system functions as handicaps do in sports like golf or horse racing, where the differences among players are so great that without some mechanism of equalization they would be divided into a few permanent winners and many permanent losers. To get the weak to continue to take part in the competition, the strong are put at a disadvantage: in golf the weakest players receive a number of strokes that do not get counted, while in horse racing the potential permanent winners have to carry additional weight. In national economies, progressive taxation performs – or is supposed to perform – something similar.[19] Seen this way, the removal of devaluation through the European Monetary Union was equivalent to the abolition of progressive taxation in national political economies, or of handicapping in horse racing.

An international economic system that permits devaluation gets by without allowing leading countries or international organizations to intervene in the economy or the way of life of other countries. It tolerates diversity and autonomy while coordinating action on the margins. It does not assume that leading countries are capable of reshaping 'backward' ones in their own image; nor does it require that the latter should grant the former a licence for this in return for financial support. Abolishing the euro in its present form would thus be equivalent to the abolition of the Gold Standard in the 1920s, which, in Polanyi's view, made it possible again 'to tolerate willingly that other nations shape their domestic institutions according to their inclinations, thus transcending the pernicious nineteenth-century dogma of the necessary uniformity of domestic regimes within the orbit of world economy'.[20] And, doubtless alluding to the postwar order then beginning to take shape, he continued: 'Out of the ruins of the Old World, cornerstones of the New can be seen to emerge: economic collaboration of governments and the liberty to organize national life at will.'[21]

---

19   The same is true of policies of regional aid, which take from the strong and give to the weak, so that at some point the latter will perhaps be able to catch up with or even overtake the former. Unlike devaluation, however, regional aid requires the consent of the donors, who in return demand that they should be allowed to supervise the uses to which their grants are put – an arrangement that typically angers the recipients. Regional policies are therefore at least officially expected to make themselves superfluous; the less they do this, the more they lose support, certainly among those who pay for them.

20   Polanyi, *The Great Transformation*, p. 253.

21   Ibid., pp. 253–4.

A flexible currency regime, such as might develop after the end of the euro, will accept that politics is more than the expert execution of rationalization measures, and will assign it a central place out of respect for the collective identities and traditions that it represents. An international economic system that permits devaluation may be defended – in line with Hayek, by the way – as a system of distributed intelligence that gets by without the 'pretence of knowledge'.[22] Hayek rightly insisted that such systems are superior to centrally planned ones; what he could not see, as an economist, was Polanyi's insight, in his debate with Hayek, that the market-obedient world shaped by transnational capitalism – which Hayek considered a state of nature to be reinstated through his liberal federation for world peace – could only take root through planning, because it presupposed the forcible annihilation of particularistic structures of social solidarity.

A devaluation regime spares countries having to negotiate over structural reforms and transfer payments; interference by 'competitive' countries in less 'competitive' ones is as unnecessary as 'growth packages', which are at constant risk of being misunderstood by their recipients as market entry charges or a form of intergovernmental taxation on economic performance, and therefore of being rejected by those who have to pay for them. International conflicts arise only if a country devalues its currency too often in too short intervals – a practice that, however, quickly loses more in trust than it would gain from the restoration of its export capacity. For this reason alone, there is no danger that countries will use devaluation in excess to improve their market position.[23]

---

22   F. Hayek, 'The Pretence of Knowledge: Nobel Prize Lecture' (1974), available at www.nobelprize.org (last accessed 26 November 2012).

23   In this and many other respects, devaluation is comparable to 'sovereign' debt reduction. Both are ways for societies at the end of the capitalist food chain to deploy their sovereignty to protect themselves from fast and far-reaching capitalist expansion.

FOR A EUROPEAN BRETTON WOODS

The European Monetary Union was a political mistake. In a eurozone marked by great heterogeneity of member-states, it eliminated devaluation without also eliminating nation-states and democracy at national level.[24] Instead of making things worse by rushing ahead to complement monetary union with 'political union' – which would in practice be nothing other than a final enthronement of the consolidation state – an attempt might be made, as long as the crisis keeps its future settlement open, to undo the euro and return to an orderly system of flexible exchange rates in Europe.[25]

Such a system, which would recognize the differences among European societies instead of trying to reform them out of existence along neoliberal lines, would be politically and economically far less demanding than monetary union. It would escape the planners' 'one size fits all' hubris and content itself with a loose connection between countries instead of merging them together. The basis for the growing envy and even hatred among the peoples of Europe would thus be removed. Politically, a more flexible currency regime would spell an end to the coalition between the export countries of the North (especially Germany) and the state apparatuses and middle classes of the South: the coalition which at present is cutting the wages and pensions of ordinary people in the Mediterranean so that its urban well-to-do can buy German luxury cars at a fixed price and its producers can count on a fixed low exchange rate – the coalition in which neoliberal modernizers in the high-debt countries of the South use the borrowed

---

24   One of those who saw this early on with amazing clarity and predicted the catastrophic consequences of the euro project was the conservative American economist Martin Feldstein. For an impressive summary of his arguments, see M. Feldstein, *The Euro and European Economic Conditions*, Working Paper 17617, Cambridge, MA: National Bureau of Economic Research, 2011.

25   In recent years, Fritz Scharpf has set out with great clarity some of the political and economic reasons for such a policy turn (F. Scharpf, 'Solidarität statt Nibelungentreue', *Berliner Republik*, vol. 12/3, 2010, pp. 90–2; F. Scharpf, 'Mit dem Euro geht die Rechnung nicht auf', *MaxPlanckForschung*, vol. 11/3, 2011, pp. 12–17; F. Scharpf, 'Monetary Union, Fiscal Crisis and the Pre-Emption of Democracy', *Zeitschrift für Staats- und Europawissenschaften*, vol. 9/2, 2011, pp. 163–98).

power of 'the markets' and of international organizations to subject their citizens to the justice of international market laws, in return for the financial and moral support of the North.

A model for a new European monetary system might be the Bretton Woods regime, created under the influence of John Maynard Keynes, with its fixed but adjustable exchange rates. In its time, it served to integrate countries like France and Italy, with their strong unions and Communist parties, into the Western free trade system, without forcing them into 'reforms' that would have endangered their social cohesion and internal peace. Its peculiar wisdom was that it refrained from imposing convergence on the internal order of member-states and abstained from forcing weaker countries to accept being governed by the stronger countries;[26] formally at least, it respected the sovereignty and the domestic politics of its member states.[27] Countries that lost competitiveness because of wage concessions or a generous social policy could offset this from time to time by devaluing at the expense of more competitive countries.[28] At the same time, as said before, devaluations could not happen too often, since that would have damaged the interests and the need for predictability of exporting countries, industries and enterprises.

The exact shape of a system of fixed but adjustable exchange rates to replace the European Monetary Union is a question worthy of the efforts of the best economists.[29] They would have a number of

---

26   The fact that the Americans, outside the monetary system, did all they could to keep the Italian Communist Party out of government, and to divide the Communist-led unions of Italy and France, is another matter. In any case, for two to three decades after the war, Washington tolerated social democrat governments in its West European sphere of influence, not least with an eye to its own New Deal tradition.

27   Not every social order earns the right to that. On the other hand, not every social order that does not earn that right deserves to be changed from outside. Only in a few extreme cases is a society so bad that other societies may have a duty to remould it – especially because, as in the numerous American nation-building expeditions, such an enterprise is usually not only costly but unpromising.

28   Voters and union members in countries with a Left political tradition thus had some scope to raise their real earnings at the expense of consumers of imported goods and foreign producers, thereby changing the distribution of income in their favour.

29   As an introduction, see F. Scharpf, 'Rettet Europa vor dem Euro', *Berliner Republik*, vol. 14/2, 2012, pp. 52–61.

past experiments as models, such as the European 'currency snake' of the 1970s and 1980s. In any event, the aim would be to come up with something looser than a single currency for all, so that democratic politics and development options may be preserved on a basis of national sovereignty. The euro would not necessarily have to be abolished; it could remain as a non-national anchor currency alongside national currencies, rather like the artificial currency called Bancor proposed by Keynes, which the United States eventually refused to accept because it wanted the dollar to play that anchoring role. Experts would also have to look for ways in which restored national currencies could be protected from speculative attacks – probably including, as both desirable and necessary, a return to capital controls of one kind or another.[30] It would also have to be made clear how expensive it would be for a country to withdraw from the euro as a single currency; there is much evidence that the short-term and long-term costs of an operation to save the euro – probably doomed to failure anyway in cases like Greece or Spain – might turn out to be rather higher.[31]

An exit from the European single currency would mean the start of a policy of drawing boundaries against so-called globalization. Anyone who rejects a sort of 'globalization' that subjects the world to a uniform law of the market, and thereby forces it into convergence, cannot want to stick with a euro that does just the same with Europe. The euro was and is a creature of the globalization euphoria of the 1990s, for which the state political capacity for action was not just obsolete but dispensable. In the context of the neoliberal turn which is today approaching completion, the call for a European Bretton Woods is what would have been seen in the

---

30 However, there have been no attacks in recent years on the Danish or Swedish crown, the British pound or other European national currencies. This contradicts the argument that only a 'major' currency like the euro can be safe from being brought down by speculators like George Soros.

31 In summer 2012, it was an open secret that the international banks and corporations had long been preparing for an eventual demise of the euro. See 'U.S. Companies Brace for an Exit from the Euro by Greece', *New York Times*, 3 September 2012.

1970s as a system-changing reform programme: a strategic response to a systemic crisis, which points beyond the crisis it undertakes to solve by showing that, in the world as it is, democracy cannot be had without state sovereignty.[32]

GAINING TIME

The call to dismantle the EMU as a socially reckless technocratic modernization project, which politically expropriates and economically divides the national peoples that make up the actually existing European people, appears as a democratically plausible answer to the legitimation crisis of a neoliberal policy of consolidation and rationalization that presents itself as being without alternative. It differs fundamentally from nationalist calls to exclude debtor countries from Euroland; its aim is not to punish but to free and recapacitate countries that are in danger of ending up in the Babylonian captivity of a politically unleashed market system, where they are assigned the role of permanent losers and supplicants. The point is not to defend inequality but on the contrary to open up a way towards political unity among the peoples of Europe – a way that is today about to be foreclosed by those who promote the project of the single market by wielding the euro as an instrument of political discipline.

The proposal for a European Bretton Woods might complement, at the level of public political discourse, the hoped-for resistance of 'the street' to market-technocratic eurofanaticism and the final institutional triumph of the consolidation state. As such, however, it can serve only to gain time for the building of new capacities for political action, in the struggle against the anti-democratic neoliberal project.

---

32   The idea that withdrawal from the euro would mean a return to parochial *Kleinstaaterei* is simply a myth: Britain and Sweden, for example, which are outside the eurozone, are among the most open societies anywhere. Even more baffling is the notion that London should be less 'European' than, say, Sofia, just because Britain does not belong to the EMU. For a 'plea for an enlightened protectionism', see M. Höpner, 'Nationale Spielräume sollten verteidigt werden', *Die Mitbestimmung*, vol. 58/3, 2012, pp. 46–9. Cf. the concluding remarks in Höpner and Schäfer, *Integration among Unequals*.

The starting-point in defending a perspective of democratic development must be that, however problematic the national organization of modern societies may be, there can be no question of overcoming the nation-state through capitalist market expansion. Rather, the aim must be to repair for now what has been left of the democratic nation-state, to an extent that allows it to be used to slow the headlong advance of capitalist 'land-grabbing'. Under today's conditions, a strategy that places its hopes in postnational democracy, following in the functionalist wake of capitalist progress,[33] merely plays into the hands of the social engineers of self-regulating global market capitalism; the crisis of 2008 offered a foretaste of the havoc this can cause.

In Western Europe today, the greatest danger is not nationalism – least of all German nationalism – but Hayekian market liberalism. Completion of monetary union would seal the end of national democracy in Europe – and therefore of the only institution that can still be used to defend against the consolidation state. If, for the foreseeable future, the historically developed differences among European nations are too great to be integrated into a common democracy, then the institutions representing those differences may possibly, as a second-best solution, be used as a stumbling block on the downhill slope into a single market state purged of democracy. And so long as the best is no solution, the second-best is the best.

---

33   Habermas, for example, speaks with astonishing assurance of a 'capitalist dynamic . . . that may be described as an interplay of functionally driven opening and socially integrative closure, each of them at a higher level' (in T. Assheuer, 'Nach dem Bankrott. Thomas Assheuer im Interview mit Jürgen Habermas', *Die Zeit*, 6 November 2008). It would certainly be nice if we could count on a dynamic like that.

Bibliography

Adorno, Theodor W., 'Late Capitalism or Industrial Society?', in Volker Meja et al., *Modern German Sociology*, New York: Columbia University Press, 1987 [1968].

Agnoli, Johannes, *Die Transformation der Demokratie*, Berlin: Voltaire Verlag, 1967.

———. Alberto Alesina et al., *The Output Effect of Fiscal Consolidations*, unpublished manuscript, 2012.

Alesina, Alberto and Roberto Perotti, 'Budget Deficits and Budget Institutions', in James M. Poterba and Jürgen von Hagen (eds), *Institutions, Politics and Fiscal Policy*, Chicago: Chicago University Press, 1999.

Assheuer, Thomas, 'Nach dem Bankrott. Thomas Assheuer im Interview mit Jürgen Habermas', *Die Zeit*, 6 November 2008.

Bach, Stefan, 'Vermögensabgaben – ein Beitrag zur Sanierung der Staatsfinanzen in Europa', *DIW Wochenbericht*, 2012, pp. 3–11.

Beckert, Jens, 'Der Streit um die Erbschaftssteuer', *Leviathan*, vol. 32/4, 2004, pp. 543–57.

———. *Die Anspruchsinflation des Wirtschaftssystems*, Cologne, 2009.

———. *Capitalism as a System of Contingent Expectations: On the Microfoundations of Economic Dynamics*, Cologne, 2012.

Bell, Daniel, *The Cultural Contradictions of Capitalism*, New York: Basic Books, 1976.

Bergmann, Joachim et al., 'Herrschaft, Klassenverhältnisse und Schichtung. Referat auf dem Soziologentag 1968', *Verhandlungen des Deutschen Soziologentags*, Stuttgart: Enke, 1969, pp. 67–87.

Block, Fred, 'Read Their Lips: Taxation and the Right-Wing Agenda', in Isaac William Martin et al. (eds), *The New Fiscal Sociology: Taxation in Comparative and Historical Perspective*, Cambridge: Cambridge University Press, 2009, pp. 68–85.

Bofinger, Peter et al., 'Einspruch gegen die Fassadendemokratie', *Frankfurter Allgemeine Zeitung*, 3 August 2012, p. 33.

Böhm-Bawerk, Eugen von, *Control or Economic Law?*, Auburn, AL: Ludwig von Mises Institute, 2012 [1914].

Boltanski, Luc and Eve Chiapello, *The New Spirit of Capitalism*, London: Verso, 2005.

Brenner, Robert, *The Economics of Global Turbulence: The Advanced Capitalist Economies from Long Boom to Long Downturn*, London: Verso, 2006.

Buchanan, James M., *Public Choice: The Origins and Development of a Research Program*, Fairfax, VA: Center for Study of Public Choice, 2003.

————. and Gordon Tullock, *The Calculus of Consent: Logical Foundations of Constitutional Democracy*, Ann Arbor: University of Michigan Press, 1962.

Bundesministerium des Innern, *Jahresbericht der Bundesregierung zum Stand der Deutschen Einheit 2012*, Berlin: Bundesministerium des Innern, 2012.

Canedo, Eduardo, *The Rise of the Deregulation Movement in Modern America, 1957–1980*, New York: Columbia University Press, 2008.

Castles, Francis G. et al., 'Introduction', in Francis G. Castles et al. (eds), *The Oxford Handbook of the Welfare State*, Oxford: Oxford University Press, 2010, pp. 1–15.

Citigroup Research, *Plutonomy: Buying Luxury, Explaining Global Imbalances*, 16 October 2005.

————. *Revisiting Plutonomy: The Rich Getting Richer*, 5 March 2006.

Citrin, Jack, 'Do People Want Something for Nothing? Public Opinion on Taxes and Government Spending', *National Tax Journal*, vol. 32/2, 1979, supplement, pp. 113–29.

————. 'Proposition 13 and the Transformation of California Government', *The California Journal of Politics and Policy*, vol. 1/1, 2009, pp. 1–9.

Commission of the European Communities et al., *Social Europe. The Social Dimension of the Internal Market. Interim Report of the*

Interdepartmental Working Party, Luxemburg: European Commission, 1988.

Crouch, Colin, *Post-Democracy*, Cambridge: John Wiley & Sons, 2004.

———. 'Privatised Keynesianism: An Unacknowledged Policy Regime', *British Journal of Politics and International Relations*, vol. 11/3, 2009, pp. 382–99.

———. and Pizzorno, Alessandro (eds), *The Resurgence of Class Conflict in Western Europe since 1968*, 2 vols, London: Macmillan, 2009.

Crozier, Michel J. et al., *The Crisis of Democracy: Report on the Governability of Democracies to the Trilateral Commission*, New York: New York University Press, 1975.

Dahrendorf, Ralf, 'Vom Sparkapitalismus zum Pumpkapitalismus', *Cicero online*, 23 July 2009.

Doering-Manteuffel, Anselm and Lutz Raphael, *Nach dem Boom. Perspektiven auf die Zeitgeschichte seit 1970*, Göttingen: Vandenhoeck und Ruprecht, 2008.

Durkheim, Émile, *The Division of Labour in Society*, London: Palgrave Macmillan, 1974 [1893].

Emmenegger, Patrick et al. (eds), *The Age of Dualization: The Changing Face of Inequality in Deindustrializing Countries*, Oxford: Oxford University Press, 2012.

Esping-Andersen, Gosta, *Politics Against Markets: The Social-Democratic Road to Power*, Princeton, NJ: Princeton University Press, 1985.

Etzioni, Amitai, *The Active Society*, New York: The Free Press, 1968.

———. *The Moral Dimension: Toward a New Economics*, New York: The Free Press, 1988.

Feldstein, Martin S., *The Euro and European Economic Conditions*, Working Paper 17617, Cambridge, MA: National Bureau of Economic Research, 2011.

Finansdepartamentet, *An Account of Fiscal and Monetary Policy in the 1990s*, Stockholm, 2001.

Flanagan, Robert J. and Lloyd Ulman, *Wage Restraint: A Study of Incomes Policy in Western Europe*, Berkeley: University of California Press, 1971.

Fritz, Wolfgang and Gertraude Mikl-Horke, *Rudolf Goldscheid: Finanzsoziologie und ethische Sozialwissenschaft*, Vienna: Lit. Verlag, 2007.

Gabor, Daniela, *Fiscal Policy in (European) Hard Times. Financialization and Varieties of Capitalism. Rethinking Financial Markets*, World Economics Association (WEA), 1–30 November 2012.

Gamble, Andrew, *The Free Economy and the Strong State*, Basingstoke: Macmillan, 1988.

Ganghof, Steffen, *Wer regiert in der Steuerpolitik? Einkommenssteuerreform zwischen internationalem Wettbewerb und nationalen Verteilungskonflikten*, Frankfurt/Main: Campus, 2004.

————. and Philip Genschel, 'Taxation and Democracy in the EU', *Journal of European Public Policy*, vol. 15, 2008, pp. 58–77.

Genschel, Philip and Peter Schwarz, 'Tax Competition and Fiscal Democracy', in Armin Schäfer et al. (eds), *Politics in the Age of Austerity*, Cambridge: Polity, 2013.

Gerber, David J., 'Constitutionalizing the Economy: German Neo-Liberalism, Competition Law and the "New Europe"', *American Journal of Comparative Law*, vol. 42, 1988, pp. 25–84.

————. 'The Transformation of European Community Competition Law', *Harvard International Law Journal*, vol. 35, 1994, pp. 97–147.

Glyn, Andrew, *Capitalism Unleashed: Finance Globalization and Welfare*, Oxford: Oxford University Press, 2006.

Goldscheid, Rudolf, 'Staat, öffentlicher Haushalt und Gesellschaft', in Wilhelm Gerloff and Franz Meisel (eds), *Handbuch der Finanzwissenschaft*, vol. 1, Tübingen: Mohr Siebeck, 1926, pp. 146–84.

————. 'Finanzwissenschaft und Soziologie', in Rudolf Hickel (ed.), *Die Finanzkrise des Steuerstaats. Beiträge zur politischen Ökonomie der Staatsfinanzen*. Frankfurt/Main: Campus, 1976 [1917], pp. 317–28.

Goldthorpe, John, 'The Current Inflation: Towards a Sociological Account', in Fred Hirsch et al. (eds), *The Political Economy of Inflation*, Cambridge, MA: Harvard University Press, 1978, pp. 186–216.

————. (ed.), *Order and Conflict in Contemporary Capitalism*, Oxford: Clarendon Press, 1984.

Gorz, André, *Critique de la division du travail*, Paris: Galilée, 1973.

————. *Strategy for Labor*, Boston: Beacon Press, 2000.

Graeber, David, *Debt: The First 5,000 Years*, Brooklyn, New York: Melville House, 2011.

Greif, Avner, *Institutions and the Path to the Modern Economy*, Cambridge: Cambridge University Press, 2006.

————. and David A. Laitin, 'A Theory of Endogenous Institutional Change', *American Political Science Review*, vol. 98/4, 2004, pp. 633–52.

Grözinger, Herbert, 'Griechenland: Von den Amerikas lernen, heißt siegen lernen', *Blätter für deutsche und internationale Politik*, vol. 9, 2012, pp. 35–9.

Guichard, Stephanie et al., 'What Affects Fiscal Consolidation? – Some Evidence from OECD Countries', conference paper, 9th Banca d'Italia Workshop on Public Finances, Rome, 2007.

Habermas, Jürgen, *Technik und Wissenschaft als Ideologie*, Frankfurt/Main: Suhrkamp, 1969.

————. *Legitimation Crisis*, Boston: Beacon Press, 1975.

————. *Zur Rekonstruktion des Historischen Materialismus*, Frankfurt/Main: Suhrkamp, 1975.

Hacker, Jacob and Paul Pierson, 'Winner-Take-All Politics: Public Policy, Political Organization, and the Precipitous Rise of Top Incomes in the United States', *Politics and Society*, vol. 38, 2010, pp. 152–204.

————. *Winner-Take-All Politics: How Washington Made the Rich Richer – and Turned Its Back on the Middle Class*, New York: Simon & Schuster, 2011.

Hall, Peter A. and David Soskice, 'An Introduction to Varieties of Capitalism', in Peter A. Hall et al. (eds), *Varieties of Capitalism:*

The Institutional Foundations of Comparative Advantage, Oxford: Oxford University Press, 2001, pp. 1–68.

Hardin, Garrett, 'The Tragedy of the Commons', *Science*, vol. 162/3859, 1968, pp. 1243–8.

Hassel, Anke, 'The Erosion of the German System of Industrial Relations', *British Journal of Industrial Relations*, vol. 37/3, 1999, pp. 483–505.

Hayek, Friedrich A., 'Full Employment, Planning and Inflation', in *Studies in Philosophy, Politics, and Economics*, Chicago: The University of Chicago Press, 1967 [1950], pp. 270–79.

———. *Die Verfassung der Freiheit*, Tübingen: J. C. B. Mohr, 1971.

———. 'The Pretence of Knowledge: Nobel Prize Lecture' (1974), available at www.nobelprize.org

———. *Recht, Gesetzgebung und Freiheit*, vol. 1, Landsberg am Lech: Verlag Moderne Industrie, 1980.

———. 'The Economic Conditions of Interstate Federalism', in *Individualism and Economic Order*, Chicago: Chicago University Press, 1980 [1939], pp. 255–72.

———. *Law, Legislation and Liberty: A New Statement of the Liberal Principles of Justice and Political Economy*, Abingdon: Routledge, 2013.

Henriksson, Jens, *Ten Lessons about Budget Consolidation*, Brussels: Bruegel, 2007.

Hessel, Stéphane, *Indignez-vous!*, Paris: Indigène, 2010.

Hien, Josef, *The Black International Catholics or the Spirit of Capitalism. The Evolution of the Political Economies of Italy and Germany and Their Religious Foundations*, doctoral dissertation, Florence: European University Institute, 2012.

Hirsch, Fred and John Goldthorpe (eds), *The Political Economy of Inflation*, London: Martin Robertson, 1978.

Hirschman, Albert O., 'Rival Interpretations of Market Society: Civilizing, Destructive, or Feeble?', *Journal of Economic Literature*, vol. 20/4, 1982, pp. 1463–84.

Höpner, Martin, *Wer beherrscht die Unternehmen? Shareholder Value, Managerherrschaft und Mitbestimmung in Deutschland*, Frankfurt/New York: Campus, 2003.

————. 'Nationale Spielräume sollten verteidigt werden', *Die Mitbestimmung*, vol. 58/3, 2012, pp. 46–9.

————. and Armin Schäfer, 'A New Phase of European Integration: Organized Capitalism in Post-Ricardian Europe', *West European Politics*, vol. 33, 2010, pp. 344–68.

————. and Armin Schäfer, *Integration Among Unequals: How the Heterogeneity of European Varieties of Capitalism Shapes the Social and Democratic Potential of the EU*, Cologne, 2012.

————. and Florian Rödl, 'Illegitim und rechtswidrig: Das neue makroökonomische Regime im Euroraum', *Wirtschaftsdienst Zeitschrift für Wirtschaftspolitik*, vol. 92/4, 2012, pp. 219–22.

————. Armin Schäfer and Hubert Zimmermann, 'Erweiterung, Vertiefung und Demokratie: Trilemma der europäischen Integration', *Frankfurter Allgemeine Zeitung*, 27 April 2012.

Illmer, Martin, 'Equity', in Jürgen Basedow et al., *Handbuch des Europäischen Privatrechts*, vol. 1, Tübingen: Mohr Siebeck, 2009, pp. 400–4.

Ingham, Geoffrey, *The Nature of Money*, Cambridge: Polity, 2004.

Judt, Tony, *Postwar: A History of Europe Since 1945*, London: Penguin, 2005.

Kalecki, Michal, 'Political Aspects of Full Employment', *Political Quarterly*, vol. 14/4, 1943, pp. 322–31.

Katz, Harry C. and Owen Darbishire, *Converging Divergences: Worldwide Changes in Employment Systems*, Ithaca, NY: Cornell University Press, 2000.

Kautto, Mikko, 'The Nordic Countries', in Francis G. Castles et al. (eds), *The Oxford Handbook of the Welfare State*, Oxford: Oxford University Press, 2010, pp. 586–600.

Kerr, Clark et al., *Industrialism and Industrial Man: The Problems of Labor and Management in Economic Growth*, Cambridge, MA: Harvard University Press, 1960.

Keynes, John Maynard, *The General Theory of Employment, Interest and Money*, London: Macmillan, 1967 [1936].

Kochan, Thomas A., 'A Jobs Compact for America's Future', *Harvard Business Review*, March 2012, pp. 64–73.

————. 'Resolving the Human Capital Paradox: A Proposal for a Jobs Compact', policy paper no. 2012-011, Kalamazoo, MI: W.E. Upjohn Institute for Employment Research, 2012.

Konrad, Kai A. and Holger Zschäpitz, *Schulden ohne Sühne? Warum der Absturz der Staatsfinanzen uns alle trifft*, Munich: C. H. Beck, 2010.

Korpi, Walter, *The Democratic Class Struggle*, London: Routledge & Kegan Paul, 1983.

Krippner, Greta R., *Capitalizing on Crisis: The Political Origins of the Rise of Finance*, Cambridge, MA: Harvard University Press, 2011.

Kristal, Tali, 'Good Times, Bad Times: Postwar Labor's Share', *American Sociological Review*, vol. 75/5, 2010, pp. 729–63.

Kuttner, Robert, *Revolt of the Haves: Tax Rebellions and Hard Times*, New York: Simon & Schuster, 1980.

Lipset, Seymour Martin, *Political Man: The Social Bases of Politics*, Garden City, NY: Anchor Books, 1963 [1960].

Lockwood, David, 'Social Integration and System Integration', in George K. Zollschan et al. (eds), *Explorations in Social Change*, London: Houghton Mifflin, 1964, pp. 244–57.

Lutz, Burkart, *Der kurze Traum immerwährender Prosperität: Eine Neuinterpretation der industriell-kapitalistischen Entwicklung im Europa des 20. Jahrhunderts*, Frankfurt/Main: Campus, 1984.

Luxemburg, Rosa, *The Accumulation of Capital*, London: Routledge & Kegan Paul, 1951 [1913].

McMurtry, John, *The Cancer Stage of Capitalism*, London: Pluto, 1999.

Maier, Charles S., 'Europe Needs a German Marshall Plan', *New York Times*, 9 June 2012.

Marcuse, Herbert, *One-Dimensional Man: Studies in the Ideology of Advanced Industrial Society*, London: Routledge & Kegan Paul, 1964.

Markantonatu, Maria, *The Uneasy Course of Democratic Capitalism in Greece: Regulation Modes and Crises from the Post-war Period to the Memoranda*, discussion paper, Cologne: Max-Planck-Institut für Gesellschaftsforschung, 2012.

Martin, Isaac William, *The Permanent Tax Revolt: How the Property Tax Transformed American Politics*, Stanford, CA: Stanford University Press, 2008.

Marx, Karl, *Capital, Volume One*, London: Penguin/New Left Books, 1976 [1867].

————. *Capital, Volume Three*, London: Penguin/New Left Books, 1981 [1894].

Maslow, Abraham, 'A Theory of Human Motivation', *Psychological Review*, vol. 50/4, 1943, pp. 370–96.

Matthes, Jürgen and Berthold Busch, 'Governance-Reformen im Euroraum: Eine Regelunion gegen Politikversagen', *IW-Positionen. Beiträge zur Ordnungspolitik aus dem Institut der deutschen Wirtschaft*, No. 56. Cologne: Institut der deutschen Wirtschaft, 2012.

Mayntz, Renate (ed.), *Crisis and Control: Institutional Change in Financial Market Regulation*, Frankfurt/Main: Campus, 2012.

Mehrtens, Philip, *Staatsentschuldung und Staatstätigkeit: Zur Transformation der schwedischen politischen Ökonomie*, Cologne: Universität Köln und Max-Planck-Institut für Gesellschaftsforschung, 2013.

Mertens, Daniel, *Privatverschuldung in Deutschland: Zur institutionellen Entwicklung der Kreditmärkte in einem exportgetriebenen Wachstumsregime*, Cologne: Universität Köln und Max-Planck-Institut für Gesellschaftsforschung, 2013.

Miegel, Meinhard, *Exit. Wohlstand ohne Wachstum*, Berlin: Propyläen, 2010.

Mills, C. Wright, *The Power Elite*, Oxford: Oxford University Press, 1956.

Milward, Alan, *The European Rescue of the Nation State*, London: Taylor and Francis, 1992.

Molander, Per, 'Reforming Budgetary Institutions: Swedish Experiences', in Rolf R. Strauch et al. (eds), *Institutions, Politics and Fiscal Policy*, Boston: Springer, 2000, pp. 191–212.

————. 'Budgeting Procedures and Democratic Ideals: An Evaluation of Swedish Reforms', *Journal of Public Policy*, vol. 21/1, 2001, pp. 23–52.

Moravcsik, Andrew, 'Warum die Europäische Union die Exekutive stärkt: Innenpolitik und internationale Kooperation', in Klaus Dieter Wolf (ed.), *Projekt Europa im Übergang?*, Baden-Baden: Nomos, 1997, pp. 211–70.

Musgrave, Richard, *The Theory of Public Finance*, New York: McGraw-Hill, 1958.

North, Douglass C. and Robert Paul Thomas, *The Rise of the Western World: A New Economic History*, Cambridge: Cambridge University Press, 1973.

O'Connor, James, 'Inflation, Fiscal Crisis, and the American Working Class', *Socialist Revolution*, vol. 2/2, 1972, pp. 9–46.

——. *The Fiscal Crisis of the State*, New York: St Martin's Press, 1973.

Offe, Claus, *Leistungsprinzip und industrielle Arbeit: Mechanismen der Statusverteilung in Arbeitsorganisationen der industriellen 'Leistungsgesellschaft'*, Frankfurt/Main: Europäische Verlagsanstalt, 1970.

——. 'Politische Herrschaft und Klassenstrukturen', in Gisela Kress et al. (eds), *Politikwissenschaft*, Frankfurt/Main: Europäische Verlagsanstalt, 1972, pp. 135–64.

——. 'Structural Problems of the Capitalist State', in Klaus Von Beyme (ed.), *German Political Studies*, vol. 1, London: Sage, 1974, pp. 31–54.

——. *Berufsbildungsreform: Eine Fallstudie über Reformpolitik*, Frankfurt/Main: Suhrkamp, 1975.

——. 'Erneute Lektüre: Die "Strukturprobleme" nach 33 Jahren', in Jens Borchert et al. (eds), *Strukturprobleme des kapitalistischen Staates. Veränderte Neuausgabe*, Frankfurt/Main: Campus, 2006, pp. 181–96.

——. *Reflections on America: Tocqueville, Weber and Adorno in the United States*, Cambridge: Polity, 2006.

——. 'Governance: "Empty Signifier" oder sozialwissenschaftliches Forschungsprogramm?', in Gunnar Folke Schuppert et al. (eds.), *Governance in einer sich wandelnden Welt*, special issue of *Politische Vierteljahresschrift*, vol. 41, 2008, pp. 61–76.

Palier, Bruno, 'Continental Western Europe', in Francis G. Castles et al. (eds), *The Oxford Handbook of the Welfare State*, Oxford: Oxford University Press, 2010, pp. 601–15.

————. and Kathleen Thelen, 'Institutionalizing Dualism: Complementarities and Change in France and Germany', *Politics and Society*, vol. 38/1, 2010, pp. 119–48.

Pierson, Paul, *Dismantling the Welfare State? Reagan, Thatcher, and the Politics of Retrenchment*, Cambridge: Cambridge University Press, 1994.

————. 'The New Politics of the Welfare State', *World Politics*, vol. 48/1, 1996, pp. 143–79.

————. 'Irresistible Forces, Immovable Objects: Post-Industrial Welfare States Confront Permanent Austerity', *Journal of European Public Policy*, vol. 5/4, 1998, pp. 539–60.

————. 'Increasing Returns, Path Dependence, and the Study of Politics', *American Political Science Review*, vol. 94/2, 2000, pp. 251–68.

————. 'From Expansion to Austerity: The New Politics of Taxing and Spending', in Martin A. Levin et al. (eds), *Seeking the Center: Politics and Policymaking at the New Century*, Washington, DC: Georgetown University Press, 2001, pp. 54–80.

————. *Politics in Time: History, Institutions, and Social Analysis*, Princeton, NJ: Princeton University Press, 2004.

Polanyi, Karl, *The Great Transformation: The Political and Economic Origins of Our Time*, Boston: Beacon Press, 1957 [1944].

Pollock, Friedrich, *Stadien des Kapitalismus*, Munich: Beck, 1975.

————. 'State Capitalism: Its Possibilities and Limitations', in Stephen Eric Bronner and Douglas MacKay Kellner (eds), *Critical Theory and Society: A Reader*, London: Routledge, 1989 [1941], pp. 95–118.

Poterba, James M. and Jürgen von Hagen (eds), *Institutions, Politics and Fiscal Policy*, Chicago: University of Chicago Press, 1999.

Putnam, Robert D., 'Diplomacy and Domestic Politics: The Logic of Two-Level Games', in Peter B. Evans (ed.), *Double-Edged Diplomacy*, Berkeley: University of California Press, 1993, pp. 431–86.

Rademacher, Inga, *National Tax Policy in the EMU: Some Empirical Evidence on the Effects of Common Monetary Policy on the Distribution of Tax Burdens*, unpublished thesis, social sciences faculty, Frankfurt/Main, 2012.

Raithel, Thomas et al. (eds), *Auf dem Weg in eine neue Moderne? Die Bundesrepublik Deutschland in den siebziger und achtziger Jahren*, Munich: Oldenbourg Wissenschaftsverlag, 2009.

Rappaport, Alfred, *Creating Shareholder Value*, New York: The Free Press, 1986.

Reinhart, Carmen M. and Kenneth S. Rogoff, *Growth in a Time of Debt*, NBER Working Paper No. 15639, Cambridge, MA: National Bureau of Economic Research, 2009.

Reinhart, Carmen M. and M. Belen Sbrancia, *The Liquidation of Government Debt*, NBER Working Paper No. 16893, Cambridge, MA: National Bureau of Economic Research, 2011.

Rose, Richard, 'Inheritance Before Choice in Public Policy', *Journal of Theoretical Politics*, vol. 2/3, 1990, pp. 263–91.

————. and Phillip L. Davies, *Inheritance in Public Policy: Change Without Choice in Britain*, New Haven, CT: Yale University Press, 1994.

Rostow, Walt W., *The Stages of Economic Growth: A Non-Communist Manifesto*, Cambridge: Cambridge University Press, 1990 [1960].

Ruggie, John Gerard, 'International Regimes, Transactions and Change: Embedded Liberalism in the Postwar Economic Order', *International Organization*, vol. 36/2, 1982, pp. 379–99.

Sachverständigenrat zur Begutachtung der gesamtwirtschaftlichen Entwicklung, *Jahresgutachten 2011/12: Verantwortung für Europa wahrnehmen*, Wiesbaden: Statistisches Bundesamt, 2011.

Sarrazin, Thilo, *Europa braucht den Euro nicht: Wie uns politisches Wunschdenken in die Krise geführt hat*, Munich: Deutsche Verlags-Anstalt, 2012.

Schäfer, Armin, 'Krisentheorien der Demokratie: Unregierbarkeit, Spätkapitalismus und Postdemokratie', *Der modern Staat*, vol. 2/1, 2009, pp. 159–83.

————. 'Die Folgen sozialer Ungleichheit für die Demokratie in Westeuropa', *Zeitschrift für vergleichende Politikwissenschaft*, vol. 4/1, 2010, pp. 131–56.

————. *Republican Liberty and Compulsory Voting*, MPIfG Discussion Paper No. 11/17, Cologne: Max-Planck-Institut für Gesellschaftsforschung, 2011.

————. and Wolfgang Streeck, 'Introduction', in Armin Schäfer et al. (eds), *Politics in the Age of Austerity*, Cambridge: Polity, 2013.

Scharpf, Fritz W., *Crisis and Choice in European Social Democracy*, Ithaca, NY: Cornell University Press, 1991.

————. 'Negative and Positive Integration in the Political Economy of European Welfare States', in Gary Marks et al. (ed), *Governance in the European Union*, London: Sage, 1996, pp. 15–39.

————. 'Solidarität statt Nibelungentreue', *Berliner Republik*, vol. 12/3, 2010, pp. 90–2.

————. 'Mit dem Euro geht die Rechnung nicht auf', *MaxPlanck-Forschung*, vol. 11/3, 2011, pp. 12–17.

————. 'Monetary Union, Fiscal Crisis and the Pre-Emption of Democracy', *Zeitschrift für Staats- und Europawissenschaaften*, vol. 9/2, 2011, pp. 163–98.

————. 'Rettet Europa vor dem Euro', *Berliner Republik*, vol. 14/2, 2012, pp. 52–61.

————. and Vivien A. Schmidt (eds), *Welfare and Work in the Open Economy, Vol. 1, From Vulnerability to Competitiveness*, Oxford: Oxford University Press, 2000.

————. and Vivien A. Schmidt (eds), *Welfare and Work in the Open Economy, Vol. 2, Diverse Responses to Common Challenges*, Oxford: Oxford University Press, 2000.

Schlieben, Michael, 'Die wählen sowieso nicht', *Zeit online*, 13 May 2012.

Schmitter, Philippe C. and Gerhard Lehmbruch (eds), *Trends Towards Corporatist Intermediation*, London: Sage, 1979.

————. and Wolfgang Streeck, *The Organization of Business Interests: Studying the Associative Action of Business in Advanced Industrial*

Societies, MPIfG Discussion Paper No. 99/1, Cologne: Max-Planck-Institut für Gesellschaftsforschung, 1999.

Schor, Juliet, *The Overworked American: The Unexpected Decline of Leisure*, New York: Basic Books, 1992.

Schularick, Moritz, *Public Debt and Financial Crises in the Twentieth Century*, Discussion Paper, No. 2012/1, Berlin: Free University, School of Business and Economics, 2012.

Schumpeter, Joseph A., *The Theory of Economic Development*, London: Transaction, 1980 [1912].

————. 'The Crisis of the Tax State', in *The Economics and Sociology of Capitalism*, Princeton, NJ: Princeton University Press, 1991 [1918], pp. 99–140.

Seikel, Daniel, *Der Kampf um öffentlich-rechtliche Banken. Wie die Europäische Kommission Liberalisierung durchsetzt*, doctoral thesis, Cologne, 2012.

Shefrin, Hersh, *Beyond Greed and Fear: Understanding Behavioral Finance and the Psychology of Investing*, Oxford: Oxford University Press, 2002.

Shonfield, Andrew, *Modern Capitalism: The Changing Balance of Public and Private Power*, Oxford: Oxford University Press, 1965.

————. and Suzanna Shonfield, *In Defense of the Mixed Economy*, Oxford: Oxford University Press, 1984.

Sinn, Hans-Werner, 'Das unsichtbare Bail-Out der EZB', *Ökonomenstimme*, 11 June 2011.

Spiro, David E., *The Hidden Hand of American Hegemony: Petrodollar Recycling and International Markets*, Ithaca, NY: Cornell University Press, 1999.

Steinbrück, Peer, 'Lobbyisten in der Produktion', *Frankfurter Allgemeine Zeitung*, 12 January 2006.

Steuerle, C. Eugene, *The Tax Decade: How Taxes Came to Dominate the Public Agenda*, Washington, DC: The Urban Institute Press, 1992.

Stiglitz, Joseph E., *The Roaring Nineties: A New History of the World's Most Prosperous Decade*, New York and London: W. W. Norton & Company, 2003.

Strauch, Rolf R. and Jürgen von Hagen (eds), *Institutions, Politics and Fiscal Policy*, Boston: Kluwer Academic Publishers, 2000.

Streeck, Wolfgang, 'Pay Restraint Without Incomes Policy: Constitutionalized Monetarism and Industrial Unionism in Germany', in Robert Boyer et al. (eds), *The Return to Incomes Policy*, London: Francis Pinter, 1994, pp. 114–40.

———. 'From Market-Making to State-Building? Reflections on the Political Economy of European Social Policy', in Stephan Leibfried et al. (eds), *European Social Policy: Between Fragmentation and Integration*, Washington DC: The Brookings Institution, 1995, pp. 389–431.

———. 'German Capitalism: Does it Exist? Can it Survive?', *New Political Economy*, vol. 2/2, 1997, pp. 237–56.

———. 'The Study of Interest Groups: Before "The Century" and After', in Colin Crouch et al. (eds), *The Diversity of Democracy: Corporatism, Social Order and Political Conflict*, London: Edward Elgar, 2006, pp. 3–45.

———. *Flexible Employment, Flexible Families, and the Socialization of Reproduction*, MPIfG Discussion Paper No. 09/13, Cologne: Max-Planck-Institut für Gesellschaftsforschung, 2009.

———. *Re-Forming Capitalism: Institutional Change in the German Political Economy*, Oxford: Oxford University Press, 2009.

———. 'Institutions in History: Bringing Capitalism Back In', in John Campbell et al. (eds), *Handbook of Comparative Institutional Analysis*, Oxford: Oxford University Press, 2010, pp. 659–86.

———.' A Crisis of Democratic Capitalism', *New Left Review*, vol. 71, 2011, pp. 1–25.'

———. 'E Pluribus Unum? Varieties and Commonalities of Capitalism', in Mark Granovetter et al. (eds), *The Sociology of Economic Life*, 3rd edition, Boulder, CO: Westview, 2011, pp. 419–55.

———. 'Taking Capitalism Seriously: Towards an Institutional Approach to Contemporary Political Economy', *Socio-Economic Review*, vol. 9/1, 2011, pp. 137–67.

———. 'Citizens as Customers: Considerations on the New Politics of Consumption', *New Left Review*, vol. 76, 2012.

————. 'Wissen als Macht, Macht als Wissen: Kapitalversteher im Krisenkapitalismus', *Merkur*, vol. 65/9–10, 2012.

————. and Daniel Mertens, *An Index of Fiscal Democracy*, MPIfG Working Paper No. 10/3, Cologne: Max-Planck-Institut für Gesellschaftsforschung, 2010.

————. and Daniel Mertens, *Fiscal Austerity and Public Investment: Is the Possible the Enemy of the Necessary?*, MPIfG Discussion Paper No. 11/12, Cologne: Max-Planck-Institut für Gesellschaftsforschung, 2011.

————. and Kathleen Thelen, 'Introduction: Institutional Change in Advanced Political Economies', In Wolfgang Streeck and Kathleen Thelen (eds), *Beyond Continuity: Institutional Change in Advanced Political Economies*, Oxford: Oxford University Press, 2005, pp. 1–39.

Taibbi, Matt, 'The Great American Bubble Machine', *Rolling Stone*, 9 July 2009.

Tarschys, Daniel, 'The Scissors Crisis in Public Finance', *Policy Sciences*, vol. 15/3, 1983, pp. 205–24.

Thielemann, Ulrich, 'Das Ende der Demokratie', *Wirtschaftsdienst – Zeitschrift für Wirtschaftspolitik*, vol. 91/12, 2011, pp. 820–23.

Tomaskovic-Devey, Donald and Ken-Hou Lin, 'Income Dynamics, Economic Rents and the Financialization of the US Economy', *American Sociological Review*, vol. 76/4, 2011, pp. 538–59.

Wagner, Adolph, *Grundlegung der politischen Oekonomie*, 3rd edition, Leipzig: C.F. Wintersche Verlagshandlung, 1892.

————. 'Staat in nationalökonomischer Hinsicht', in Ludwig Elster et al. (eds), *Handwörterbuch der Staatswissenschaften*, Jena: Fischer, 1911, pp. 727–39.

Wagschal, Uwe, *Staatsverschuldung: Ursachen im internationalen Vergleich*, Opladen: Verlag für Sozialwissenschaften, 1996.

————. 'Staatsverschuldung', in Dieter Nohlen et al. (eds), *Kleines Lexikon der Politik*, Munich: C.H. Beck, 2007, pp. 547–52.

Weber, Max, *Economy and Society*, 2 vols., Berkeley: University of California Press, 1978 [1956].

Weizsäcker, Carl Christian von, 'Das Janusgesicht der Staatsschulden', *Frankfurter Allgemeine Zeitung*, 5 June 2010.

Werner, Benjamin, *Die Stärke der judikativen Integration. Wie Kommission und Europäischer Gerichtshof die Unternehmenskontrolle liberalisieren*, Economics and Social Science Faculty, Cologne University, 2012.

Western, Bruce and Jake Rosenfeld, 'Unions, Norms, and the Rise in US Wage Inequality', *American Sociological Review*, vol. 76/4, 2011, pp. 513–37.

Williamson, O. E. et al., 'Understanding the Employment Relation: The Analysis of Idiosyncratic Exchange', *Bell Journal of Economics*, vol. 6, 1975, pp. 250–78.

Wright, Erik Olin, *Classes*, London: Verso, 1985.

Index

Christian Democrats, 12, 137n67,
145n75, 148, 157n91
Ciampi, Carlo Azeglio, 167
Citibank, 6n12
citizen political participation. *See*
political participation
citizenry. *See Staatsvolk* (citizens)
class, 4–6 passim, 18n35, 21, 84, 92,
162. *See also* capitalist class;
middle class; working class
class struggle, 60
clientelism, 91, 137, 143, 145n75, 151,
167
Clinton, Bill, 36, 40, 51, 53, 67, 123
coalition government: Germany. *See*
'Grand Coalition' (Germany)
Cold War, 57, 145n75
commercialism and consumerism. *See*
consumerism and commercialism
commons, 47–8
communism, 12, 59n25, 111, 143,
186; renunciation/discrediting of,
127, 140. *See also* anti-
communism
'consolidation state', 97–164 passim,
181, 189
constituency. *See Marktvolk*;
Staatsvolk (citizens)
constitution of Europe (proposed).
See European constitution
(proposed)
consumerism and commercialism,
16–17, 18, 31, 45, 117
courts, 60n27, 105, 109, 158
credit. *See* private debt; public debt
creditors as constituency. See
Marktvolk
crisis theory, vii–5 passim, 10, 14–21
passim, 27, 32, 72, 73, 84
Crouch, Colin, 38, 74
*The Cultural Contradictions of
Capitalism* (Bell), 15n25
currency. *See* money

currency devaluation. *See* devaluation
of currency
thecurrentmoment (blog), 167n2,
170n6

debt. *See* private debt; public debt
debt ceilings, 62, 86, 108, 117, 122n49
debt-financing, 76–82 passim, 86–9
passim, 93, 120n43, 124, 130. *See
also* public debt: refinancing
'debt state', xviii, 72–97 passim, 112,
134
Debt: The First 5,000 Years (Graeber),
161
deficits. *See* budget deficits
deflation, 34, 36
Delors, Jacques, 104, 149n78
democracy, 46–63 passim, 78–86
passim, 90–1, 96, 162, 172–4, 189;
failure of, 74–6 passim; Hayek
views, 101, 103n19; in intrastate
federation/EU, 101–4 passim,
112–7 passim, 134, 155, 159–61
passim, 167, 177–81; state
sovereignty relationship, 188;
workplace, 16. *See also* social
democracy
The Democratic Class Struggle (Korpi),
27
Denmark, 50, 149, 179, 187n30
depressions, xi, 13
deregulation, 2, 20, 28, 49, 134; of
finance markets, xii, 38n70, 51, 69,
73, 159; of labour markets, 17, 29
Deutsche Bundesbank. *See*
Bundesbank
devaluation of currency, 106, 111,
114, 147, 150, 174–5, 181–4, 186
dictatorship, 57, 76n56, 143, 172
distribution of wealth, 76–9 passim
dollar, 187
Draghi, Mario, 132, 153, 156n90, 166,
168, 169n4

private enterprise: Schumpeter view,
72n47. *See also* public-private
partnerships (PPPs)
private ownership. *See* ownership,
private
'privatized Keynesianism', 38–9, 127
privatization, 3, 29, 40, 73, 124; of
commons, 47; EU, 104, 121; of
pensions, 90; of public services, 45,
73, 88, 113, 121
productivity, 15, 45n76, 52–3, 58, 174
profit, xiii (n12), 20–8 passim, 71, 75,
111, 159
profit-dependent class. *See* capitalist
class
protest and resistance, 5–6, 109,
160–5 passim, 172–3, 175–6, 188
public choice theory, 27n48
public debt, xiv, xvii–xviii, 7–9 passim,
34, 36, 43–52 passim, 72–96
passim, 176; blamed on workers,
26n47; comparative figures, 8, 41,
50; EU, 106, 113, 121, 126, 134, 141,
149, 153, 166; Germany, 8, 32n59,
42–4 passim, 50, 87, 125, 156, 171;
Greece, 50, 89n76, 126–32 passim,
152; refinancing, 82, 84, 89n77, 90,
121, 128, 153, 154, 162, 166;
relationship to private debt, 39;
Sweden, 8, 41, 43, 44, 50, 124n51,
125; United States, 8, 40–2 passim,
50, 67n35, 68, 82n65, 165, 170–1.
See also debt ceilings; state
bankruptcy
public employment, 29, 42, 113
Public Investment Management
Company. *See* PIMCO (Public
Investment Management
Company)
public-private partnerships (PPPs),
123n49
public spending, 9, 36, 68–9, 74, 123–4;
compared to taxation, 63, 66; EU,

109, 118–20 passim; Germany,
120, 123, 125; Greece, 130; legal
limits, 87; on social services, 45,
51, 52, 68–9, 74, 86, 88, 113, 119–20
passim; Sweden, 120, 123, 125

rage. *See* anger
rating agencies, 83n68, 88
rationality and irrationality, 59, 160,
161, 164, 172
Rattner, Steven, 53
Reagan, Ronald, 34, 36, 49, 114
recession, 9, 34, 118n41
redistribution, 52, 62, 169
refinancing of public debt. *See* public
debt: refinancing
regional growth programmes, 134–46,
183n19
rentiers, 113
'reservation profit' and 'reservation
wage', 75n54
resistance and protest. *See* protest and
resistance
retirement pensions. *See* pensions
revolts, 19
rich people, 95–6, 182; taxation and
tax avoidance, 76n56, 108n2,
119n42, 162. *See also* executive pay
rights, 28, 29, 45, 50, 58, 73–4, 89n76,
159
risk propensity, 22, 69n40, 81
Romney, Mitt, 124n50, 158
Rosenfeld, Jake, 52
Rösler, Philipp, 86–7n71
Rubinstein, David, 173n8

Sallusti, Alessandro, 92–3n81
Sarkozy, Nicolas, 110, 126, 170n6
Sarrazin, Thilo: *Europa braucht den
Euro nicht*, 92
savings, 45, 77, 78n59, 154
Scandinavia, 29–30, 38, 39, 50. *See
also* Denmark; Sweden